INTRODUCING US

Anne Stewart is an experienced consultant psychiatrist who has set up services for young people who struggle with eating, as well as doing teaching and research at the University of Oxford. Anne has lots of experience doing CBT with young people as well as training others in CBT. She is keen to help young people deal with worries about eating and body image early on so that they can get on with their lives.

Caz Nahman is a consultant psychiatrist who has worked with young people with an eating disorder both in the community and in hospital. She has an interest in athletes with eating disorders, boys who are struggling with eating difficulties and young people who have problems with their body image. She is keen on helping young people build a healthy relationship with exercise.

Joanna Adams is a clinical psychologist with lots of experience of working with young people with eating disorders, both individually and with their families. As well as doing therapy, Jo teaches professionals about CBT and is also involved in research to better understand eating disorders. She really wants to help young people to feel good about themselves and their bodies and to try and stop eating disorders from taking hold

Overcoming for Teenagers is a series to support young people through common mental health issues during adolescence, using scientific techniques that have been proven to work.

Series editors: Dr Polly Waite and Emeritus Professor Peter Cooper

Titles in the series include:

Overcoming Social Anxiety and Building Self-confidence

OVERCOMING WORRIES ABOUT BODY IMAGE AND EATING

A SELF-HELP GUIDE FOR TEENAGERS

Anne Stewart, Caz Nahman and Joanna Adams

Illustrated by Juliet Young

ROBINSON

ROBINSON

First published in Great Britain in 2024 by Robinson

1 3 5 7 9 10 8 6 4 2

Copyright © Anne Stewart, Caz Nahman and Joanna Adams, 2024
Illustrations by Juliet Young

The moral right of the authors has been asserted.

Important Note
This book is not intended as a substitute for medical advice or treatment.
Any person with a condition requiring medical attention should consult
a qualified medical practitioner or suitable therapist.

A CIP catalogue record for this book
is available from the British Library.

ISBN: 978-1-47214-758-5

Typeset in Palatino by Initial Typesetting Services, Edinburgh
Printed and bound in Great Britain by Clays Ltd, Elcograf S.p.A.

Papers used by Robinson are from well-managed forests
and other responsible sources.

Robinson
An imprint of
Little, Brown Book Group
Carmelite House
50 Victoria Embankment
London EC4Y 0DZ

An Hachette UK Company
www.hachette.co.uk

www.littlebrown.co.uk

This book is dedicated to all the young people and their families with whom we have worked who have taught us so much about eating disorders, and to our families for supporting us during the writing process.

Contents

Part 3
Getting Help from Others

Preface

Dear reader

Thank you for picking up this book. Whether you are a young person who is struggling with eating difficulties and body image concerns, or a parent or carer who is worried about a young person in your life, we hope that you will find this book helpful.

We have written this book because we know that lots of young people feel worried about food and eating and the effect that has on their bodies, particularly during the teenage years. Most teenagers worry about their body and appearance at some point, and some may alter their eating to change their weight or shape.

We are clinicians who have many years of experience working in specialist eating disorder services for children and adolescents. We have met lots of young people who are referred to our clinics at a point where an eating disorder has really taken hold.

Eating disorders can have a huge and negative impact on your physical health, your emotional wellbeing, your relationships and social life. Eating disorders can take control of your mind and body, making it difficult to feel motivated to recover. Getting back on track can be a long and difficult journey. Eating disorders often start in small ways, so if we can help you to recognise and cope with the early warning signs this might stop the problem from taking hold, affecting your wellbeing and interfering with your life.

We know that being a teenager isn't easy, and there are lots of challenges that you may have to face. By writing this book, we'd really like to help you to develop a healthy relationship with eating and with your body, so that you can feel strong, healthy and good about yourself.

This book follows an approach called cognitive behavioural therapy (CBT), which was devised by Aaron Beck, an American psychiatrist. CBT is a really useful way of helping us to make sense of our experiences and overcome the difficulties that we face. It is an evidence-based approach, which means that lots of research has been done to evaluate it and show that it can be helpful.

The chapters are based on the works of a number of well-known researchers who have applied CBT to particular problems, like eating disorders and self-esteem. We have learned a lot from these researchers, and they have helped to shape the ideas presented here. If you'd like to find out more about them, and their work, their details are listed at the end of the book. We also draw on our own clinical experience of working with lots of young people and helping them put CBT into practice.

You don't need to read this book from cover to cover, but you can if you want to! Some chapters will be more relevant to you than others. You can dip in and out or come back to sections at another time. There are lots of extra resources (including books and websites) listed at the end of the book if you would like to find out more about some of the topics we discuss in the chapters.

We hope this book helps you with your own journey.

With warmest regards

Anne, Caz and Jo

Introduction

Ella

I can't get to sleep. It's my dance performance tomorrow and I just can't stop thinking about it. Am I going to remember my steps? Will I look OK? Have I put on any weight? Should I skip breakfast? Am I eating the right things? Should I cut down on fats? What do my friends think of me? What if I make a fool of myself? I can't stop these thoughts crowding in on me and I can feel my heart beating fast. I really need the sleep – but there's too much going round my head.

What the Introduction will cover:

- What this book is about.

- Introducing seven young people.

- How the book is structured and how to use it.

What is this book about?

Have you ever worried about your weight or appearance or what food you should, or should not, be eating? Most people think about how they look and what they are eating; but if you end up spending a lot of time worrying it can have a big impact on your life, just like Ella (above), who couldn't get to sleep because of her concerns. The aim of this book is to help you to understand a bit more about these worries, what you can do about them and, most importantly, how you can develop a healthy relationship with your body and with food.

Being concerned about eating, weight or body image is common in the teenage years. But if these worries take hold, there is a risk of developing a full-blown eating disorder or becoming depressed. In this book we follow seven young people, and one of their friends, who have worries about their eating and body image but learn to get the better of these and get their lives back on track. They all live in the same town and go to the same school. Their characters are fictional, but their stories are similar to those of many young people we have met in our work.

Introducing the teenagers

Ella (age 15) is a keen dancer and is involved in various kinds of dance and drama most days. She is attractive and slim and very aware of 'healthy eating'. She is very active on social media and has a large following which makes her feel valued, although, at the same time, she finds this a pressure.

She posts photos of her healthy food choices on social media and is critical of people who have what she considers unhealthy eating habits. Ella's whole family is very health conscious and her mum frequently diets. Many younger students in the school follow her on social media and try to copy her.

Chloe (age 13) is very tall; she started her periods when she was ten and was teased about wearing a bra in primary school. Her parents are divorcing and frequently argue. The family are on a waiting list for housing, but until then her parents have to live in the same house. Her mum cries a lot. Chloe worries a lot about money. There are no set meals at home, and she has started to comfort eat. She feels miserable because she is gaining weight and has started to try to restrict her food intake. She skips breakfast but ends up bingeing on crisps, biscuits and chocolates every night. After a binge she feels gross and ashamed of herself and plans to skip the next meal. However, she is still putting on weight and feels increasingly unhappy. She follows Ella on social media but feels she will never be as popular as Ella.

Wesley (age 16) is tall, good-looking and popular at school. He is on the rugby team and works out a lot at the gym; his school friends admire the personal bests he is hitting. He posts his gym workouts on social media and has lots of followers. He looks confident on the outside but inside he is worried about not being muscular enough and having to keep performing well for others. He spends more and more time in the gym and has become obsessed with protein powders, bars and shakes. Despite taking

lots of these, he is beginning to lose weight. His friends feel concerned as he never has time just to hang out with them. His parents wonder if they should talk to the coach about him.

Jake (age 12) hates school, struggles with friendships, is lonely and worries a lot. He has been diagnosed with an autism spectrum condition (ASC) and attention deficit hyperactivity disorder (ADHD) and feels different from the others

in his class. He has been a fussy eater for many years, preferring soft food and avoiding anything green. When he is upset or worried, he finds it hard to eat. He feels sick much of the time and finds it difficult to eat because of his worries about being rejected and teased by his classmates. He can't eat in front of others and never puts up his hand in class because he is self-conscious. His mum is worried because he is losing weight and says he is not hungry.

Jen (age 14) really looks up to Ella. Jen excels at her school subjects and is always trying to be the best in the class. She is also an exceptionally successful tennis player, but puts pressure on herself to achieve and wants to be faster at the game. Her coach has suggested that if she lost a bit of 'puppy fat' she would improve, so she is on a strict diet. However, her mood is low, and she is tired and irritable all the time. Her friends are worried about her as they see she has lost weight and is not her usual

bubbly self. She gets irritated when they ask her whether she might have an eating disorder. Jen really wants approval from her coach and her father and is scared of failure.

Aisha (age 15) comes from a family where her parents are quite overweight. She is aware of putting on weight in puberty and is very self-conscious about this. She is determined to lose weight and goes on a strict diet. She begins

to lose weight, posts pictures of herself on social media and has lots of likes. However, she has no energy, her mood is down, and she begins to avoid going out with friends because she wants to avoid eating socially. When it comes to Ramadan, she is determined to keep to strict fasting during the day but does not make up for this in the evening. Consequently, her weight drops further. Aisha has two younger siblings,

Rashmi and Aadesh, and has always got on with them, but since her eating problems started she has become quite distant from them.

Sam (age 14) identifies at times as a boy but is also unsure whether they are non-binary. They worry about fitting in with others. They also worry how puberty, looking female and starting periods will make them feel about their identity. They want to be tall and strong and good at sport and have friends. They worry about being teased and they worry about who to talk to. Sam's parents split up when they were young, and they have a stepfather and two young half-siblings who take up a lot of their mum's time. They sometimes feel they don't belong in the family at all.

Zoe (age 14) is Jen's best friend at school. She sometimes becomes frustrated that Jen won't come out with her and their group of friends. She is worried that Jen doesn't like her but at the same time realises that Jen looks unhappy and tired all the time and has become a bit snappy. When she asks if she's OK, Jen seems to get cross with her. She is worried about Jen and not quite sure who to talk to or what to do about it.

How to use this book

These examples are taken (and adapted) from real-life situations. However, we are aware that we can't cover every situation and the examples may not apply in the same way to all cultures and contexts. Every young person and family is unique! So, as you go through the book, you may need to adapt the ideas to suit your own context.

The book is divided into three sections:

1. The first section covers general stuff about adolescent development, how we make sense of our experiences, healthy eating, body image, information about eating disorders and how to look after yourself during the teenage years.

2. The second section goes into more detail about eating and body image difficulties and how you can stop them taking hold. It includes ideas for feeling good about yourself and your body, dealing with stress and managing social media. One chapter focuses on issues for boys/young men. Boys and men can have different difficulties with weight and body image compared to girls and young women, and some of the current myths stop teenagers who identify as boys from seeking help. We have not written a chapter specifically for gender diverse teens, but acknowledge that when a teen is in a different body from how they identify it can result in even more difficulties around body image, self-esteem and self-confidence. Some of the principles in the book

will be relevant and helpful, but this group of teens may need specialised services which go beyond the early intervention strategies covered here.

3. The final part is about how to get help from family and friends if you are struggling with these concerns, and there is a chapter for parents/carers and families with suggestions on how they can help. The last chapter discusses what to do if the problems just don't go away and you need professional help.

Some chapters may be more relevant to you than others, and it's fine to focus on the parts that most interest you. We mention parents throughout the book but are aware that some young people may live with carers, or may have left home and are living independently. If this is the case, you may want to ignore the bits that are not relevant to you and your situation.

Throughout the book we suggest things to try out or think about, so grab a pencil and paper so that you can jot things down as you read through.

There are also worksheets that you can access online from https://overcoming.co.uk/715/resources-to-download.

Part 1

Understanding Eating Difficulties and Body Image

Chapter 1

What Is Adolescence All About?

Jake

It's not fair, some of the boys in my class have grown really tall and strong and I feel such a wimp compared to them – I haven't started growing yet and I am no good at sport. Why can't I grow like them? The other boys tease me and call me Titch.

What this chapter will cover:

- What are the developmental changes in adolescence?

- How the brain develops in adolescence.

- How concerns about eating and body image develop in adolescence.

What are the developmental changes in adolescence?

Check it out: Developmental changes in adolescence

- Starting puberty
- Learning to do things by yourself
- Making friends
- Developing knowledge and skills
- Developing your own identity

Research has shown that eating disorders often start in adolescence. Why might this be? During adolescence, young people go through a number of challenging physical, social and emotional changes which can trigger difficulties with eating and body image. So, what are these changes?

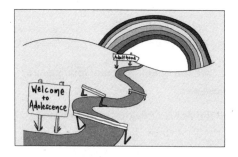

Welcome to adolescence – an exhilarating journey lasting several years with some hurdles and obstacles, but also exciting times

Puberty

Ella was twelve when she looked in the mirror and noticed spots on her face, hairs under her arms and her body beginning to change shape. This was the beginning of puberty, when levels of sex hormones rise and emotions can suddenly be all over the place.

This normally happens around the age of ten to thirteen in girls and a bit later in boys (can be earlier or later too). Although most teenagers get through it OK, some find it particularly challenging. They can become irritated with family and friends or find school difficult. Chloe went into puberty quite early and found this a challenge as she was much taller than her peers and was laughed at for having to wear a bra at primary school. She became quite self-conscious of her weight and how she looked, and this made her feel unhappy.

Wesley also went into puberty a bit younger than his peers; he became tall and muscular and was good at sport, which meant that people looked up to him. However, hormonal changes contributed to his swinging emotions.

Jake is going through puberty a bit later than his peers, is smaller than his friends and his voice hasn't changed yet. He is teased at school and is called 'small and weak' by his classmates.

Sam is fourteen and hasn't yet started their periods. They feel confused about their identity and are not sure how they identify but are anxious about periods starting and physically developing as a female.

Independence

Many teenagers can't wait to go out on their own, or with friends, without having their parents/carers trailing along behind. This is the time of life when young people learn to become independent. They may find that they spend less time with their parents/carers and want to do things with their friends instead. There can be tensions at home, with parents wanting to set boundaries, for example coming home at a certain time, having family meals or getting homework done before going out.

Most teenagers get into conflict with their parents or carers, but usually this resolves as families find ways to communicate and negotiate. At times, you may be relieved that your parents set limits as it can be scary doing things for the first time on your own. Parents and carers are usually there to fall back on if you need support. However, it can be difficult if your parents/carers are thinking about other issues and have less time for you. Chloe's mum was in the process of splitting up from her partner and was stressed and preoccupied, leaving less time to focus on her daughter at a time when she needed her mum's support.

Friendships

Adolescence is a crucial time for making friends. However, it can be stressful when friends let you down or exclude you, or you feel like you don't fit in. Some young people find it hard to make friends and can feel very lonely. Jake finds it difficult to relate to others and feels very much on his own.

He doesn't get invited to birthday parties like the other kids in his class and is bullied because he is seen as different from others. This makes him feel distressed – and he tends to keep this to himself as he finds it difficult to talk about his feelings.

Identity

An important process in adolescence is learning who you are and what sort of person you want to be, and developing a sense of self-esteem is a crucial part of this. Learning to value yourself shouldn't just depend on whether you are good at sport or at your work, or whether you are good-looking. However, sometimes this is the way it feels. Teenagers frequently compare themselves with others, which can be made worse by viewing what is shared on social media.

Chloe struggles to be herself. She follows Ella on social media and desperately wants to be like her. She doesn't feel that she has any good qualities herself. Ella also feels under pressure to always show her best side and maintain the image that she feels people expect, even when she doesn't feel good about herself inside. Sam feels unsure of their identity and this can change from day to day. This means Sam might worry a lot around body image, self-esteem and eating.

Skills and knowledge

Adolescence is also a time when you are developing skills and knowledge. School can be interesting and fun for some young people but an anxious or frustrating experience for others. Some young people set themselves extremely high goals or feel that school or parents expect a lot of them and worry excessively if they don't achieve those goals. Jen is a perfectionist and wants to be the best academically and at tennis. But this leads to considerable worry, particularly if she doesn't come top in class or loses a tennis match. We will see later how she managed to put her worries into perspective.

How is the brain developing in adolescence?

In the same way that a young person's body is changing, their brain is also going through some pretty big changes. The way teenagers feel and behave is very much linked to how their brains are developing.

Although much of brain growth occurs in the first year of life, a huge amount of growth and development takes place during adolescence. Growing brains need up to a quarter of the oxygen we breathe and thrive on the energy we feed them. Our brains (compared to other animals) need and use a huge amount of energy.

Check it out: Facts about our amazing brains

- Our brains contain about 100 billion neurones. Neurones are cells which carry information across and from the brain to different parts of our bodies.

- Information in our brains travels at about 431 kilometres per hour.

- When you touch something, sensory neurones carry information back to the brain. Sensory neurones can be as long as 1 metre (e.g. the neurone reaching from the base of the spine to the toes).

- An adult brain weighs 1.1–1.4kg but uses a quarter of the oxygen we breathe and 20 per cent of the energy we eat.

- Our brains are extremely busy and need lots of energy (food) and oxygen to work efficiently.

The brain is developing fast in the teenage years, but many areas do not fully develop until adulthood. This can contribute to some thoughts or feelings which adults (who might not understand) call 'typical adolescent behaviour'. We'd like to discuss what's going on in the teenage brain which might explain how you might behave, think or feel in the way that you do.

On that note, let's look at some areas of the brain, and think about what they do.

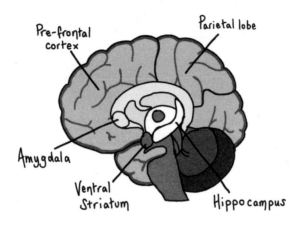

Our amazing brain – our brains change throughout adolescence – here are some parts which are developing rapidly during the teenage years (and beyond)!

Hippocampus This is the centre for memory and learning. There is lots of activity in this part of the brain as you are learning so much at school, preparing for exams and, importantly, learning about the world.

Ventral striatum This is the reward centre of the brain. It is normal for teenagers to be more influenced by reward than by consequences, particularly in the short term. It is much harder to think about future consequences.

Amygdala This part of the brain is responsible for emotional states, for example fear, anger, passion, excitement. Adults rely less on this area, using the pre-frontal cortex more in decision-making. However, as a teenager you tend to be guided more by your emotions and take your lead from this part of the brain.

Parietal lobe This part of the brain is involved in the experience of the senses, for example touch, sight, hearing. It is not fully developed until around the age of twenty, which can make it more difficult for young people to process this information effectively. As a result, they may miss cues which help with decision-making.

Pre-frontal cortex This area of the brain is involved in planning and reasoning. It is not fully mature in young people, which is why they often do things without thinking fully about the consequences or the pros and cons of certain actions.

There is lots going on in an adolescent's brain, and intense emotion may be experienced due to the activity of the amygdala. This can make adolescents passionate about the things that are important to them. On the other hand, they can become easily embarrassed and may struggle to read the feelings and intentions of others.

There are also a greater number of connections between the nerves (synaptic connections) at this time of life and greater possibility of change in the brain. This makes young people open to learning new things, stepping out of their comfort zone and taking risks. Part of that creativity and openness can mean doing things impulsively, without thinking about what might happen next. This can work brilliantly – you may discover, for example, a new hobby – but it can also get teenagers into trouble, or their intentions may be misunderstood by adults.

In adolescence, emotions can feel intense but the ability to regulate them has yet to mature. Young people are more likely to behave in risky ways, perhaps to fit in with friends or because they haven't thought about the consequences. This does not apply to all teenagers, but can be relevant to those teenagers who are self-harming, taking drugs or skipping meals. They might find it harder to think about the longer-term consequences of these behaviours and focus more on the immediate rewards. Jen is like this; she goes on a strict diet because she feels unhappy about herself but doesn't think about how this might affect her mood and physical state.

Why do concerns about eating and body image develop during adolescence?

In adolescence the body is changing rapidly. It is natural for young people to grow in height and put on weight throughout this period. The graph below shows the rapid increase in weight that occurs in adolescence, reaching adult weight around the age of eighteen. This happens at different rates and at different times, as shown by the different lines on the graph; not everyone will look the same. The graph represents the way weight will change depending on your weight when you go into adolescence.

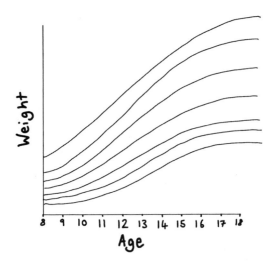

This graph shows an example of the normal changes in weight that happen during the pre-teen and teenage years that are part of normal growth and development

This is a normal part of changing from a child to a young adult, but in some cases the weight gain is uneven. Just before a growth spurt, teenagers might store some energy that is needed for growing quickly, and if you pay too much attention to this you may worry that you are getting 'fat'. Many young women find it uncomfortable when they notice that they are beginning to have a rounder shape. After a growth spurt, some teenage boys might worry about looking too thin and with less muscle than they would like.

At the same time, the chance of experiencing mood swings or low mood and depression increases due to all the emotional and biological changes, as well as expectations and challenges, that teenagers face. In today's society, we are bombarded by images from the internet, TV, magazines and social media which can also play a part in increasing dissatisfaction about your body. We are exposed to celebrities who have had various body alterations to achieve a certain look or body shape. In addition, photographs and videos can be photoshopped to:

- change body shape
- lengthen legs
- remove blemishes
- iron out flaws
- enhance colour

You name it: anything can be done to create a perfect image. Using social media and the internet makes it easier to compare yourself with others – and you can end up feeling bad about yourself, particularly as the images you see are all perfect!

The internet and social media are an invaluable part of everyday life for teenagers, providing entertainment, help with learning and a way to connect socially with others. However, you may feel under pressure to present the 'perfect' person on social media, even though no one is perfect. It may be tempting to measure your value from the number of likes, followers or shares that you get in response to a post.

There may be other stresses in adolescence too, linked to friendships, school or family life. Some young people, like Jen, may decide to diet to feel better about themselves.

Others may turn to food for comfort, but their increased weight makes them feel ashamed and worse about themselves. Chloe gained weight in puberty and struggled to feel good about herself and at the same time experienced a lot of stress in her family. She began to comfort eat to try and distract herself from her feelings of distress.

You might want to take a look at Chapter 6 which thinks about strategies for taking care of yourself, Chapter 12 which discusses social media in more detail, Chapter 9 which is about building self-esteem, or Chapter 10 which covers feeling good about your body.

Check it out: Facts about weight and bodies

- It is natural to gain weight in adolescence, along with growth in height.
- The perfect body doesn't exist!
- Images of models are altered digitally to make them look perfect.

So how will you manage to get through adolescence with all these pressures? The good news is that most adolescents do get through OK! It really helps to talk about worries with family, friends or someone you trust. The aim of this book is to help you think about the challenges of the teenage years and find a way through, and, importantly, end up feeling happy about yourself and your body image.

Summary

- Adolescence is a time of great change.

- Going through puberty early can be difficult for some teenagers.

- The brain is developing rapidly in the teenage years.

- Adolescents can be impulsive and risk-taking.

- Images of perfect models can cause pressure for young women and men.

- The internet and social media can be both helpful and unhelpful.

- Most young people get through adolescence pretty well.

Chapter 2

Making Sense of Experiences

The crowd falls silent. I bounce the tennis ball once, twice, on the ground, then toss it high up into the air. I slam my racket down with all my might, feeling the strings make contact with the ball. The ball shoots over the net and bounces in the far corner of the court out of my opponent's reach. The crowd goes wild! I have won the match!

The daydream evaporates. The joy and excitement that was tingling through my body fades away, and I'm back in the school lunch hall. My shoulders slump and the heavy feeling in the pit of my stomach returns. I'll never be good enough to win the match. I'm too fat and too slow. If only I could lose weight then I wouldn't be such a failure on the court. I push the salad around my plate but don't eat it – I feel sick and have no appetite. I should probably go for a run after school before tennis training, but I just don't have any energy – which proves what a fat, lazy loser I am.

Jen

What this chapter will cover:

- Understanding thoughts, feelings, sensations and behaviour, and how they link together to help us make sense of our experiences.

- How we get trapped into a vicious cycle of responding, and how we can break out of the trap.

- Understanding different perspectives.

The situations we find ourselves in can provoke a whole range of reactions. Sometimes these can feel positive, like in Jen's daydream, whereas at other times they can feel negative, overwhelming or confusing. This chapter is about helping you to make sense of your experiences and understanding why you react to situations in particular ways.

Our reactions are made up of our thoughts, feelings, physical sensations and behaviours. Breaking down our experiences into these different parts can really help us to understand why we respond to situations in particular ways. Understanding experiences through the framework of thoughts, feelings, physical sensations and behaviours is based on an approach called cognitive behavioural therapy, where cognitions is just another word for thoughts. Cognitive behavioural therapy, or CBT, is based on the idea that how we *think* about a situation influences how we *feel* and the *sensations* we experience in our body, and what we do (our *behaviour*). Let's look at what we mean by thoughts, feelings, sensations and behaviour, and how they fit together to help make sense of our experiences.

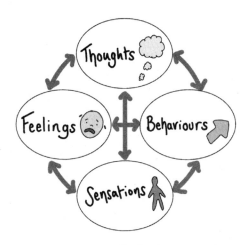

Cognitive behavioural therapy (CBT) helps us to make sense of our experiences by looking at the links between our thoughts, feelings, physical sensations and behaviours

Thoughts	Feelings	Sensations	Behaviours
'I will never be good enough to win the match' 'I'm too fat and slow' 'I am so lazy' 'I am such a loser'	Overwhelmed Anxious Sad	Shoulders slump Heavy feeling in stomach Feel sick, no appetite No energy	Eat low-calorie food Avoid junk food Exercise more

Jen's thoughts, feelings, physical sensations and behaviours

Thoughts

We all have a constant stream of thoughts going through our heads, but we may not notice them all the time. It's a bit like looking at your social media feed: some posts you pay attention to and read, others you skim over and ignore. Similarly, your thoughts are there all the time, but you pay more attention to some than to others. Our thoughts tend to be automatic. We don't always choose to have them: they often just pop into our heads.

Our thoughts are important because they help us to make sense of the situations that we encounter by providing an interpretation of their meaning and significance. Our thoughts tell us what we think about ourselves, about other people and about the situations we are in. Sometimes our thoughts are positive (*'I won the tennis match!'*), sometimes they are neutral (*'This tennis ball is yellow'*), and sometimes they can be negative (*'I am such a loser'*). We tend to accept our thoughts as true, without really questioning them.

Our thoughts tend to be shaped by past experiences and the values and influences of our family, society or culture. These experiences lead us to develop beliefs and expectations about ourselves, about other people and about the future. It's a bit like having a rule book that tells us how we 'should' think or what we 'must' do. Jen's thoughts about being successful at tennis were shaped by growing up in a family and culture that valued hard work and doing your best. Her rules for life would include things like, *'I <u>must</u> always do my best'*, *'I <u>should</u> work as hard as I can'*, *'I <u>must</u> be successful'*.

We all have an internal rule book which tells us
how we should think and behave

It can be helpful to learn to identify the thoughts that you
have.

Ask yourself:

- What was going through my mind when that happened?

- Imagine yourself as a character in a comic book – what would be in your thought bubble in any given scene?

- Are there any rules that might influence your thoughts?

- Are there any 'shoulds' or 'musts' in your rule book?

Feelings

 Feelings, or emotions, are a normal part of life and part of what makes us human. Some can be really positive and enjoyable – such as feeling happy, excited or proud – but others can feel negative, like anxiety, sadness, disgust or shame. Sometimes we experience a mix of emotions: we might enjoy eating a slice of cake, but then feel guilty and worried about gaining weight. Sometimes we just feel numb. Like Jen, the highs and lows of different feelings can seem like an emotional roller coaster.

It can often feel really difficult to make sense of why we feel a particular way. However, the feelings we experience tend to follow logically from the thoughts that we have. When Jen imagined winning the tennis match (positive thought), she felt elated and happy (positive emotion). But when she thought about losing at tennis (negative thought), it made her feel anxious and overwhelmed (negative emotion). It works in the other direction too: how we feel influences our thoughts. So for Jen, feeling anxious and worried increased her perception that she wouldn't be able to cope and was likely to fail.

Ask yourself:

- How do your thoughts make you feel?
- What effect do your feelings have on your thoughts?

Physical sensations

When we have strong feelings, our bodies often respond in particular ways. Imagine how your body would react if a blood-thirsty zombie was coming towards you! It's likely that your heart would start beating really fast, and your breathing would become quicker and shallower. You might notice your muscles becoming tense and have a sudden urge to go to the toilet. You might feel hot and sweaty. This is called your 'fight-flight-freeze' response and makes sense when faced with a threat because your body is preparing to take action to keep you safe. This response has evolved over many thousands of years to keep us safe from danger.

We might not encounter any zombies in our day-to-day lives, but there are lots of things that we might view as threatening to our wellbeing. Failing a test, saying the wrong thing in front of our friends or being dissatisfied with our appearance . . . all of these can activate our fight-flight-freeze response. Our bodies can feel very different depending on the emotion we are experiencing. Feeling excited can feel like a milder version of feeling scared, while feeling sad can make our bodies feel heavy, tired and lacking energy. You might feel warm and relaxed when you feel calm. When Jen felt sad and anxious about her tennis match, her body felt sick, tense and lacking energy.

Ask yourself:

• What do you notice in your body when you feel happy, sad or anxious?

Behaviours

The thoughts we have and the way we feel can affect our behaviour. If that zombie was coming towards you, bopping it on the head, running away as fast as you can or freezing and hoping that it doesn't notice you would be very sensible courses of action if you want to survive. Our behaviours tend to be logically connected to our thoughts and feelings and are usually our best attempt to cope with the situation we are faced with.

For example, when Jen feels anxious about her performance in tennis and has thoughts about losing the match because she is too heavy, she responds by training even harder to improve her fitness and eating less to try and lose weight. She stops seeing her friend Zoe so regularly and spends all her free time working out. Jen feels tired and sluggish when she wakes up in the morning, which makes her want to stay in bed. Jen's behaviour makes sense because she is responding to her thoughts and to how she feels: by dieting and exercising more, she is trying to improve her tennis performance and prevent her worries about losing coming true. It might seem obvious to us that dieting and training so hard is likely to make Jen's performance worse, but Jen doesn't see it this way because she really believes that her thoughts are true.

When we're faced with situations that trigger negative thoughts and feelings, our behavioural responses tend to follow one of the following strategies:

Avoid We might go out of our way to avoid situations that trigger negative thoughts and feelings to prevent the possibility of our worry coming true. If Jen feels worried about playing badly, she might avoid entering any tennis tournaments so as not to lose any matches. Avoidance can also happen when we feel sad, tired, or are struggling to feel motivated.

Escape If we're already in the situation, we might try and leave as quickly as we can. If her opponent is in the lead, Jen might try to cut her losses and quit the match rather than risk failure.

Use safety behaviours These are behaviours that we do to try and prevent our worries coming true or to help us to cope in difficult situations. Jen's tendency to train excessively hard without taking any breaks is an example of a safety behaviour as it helps her to cope with her worry about losing and to try and reduce the likelihood of it coming true.

How we behave can also influence our thoughts and feelings. So, while avoiding the tennis tournament might be driven by Jen's worry about losing, it's very likely that she would view dropping out as a sign of failure too.

Ask yourself:

- How do you behave when you feel happy, sad or
  anxious?

Putting it all together: vicious and virtuous cycles

As we have discovered, our thoughts, feelings, sensations and behaviours are all part of how we respond to different situations. What we think about a situation affects how we feel (our emotions and sensations) and what we do (our behaviour). Each part is connected and influences the other parts, as shown in the diagram opposite.

The problem is that our reactions can often trap us into an unhelpful cycle of responding. Our responses might seem helpful in the short term, but they often don't solve the problem completely, and can create additional problems. For example, it will be difficult for Jen to keep restricting her diet and training so hard all the time; following such a strict regime may result in her feeling even more exhausted and lacking in energy, which might then make her performance in tennis even worse – the very thing that she is trying to prevent. When Jen feels tired and sluggish in the mornings and doesn't want to get out of bed because she is so exhausted, it triggers further negative thoughts: *'I am lazy. I will never achieve anything'*. Her thoughts, feelings, sensations

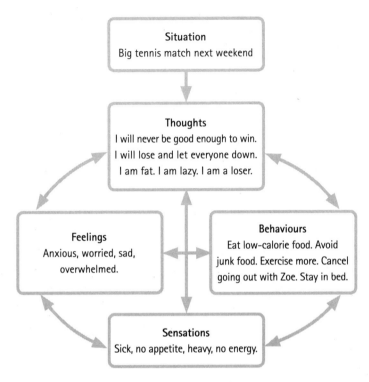

Jen's cycle of thoughts, feelings, sensations and behaviours

and behaviours have created a vicious cycle that can make everything seem worse and keep her stuck in an unhelpful cycle of responding.

The good news is that, because our thoughts, feelings, sensations and behaviours are all connected, we can break out of the cycle by learning how to change any part of our response system. Developing more helpful thoughts, changing our behaviours, and learning to cope with difficult feelings and sensations can transform the vicious cycle to a more positive virtuous one. There are lots of ways to do this, and throughout the book we will be showing you how.

Ask yourself:

- When you feel sad or worried, how do you behave?

- Does the way you behave make the problem better, worse or stay the same?

Facts, opinions and different perspectives

One afternoon after school, Jen goes to her friend Zoe's house to do homework. The pair are sitting at the kitchen table working on some science problems. Zoe's mum puts a plate of biscuits on the table. Zoe enthusiastically reaches for one, starts eating and carries on calmly with her homework. Jen starts to feel very anxious. She pushes the plate far away but keeps looking at the biscuits and can't concentrate on her work.

Jen and Zoe are in the same situation, but why are their reactions so different? The key is that they have different thoughts about the plate of biscuits. Zoe thinks, *'Oh yum! I love biscuits!'*, and so feels happy and eats one. Jen, on the other hand, experiences a stream of negative thoughts: *'I really want one, but biscuits are so bad for you. If I have one, it will make me fat. If I put on weight, my tennis will get worse, and my coach and Dad will be disappointed with me'*. Given Jen's thoughts, it makes sense that she feels very anxious and pushes the plate away. We can map out Jen and Zoe's responses in the cycles below.

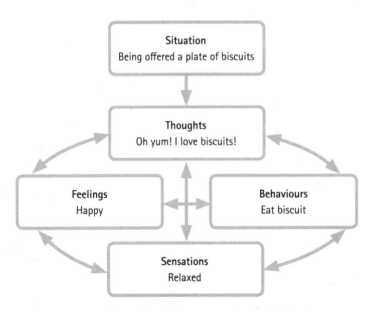

Zoe's cycle of thoughts, feelings, sensations and behaviours

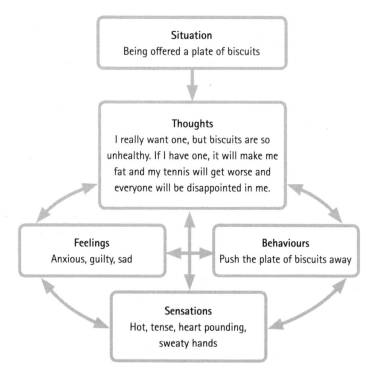

Jen's cycle of thoughts, feelings, sensations and behaviours

This example shows us that different people can have different perspectives about the same situation, and that those different perspectives lead to different emotional, physical and behavioural responses. The important thing to remember is that Jen and Zoe's thoughts tell us about their *opinions* about the plate of biscuits, but their thoughts are not *facts*. When we treat our thoughts as facts, we tend to assume that they are true and do not question them. But often our thoughts are only our opinions about what is going on, which means that there might be another way of thinking about the situation. This is the key to breaking out of the vicious cycle trap.

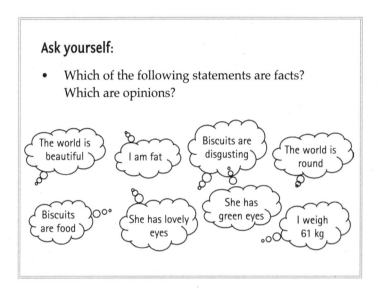

Ask yourself:

- Which of the following statements are facts? Which are opinions?

As you go through this book, you may start to notice how your thoughts, feelings, sensations and behaviours link together. Learning to notice these four response systems can help you to make sense of difficult situations. Perhaps you sometimes find yourself trapped in a vicious cycle like Jen? The good news is that once you start to identify your vicious cycles, you can also learn how to exit them and create more positive virtuous cycles.

Summary

- When we encounter a situation, four response systems are activated: our thoughts, feelings, physical sensations and behaviours.

- Our thoughts have a particularly important role because they influence how we feel, how our body responds and how we behave. Our feelings, sensations and behaviours can also influence our thoughts.

- It's important to remember that thoughts are just opinions, not facts.

- Because different people can have different thoughts, or opinions, about the same situation, their feelings, sensations and behavioural responses will be different.

- Because our thoughts, feelings, sensations and behaviours link together, sometimes we can get trapped in vicious cycles of responding that can keep problems going.

- Noticing your own thoughts, feelings, body symptoms and behaviours is the first step towards learning how to exit the vicious cycle.

Chapter 3

What Is Healthy Eating?

Aisha

'Coming Mum . . .' I reply when Mum calls me down to dinner. I wish our home was more like my friends' – Ella eats such colourful salads and makes her own meals, Chloe gets to eat in front of the TV, Zoe often has a takeaway or eats out on her way home from sport.

My mum and dad insist we all eat at the table and Mum spends hours making dinner every evening. I like my mum's cooking, but it is quite heavy and rich.

My parents are a bit overweight, and I don't want to look like them when I'm older. I'm also embarrassed that the way we eat is so different from other families. We have to leave our phones upstairs during dinner and the meal seems to take forever.

I worry about being so different from my friends. Is my mum's cooking healthy? Are the portions too big? What should I be eating?

What this chapter will cover:

- Why nutrition is so important for teenagers.
- What teenagers need to be healthy and strong and grow to their full potential.
- Social eating.
- Fuelling sports.
- Food fads.
- Impact of poor nutrition.
- What is normal eating?

Ask yourself:

Before reading this chapter, think about what you ate yesterday.

- Who were you with?
- Where did you eat?
- How did you feel?

Think about the last week.

- Were there days that were very different, and if so, why?

We will ask you to think about similar questions at the end of this chapter.

Why is nutrition important for teenagers?

In the teenage years your metabolism (the chemical changes that convert food into energy) is the fastest it will be for the rest of your life. Energy is needed for this metabolism in the form of food. If we don't eat well in the teenage years, growth and development will be stunted. Our growing brains need up to a quarter of the oxygen we breathe and a huge amount of energy to grow and thrive.

What do our bodies do with the energy that comes from our food?

Basal metabolic rate (BMR)

This is the rate of energy our body uses just to stay alive – to breathe, to maintain our body temperature, keep our hearts beating, build new cells and ensure our brains are working. We need this energy from our food even if we stay in bed and don't move at all. How much energy we use (BMR) varies depending on our age, gender and the amount of muscle we have.

If we don't eat enough our BMR can slow down by up to 30 per cent to try and keep us alive. When we eat well our BMR will speed up so our body can function fully.

The body has a very clever process for storing energy and then using it when needed. The food we eat is converted into energy (called glycogen) that can be stored in the liver and muscles (this process is known as 'anabolism').

When we need energy, these compounds are broken down to release the energy (known as 'catabolism'). Most of our energy comes from carbohydrates in our diet (more about these later). If we are short of carbohydrates the body can get energy from protein, for example from muscle fibre – which is why people who don't eat enough often notice their muscles have become smaller.

The brain needs lots of energy to function – it uses up to 20 per cent of the energy that comes from our food, even though it makes up less than 10 per cent of our body weight. Teenage brains in particular use a lot of energy as there is considerable brain growth and development during the teenage years.

BMR is faster in teenagers than in older people and accounts (depending on activity levels) for up to 70 per cent of the energy used. In very active teenagers it can be a smaller percentage – but more about this later.

Thermal effect of food

When we eat, our metabolism speeds up as our body needs to use energy to digest, absorb and store some of the nutrition we have taken in. Up to 10 per cent of the energy we take in is used in this way.

Physical activity

This is the most variable part of how energy is used by our bodies. As a teenager, you are likely to be quite active and busy – getting to and from school, carrying bags of books, moving between lessons as well as doing specific sports and activities. Some teenagers do a lot of sport and can have high energy needs. It is particularly important to make sure you are fuelling your sport sufficiently if you want to have energy to get through games and matches and to avoid injuries to your muscles, tendons and bones.

Energy for growth and development

During the teenage years our requirements for growth are high. Girls do most of their growing between the ages of eleven and fourteen, and boys between the ages of thirteen and sixteen, but it can happen earlier or later. Growing is not always even – it is normal to gain some weight to store energy for growth in height. It is also quite normal to feel starvingly hungry before and during a growth spurt.

When we grow, we can become a bit clumsier and may sometimes struggle a bit with sport. For some young people it is hard to feel like you have less control over your body, but keep reminding yourself that everybody (and everyone's body) is unique, and that we all grow and develop differently.

When a teenager goes through a growth spurt, the body needs lots of energy, so you can feel very hungry. Having good nutrition helps to fuel the growth and development of the body in puberty, but many teenagers worry about their weight and changes in appearance. It is important to talk to an adult if you have worries about this.

I arrange my beautiful colourful salad and try another photograph. I make sure there isn't anybody in the background and that the photograph looks just right. I try another photograph from a different angle to see if that looks better. I quickly check whether this would fit in with my favourite online influencers or not. I worry that there is too much brown rice, or how I should slice the chicken on my plate.

My thoughts are interrupted by Mum's nagging: 'Ella – stop playing with your food and eat it. And take a bit more rice – you've done lots of dance today.'

Ella

I ignore her – she is so irritating and annoying – what does she know anyway? – and she is always on a diet and sometimes she doesn't even eat rice.

I choose a picture and post it on my feed, tagging it with #healthyeating and #superfoods and #balletdiet. I feel proud of how healthily I eat and smile when my phone starts pinging notifications when everybody starts liking my post.

What do teenagers need?

The internet and social media are full of advice about what and how we should eat. Fashions about food also change. Food is sometimes labelled as 'good', 'bad', 'healthy' or 'unhealthy', which can be confusing for teenagers who are struggling to work out the right things to eat.

Aisha feels her family eat differently from her friends. Ella is heavily influenced by her social media feeds, and makes her food choices based on this. She wants her friends to see that what she is eating is 'healthy' – but is it?

Every teenager is different – but there are some basic important principles.

Regular eating

We need to eat regular meals during the day which include the basic food groups: proteins, carbohydrates and fats, plus fruit or vegetables. It goes without saying that it is a good idea to try and hit at least five portions of fruit and vegetables a day.

We know that skipping meals can make anybody (but especially teenagers) a bit grumpy and hungry ('hangry'), so try to make sure that you don't go for too long without eating. Up to a third of teenagers skip breakfast and this age group finds it much harder to get up in the morning in time (see Chapter 6 for more on teenage sleep patterns).

We also know if we eat too much of one food type, we can miss out on other important foods, so variety is important. Ella might be having too much salad on her plate and could therefore miss out on protein, fats and carbs which her body needs to fuel her activities, like dancing.

Energy requirements

Energy requirements vary from person to person, so it is impossible to say what an average teenager needs. The seven young people we have spoken about would all need different snacks, different lunches, different drinks and different dinners. The important thing during the teenage years is to understand when your body is hungry and to eat appropriately.

Carbohydrates (or 'carbs')

Examples of food high in carbohydrates include all different types of bread (including pitta, bread rolls, etc.), pasta, rice, cereals, oats, quinoa, couscous, potatoes, sweet potatoes, biscuits, cakes, honey, jam, sweets and sugary drinks.

Carbohydrates are one of the three main sources of energy in our diets (macronutrients) and are broken down by digestion into glucose, which is absorbed, transported around our body and used as an energy source. Glycaemic index (GI) is a measure of how fast or slow a type of carbohydrate is digested – the lower the GI number, the more slowly it enters our bloodstream, and the higher the number, the more quickly it is digested and absorbed.

Examples of high GI foods include sugary drinks and snacks, white bread, cakes and biscuits, all of which are easily and quickly absorbed by the body. Examples of low GI foods are whole-grain foods, some fruits, oats and porridge. The foods we eat at the same time as carbohydrates (like fats and proteins) also influence how quickly the carbohydrate is digested and absorbed.

We should eat some low GI foods for a longer steadier supply of energy, but at times a high GI food can give a quick energy boost which could be important during, for example, a sports event or school break time.

Carbohydrates are the body's preferred and most efficient source of energy, especially providing fuel for muscles and brains. They are also considered to be 'protein sparing' – carbohydrates protect muscle from being broken down. If we don't eat enough, our body will break down muscles to provide a source of energy to keep functioning. Carbohydrates also help our bodies absorb water and encourage healthy bacteria in our bowels. They also increase the production of serotonin – a chemical in our brains that helps with mood, appetite and sleep.

Carbohydrates provide the energy for us to learn and play and enjoy ourselves and sleep well. The amount needed by a teenager varies according to age, growth spurts and activity levels. Having insufficient carbohydrates can make us moody, irritable and low on energy. It can also make it hard to focus and learn and can cause poor sleep.

Fibre is a type of carbohydrate that our bodies can't digest or use for energy but is important to keep our bowels healthy.

Carbohydrate intake should be around 50 per cent of your daily food intake. The exact amount depends on whether you are biologically male or female, whether or not you are having a growth spurt and how active you are.

Fats

We obtain fats from many different food sources: for example, cooking oils, salad dressings, nuts, seeds, milk and dairy products (or plant-based dairy alternatives), cakes, biscuits, olives, avocados, cheese, meats, some fish and chocolate.

Fats are another essential macronutrient in our diets – we all need fats to provide an energy source that our bodies can use if needed. Fat provides protection for our internal organs and is an essential part of every cell in our body. Fats are used for making hormones and play an important role in our brains. White matter, which insulates our brain cells, consists of fat and protein combined – 60 per cent of our brain's matter is fat. Without enough dietary fat we are unable to absorb some vitamins (Vitamins A, D, E, K) which are essential for healthy hair, skin and eyes.

Fats make our food taste good but also help us feel full after a meal and they slow down the release of energy into our blood. Fats and oils are an important part of cooking and baking.

In a healthy teenage diet 25–35 per cent of the overall energy intake will come from a wide variety of different sources of fats and oils.

Proteins

About half a teenager's body weight is protein, and the amount needed depends on height, weight and activity levels. Protein helps maintain, repair and build healthy muscle and bone and is needed for growth and development. It helps build hair, nails, skin and heal wounds. Proteins are made of strings of amino acids and essential amino acids which can't be made by the body and therefore need to come from the food we eat.

Animal sources high in protein include meat, chicken, fish, eggs, milk, cheese, yoghurt and other foods made from milk. Plant sources of protein include soya, peas, beans, lentils, tofu and other meat substitutes, dahl, chickpeas, baked beans, mycoproteins (for example Quorn), nuts and seeds, as well as some plant-based milks, yoghurt and cheese (some of these may only contain small amounts of protein). Some plant-based proteins are low in some amino acids but by having variety it is possible to take in enough complete protein. Good combinations include, for example, lentils and rice, or peanut butter on toast, both of which provide the perfect balance of amino acids.

Most people in the Western world eat more protein than their bodies need, but those following a plant-based diet need to make sure they are getting enough protein. Some teenagers use protein shakes and supplements in the hope of becoming more muscular. However, having too much protein doesn't increase muscle but can cause the kidneys to overwork, which can be dangerous.

Fruit and vegetables

Teenagers should aim for at least five portions of fruit and vegetables per day. Fruit and vegetables provide many essential vitamins, minerals and fibre as well as antioxidants which protect your body from all sorts of diseases later in life. It is estimated that less than a third of teenagers eat enough fruit and vegetables.

Research shows that if fruit and vegetables are regularly eaten as part of your family's diet, and you like these foods, you are more likely to eat them regularly. It helps if they are easy to access (school dinners, vending machines, nearby shops). However, teenagers are often busy, buying food in a hurry, and the importance of eating enough fruit and vegetables can be the last thing on their mind.

If you try to include some fruit or vegetables at every meal you are more likely to meet your daily requirements. If you haven't eaten a particular food for a long time, you might have forgotten how much you like it – do try foods you might not have had for a while.

Dried fruit, smoothies, tinned fruit, frozen fruit, fruit juice, soups, frozen vegetables and tinned vegetables can all help you to meet your daily requirements.

Check it out: Facts about fruit and vegetables

- Pumpkins and tomatoes are fruits, as are peppers, cucumbers, aubergines, olives and green beans.

- Strawberries are not a berry; examples of berries include tomatoes, avocados, kiwi fruit, cucumbers, aubergines and bananas. Strawberries are sometimes called 'false fruit' or an 'aggregate fruit' and are actually made up of many tiny different fruits.

- Not all oranges are orange. Same with carrots!

- The first vegetable grown in space was a potato; potatoes (while technically a vegetable) are counted as one of your daily portions of carbohydrate.

Vitamins and minerals

It is particularly important in the teenage years to make sure that you get enough vitamins and minerals for the body to function, grow and develop (there are comprehensive lists covering the role of different vitamins and minerals in the resources section at the end of the book). It is common for teenagers to be short on Vitamin D, calcium and iron.

Vitamin D Vitamin D contributes to the growth of strong healthy bones as well as a healthy immune system (the system that fights disease) and a well-functioning heart.

Although Vitamin D is found in some foods such as oily fish, the main way we get Vitamin D is through the action of UV sunlight on our skin, especially during summer when the sun is strong. So, in the winter months (or in the summer if you don't go outside much) it is easy for teenagers to become low in Vitamin D.

Calcium During the teenage years, especially when growing rapidly, there is a need for plenty of calcium to build strong and healthy bones – the recommended calcium intake is higher than for any other age group. In addition to increasing height, bones also become stronger during the teenage years. Only about half of British teenagers get enough calcium. Rich sources of calcium are dairy products, some plant-based milks with calcium added, soya products and leafy green vegetables. If you don't drink milk, it is hard to meet your calcium requirements without eating lots of other foods containing calcium. You might not like the taste or smell of milk, but how about drinking flavoured milk with a straw (maybe in a container with a lid), having smoothies made with milk or yoghurt, lattes, chai tea and other interesting drinks (but watch out that you don't have too much caffeine as it causes other problems). Some teenagers like yoghurts, mousses, custards, cheese, cheese sauces and yoghurt drinks. Cereal with milk, overnight oats (porridge oats soaked in milk overnight), porridge made with milk or yoghurt can be useful at any time!

Iron This is another important mineral needed to release energy from cells, to transport oxygen about the body and to maintain a healthy immune system. Many enzymes in our body require iron to function well. Lack of iron can cause tiredness, poor concentration and weakness. The two main types of iron are 'haem iron' which our bodies absorb easily and comes from animal products (such as red meat, chicken) and 'non-haem iron' which comes from fortified cereals, dried fruit and leafy green vegetables, and which is harder for our bodies to absorb. Many teenagers – especially girls – can be iron deficient and not be aware of this.

Fluids

Up to two-thirds of our body is made up of water, and having enough body water is essential in keeping us alive. Blood is an important liquid which carries oxygen to, and waste from, our cells. Kidneys need fluid to flush out waste. We also need enough fluid to maintain a stable blood pressure (so we don't get dizzy when we stand up), to manage body temperature (we cool ourselves by sweating) and to keep our digestion healthy. We need to drink enough fluid to maintain these functions.

Fluid requirements vary depending on activity, how hot it is, genetics and many other things. In general – if you are thirsty and your mouth feels dry, you need to have something to drink. Having a bottle of fluid with you when you are out and about can be a helpful reminder.

Variety is important, but some of what you drink should be water. Fizzy drinks can have poor nutritional value and are not great for your teeth, as well as causing you to feel bloated, so are better as an occasional treat.

Many drinks (such as coffee, colas and energy drinks) contain caffeine, a type of drug known as a 'stimulant' – meaning it gives people the feeling of an energy boost. However, it can cause restlessness, nervousness and a racing or irregular heartbeat, especially in children and teenagers. Studies suggest that it can affect a teen's concentration and ability to sleep which may potentially slow down brain development. It is recommended that teenagers should not have more than the equivalent of one cup of coffee per day. Energy drinks can contain large amounts of caffeine and some teenagers have become unwell from having too much caffeine.

Avoiding 'hanger'

'Hanger' is a word used to describe when you are feeling grumpy, irritable and hungry. If you go for too long without eating, hanger is quite common – not just in teenagers but in everyone. Too long is anything longer than three to four hours! This is because our brains and bodies work best when we regularly get energy.

It is quite normal as a teenager to feel hungry between meals. As long are you are having all your important food groups and getting all the nutrients you need from your meals, then snacks can serve as an additional source of energy, particularly on days when you are physically active. It is important to listen to your body and recognise when you need food and to eat a range of different foods that you enjoy.

Social eating

Food should be fun and enjoyable. Sometimes we might eat more than we need (at Christmas or a birthday party), but in general these balance with other times when we eat less so that, overall, we eat consistently. Teenagers (and some adults) are unlikely to have to compensate for times when they eat more because they are using up energy all the time. Nutritional requirements vary between teenagers, and every family has different habits around food – there is no right way to eat.

We learn a lot about celebrations and customs from our families and friends and this brings people closer together and can help us feel like we belong.

Worries about weight

We know that many teenagers worry about weight and try to avoid particular foods, or food groups, or even go on a diet to lose weight. Some young people use BMI calculators to work out if their weight is healthy. BMI stands for Body Mass Index and gives you a value based on combined weight and height. However, it can be misleading as it varies depending on age, ethnicity and how muscular you are.

Remember this is a time in your life when you are growing and developing, and energy requirements are high. Food is an essential source of energy and nutrients. Avoiding foods or dieting can have an adverse impact on the way your body and brain develop.

There are studies which look at teenagers who diet, and these show some worrying trends. Teenagers who go on a diet tend to have lower mood and increased anxiety; they are more likely to develop an eating disorder; and are more likely to end up with out-of-control episodes of binge-eating. Dieting frequently can lead to patterns where teenagers avoid eating for long periods of time (becoming very grumpy, and less able to learn), followed by out-of-control binges; and this can lead to unintended weight gain.

We know that teenagers often talk about dieting, and sometimes it can be unfashionable to eat when at school; it can be hard if others around you are skipping meals.

If you have developed an unhealthy pattern of dieting it can be hard to break out of this. You may have got into a pattern of fighting your body and not allowing yourself certain foods. See Chapter 7 for some ideas on how to manage worries about weight and eating and how to break the diet cycle.

How our feelings can affect how we eat

Everybody has a bad or upsetting day sometimes. Some teenagers might not feel like eating if they are really upset; others can feel they are about to be sick when they are very worried about something. Others, when they're upset, will comfort themselves with food to feel happier.

If this is something that happens very occasionally, and only for a short period of time, it might not affect your physical health, but if it is happening really often it will be important to get some help. For more information around some ways of managing stressful periods look at Chapter 6 and Chapter 7.

Fuelling sport

Wes

Just completed another hard session at the gym. I think I'm starting to see some results, although I have a way to go before I'll be happy with how I look. I ache all over, but feel good about how hard I've worked out. I'm craving chocolate but that won't help me build any muscle, so I'll have one of the muscle gain shakes. I really want to excel at rugby and hope I can get into the academy team and also hopefully (one day) play for my uni.

Mum arrives and as usual she has to nag about the cost of the shakes and has a go at me about how much I'm spending on them. I really want to get this right and I don't think she understands me.

Sports and exercise can use up a lot of additional energy. It is important to fuel your body with carbohydrates both before and after sport to give you the energy needed for your muscles. This helps you to grow and develop, become stronger and avoid injuries. It is also important to drink enough fluid.

There can be lots of confusing information online, and it is hard to work out the right thing to do. There are many 'post-workout' sports drinks which promise to help build muscle, but these can be expensive. In general, any carbohydrates and proteins can help restore energy and repair muscle. This can vary from a cereal bar and a milky drink to something like a tuna sandwich or a bagel with peanut butter and a glass of milk.

Although taking part in sports is healthy for teenagers, some (especially boys) may worry about not gaining enough muscle or gaining too much muscle. It is important to make sure that taking part in sports stays fun but – as well – remembering that looking a particular way does not always make you faster and stronger.

Finally, muscle weighs more than any other body tissue so if you are building muscle or doing a lot of sport you may well notice that your weight increases. So, it is important to remember the reason behind this and not get hung up on measurements like your weight.

Look at Chapter 13 for more information about exercise and activity. Chapter 14 focuses on common problems in boys, including worries around muscle development.

Food fads

There is a lot of information out there referring to 'good foods' and 'bad foods' and 'healthy foods' and 'unhealthy foods'. However, in general, there are no good foods or bad foods. Variety is key: make sure you eat regularly, get a balance of all your nutrients, and eat foods that you enjoy.

What is healthy eating?

Is it healthy to spend a lot of time worrying about what you should eat, or could it be better to eat in a fun and flexible way, making sure you have variety and eat regularly?

Some teenagers decide to become vegetarian or vegan or follow other particular ways of eating, which may be due to the influence of friends, social media or other family members. Modern society would have you believe that who you are as a person is closely related to how you eat, and that your food choices say a lot about you. Sometimes we can be tempted to make food choices to fit in with our friends, or because one way of eating is seen as superior or fashionable. We are bombarded by so many messages about how we should eat that it can be difficult to work out what to do for the best.

It is important to think carefully about the reasons for your choices. Have conversations with your family about whether they can support you to stay healthy while following a particular way of eating. If you are thinking about making a big change, for example, becoming vegetarian or vegan, it will take a bit of planning and will require family support. It is particularly hard if you become vegan as a teenager to ensure that you have all the nutrients you need to meet your energy needs and grow and develop. It is also important to be honest with yourself about your reasons for changing: is this an ethical choice, or is it to fit in with your friends or to try and lose weight?

To find out more about how social media can influence us, have a look at Chapter 12.

What might be a consequence of poor nutrition?

Planning and organising food can be low down on a teenager's list of priorities. Sometimes teenagers will just grab what they can get hold of (so long as it doesn't cost too much). You might eat erratically, not necessarily having a balanced diet yet feel 'just fine' – and find all this dietary advice annoying.

Some teenagers with poor nutrition somehow manage to grow and get by, even though they may be lacking in energy and feel stressed. However, if you don't have enough overall nutrition, you may not reach your full height potential, or you may end up with weaker bones and less muscle.

Improving nutrition in adolescence avoids this becoming a long-term problem and affecting your health in adult life.

When you're not eating regularly or getting everything your body needs, this has an adverse effect on your mood, irritability, decision-making, learning, energy levels, sleep, friendships and ability to have fun.

If you are an athlete and trying to do well at sport, not eating regularly can impair your performance, and you are also at higher risk of being injured.

Ask yourself:

- Am I eating the way I do because of my own beliefs or because of how my friends might see me?

- Am I eating the way I do to fit in with my friends or because I think it is healthier?

- Am I choosing food because I am worried about my appearance or about my weight?

- What are the advantages of eating in this way?

- What might be the disadvantages of eating in this way?

- Am I sometimes skipping meals and snacks because I'm struggling to be organised, and is there a way I can get into better habits?

Ask yourself:

Have a look at what you wrote before reading this chapter.

- How would you rate your current way of eating?

- Are you eating a balance of food groups and nutrients?

- Is there anything that you feel that you might want to change or do differently?

- Is there one change you would like to make in how you eat and drink in order to be healthier?

Check it out: Normal eating

- Eating regularly and not going too long without food.

- Sometimes you might eat more than on other days, e.g. at celebrations and parties.

- Eating food that you enjoy.

- Saving some of your favourite food to make it last longer.

- Sometimes eating differently because of being unwell (for short periods only).

- Eating a wide variety of foods without feeling guilty.

- Eating in a flexible way which fits in with your work and social life.

- Eating socially with friends.

- Not having food rules.

Summary

- Teenagers need to have enough energy in their daily food intake to grow and develop normally.

- Variety is important to make sure you are getting enough of all the main nutrients.

- Although there are common principles that we need to follow (e.g. having enough carbohydrates, fats, proteins, vitamins and minerals), there is no right way of eating.

- The amount of energy teenagers need is individual and depends on growth, activity and many other factors, so it is important to understand when you are hungry and to listen to your body.

- Getting enough fluids, particularly water, is important to help various body systems function.

- Social eating is important, and many celebrations that bring people closer involve a particular way of eating.

- There is a lot of misinformation around about 'good' or 'bad' foods or particular ways of eating.

Chapter 4

Eating Difficulties in the Teenage Years

I can't stop thinking about calories. I work out how many calories there are in every meal just to make sure that I don't go over my limit. I worry about the next meal, and I weigh myself several times a day just to make sure I am not putting on weight. I can't stop looking in the mirror to check the areas of my body that I don't like.

Jen

But I still feel really anxious, and everything is more difficult than it used to be. My school grades have begun to drop, and my tennis coach told me that my game has deteriorated, and that I will have to put in more practice. I am gutted by this. I am working late into the evening to try and improve my grades and I now stay behind at tennis club after the others have gone to practise my strokes. I find it really hard to concentrate and just have no energy. I often wake up at night and find it really difficult to go back to sleep. Everything is going wrong.

Chloe

Things are so difficult at home with my parents arguing all the time. I don't want to spend time with them so I creep up to my bedroom where I have a stash of biscuits. I feel really upset and eat all the biscuits really quickly and then feel so guilty. I will skip the evening meal. It is no fun anyway having a meal when my parents are just complaining at each other and at me.

What this chapter will cover:

- Food in the teenage years.

- What are eating difficulties and eating disorders?

- What are the consequences of eating disorders?

- How do eating disorders start?

- Who is at risk of developing an eating disorder?

- Spotting the signs of an eating disorder developing.

- What you can do about it.

You may be thinking: what sort of eating difficulties do teenagers get into, and how does this relate to eating disorders?

How do you know if you have an eating disorder? Does Jen have an eating disorder? In this chapter we will look at different types of eating difficulties and eating disorders, and how poor eating might adversely affect a teenager's health and wellbeing. We will also look at how eating disorders start, who is at risk, and how to spot an eating disorder developing. But, before we do that, let's think about why food is so important in the teenage years.

Why food is important in the teenage years

As previously discussed, the teenage years are a key time for growth and development. Young people increase in height and weight, develop their muscles, lay down a healthy strong bone structure, increase their brain capacity and go through the changes of puberty. All these processes need fuel to make them happen – and the fuel is the food we eat.

Our health and wellbeing depend on regular eating; if we don't eat regularly we can start feeling a lack of energy and a drop in mood, just like Jen. In addition, the normal processes of development and growth are put on hold while the body tries to survive. It's a bit like your phone or device going into 'power-saving mode' when it's running out of battery. You may notice that the processing is slower, and some apps may not work at all until it is properly charged. Your body is exactly the same: if you don't eat enough, it won't work effectively.

Getting back on track with growth and development requires a return to regular eating with a healthy balance of the different food groups, vitamins and minerals (there's lots of information in Chapter 3 about healthy eating in adolescence).

Eating difficulties and eating disorders

Eating difficulties are common in the teenage years and can present in lots of different ways. They can creep up gradually and not be noticed initially; they may be quite minor and quickly resolved; they can also become more serious and develop into a diagnosable eating disorder.

So why do eating difficulties occur? Sometimes, just having a *physical illness*, when you go off your food, can make it difficult to eat after you recover. If you don't feel like eating, check out your physical health. For example, poor appetite can be a sign of anaemia (when the number of red blood cells in the body is too low), a gut problem or some other illness that needs attention.

It may be that you are eating less, or eating more, because you are *anxious* or *worried*. Some people eat more when they are stressed, and others eat less. It is difficult to eat if you are really anxious about something. You might also notice your heart beating fast, feeling sick, sweating or breathing more quickly.

Alternatively, you may be *depressed*, which can cause a loss of appetite, resulting in weight loss. Other signs of depression are low mood, difficulty in sleeping, failure to find enjoyment in usual activities, withdrawal from friends or family and loss of concentration. Some young people also have thoughts of harming themselves when they feel really depressed.

Almost 10 per cent of young people suffer depression at some stage during adolescence. If you feel that you might be depressed, it is important to talk to someone you trust so that you can get some help. There are well-researched treatments that can be effective in helping young people recover from depression – this includes talking therapies such as CBT, or anti-depressant medication.

Check it out: Signs of depression

- Low mood
- Poor concentration
- Feelings of hopelessness
- Difficulty in sleeping
- Loss of interest/enjoyment in usual activities
- Irritability
- Withdrawal from friends/family
- Self-harm

Some teenagers develop a *fear of vomiting* (emetophobia) which may occur after an experience when they vomited and found it unpleasant. This can result in reluctance to eat certain foods which they believe may lead to vomiting. This can be very restricting to a young person's life as it makes eating with other people difficult. It can also lead to a loss of weight and development of an eating disorder.

Another specific eating difficulty which can be very serious is *Avoidant Restrictive Food Intake Disorder* (ARFID). This is where a young person avoids certain foods, such as crusts of bread or green vegetables, or restricts the amount they eat. As a result they can get into trouble with their health because of poor nutrition. This can be due to anxiety or difficult thoughts about food, or disliking the sensation or texture of certain foods, rather than a concern about weight. There is often a long-standing history of being picky with food and avoiding food of certain colours or textures. Take Jake, for example: he has always been fussy about his food and finds hard textures difficult to manage. Teenagers who have this problem may need professional help to make sure they are getting the nutrition they need.

For some young people, eating patterns change because they start to feel worried about their weight, shape and size. They might start to eat a bit less, exclude certain foods from their diet, or develop rigid rules around eating, such as counting calories. Controlling your food intake can also be a way of coping with distress. The problem is that these habits can settle in, which can take you down the path of an eating disorder.

This diagram summarises some of the main causes of eating difficulties:

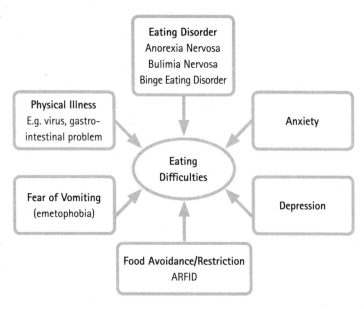

Eating difficulties can be caused by lots of different things

So what exactly are eating disorders? There are three main types: anorexia nervosa, bulimia nervosa and binge eating disorder.

Anorexia nervosa Teenagers become concerned about their weight and shape and make continued efforts to lose weight even when they are very thin, and people around them are worried. Losing weight quickly, even if you are still in the healthy weight range, can be a worrying sign. In some females, periods can stop (or not start) due to the loss of weight. Males may stop growing in height and fail to go into puberty. As weight drops further, they can become more and more preoccupied with losing weight until it starts to take over their life.

It looks like Jen may be in the early stages of anorexia nervosa. She worries about her weight and is restricting her diet, constantly weighing herself, counting calories and looking at herself in the mirror a lot.

Anorexia nervosa commonly starts in the mid-teens but can occur even earlier. Once it has taken hold, it can feel like it has a life of its own. Losing weight feels like an achievement, and keeps the anorexia happy. At other times the anorexia can feel like a punishing bully, telling you that you are not trying hard enough and must do better.

Bulimia nervosa This generally starts in older teens but can develop earlier. There are similar worries about weight and shape and the young person starts by restricting food and eating (sometimes including a cycle of fasting) but, at some point, can lose control and eat a huge amount of food in a short time: bingeing. Young people often feel really guilty and ashamed about what they have eaten in a binge, and so may attempt to get rid of it by vomiting (purging) or over-exercising. This cycle then starts again, and it can be hard to stop. People with bulimia nervosa usually have a normal weight.

It looks like Chloe may be developing the early signs of bulimia nervosa as she restricts her food intake, binges secretly and then tries to make up for what she has eaten by skipping meals or exercising.

Binge eating disorder This is a cycle of restricting intake then bingeing, but without vomiting, so weight gradually increases.

Although we talk about three different eating disorders, the distinction between them is not necessarily clear-cut. People can have different eating disorders at different times in their lives. For example, someone with anorexia can develop bulimia at a later stage of life to compensate for a body seriously depleted by long-term under-eating.

Check it out: Signs of eating disorders

Anorexia nervosa

- Worries about weight and shape which take over your life

- Excessive loss of weight

- Determination to lose weight

Bulimia nervosa

- Worries about weight and shape

- Bingeing (eating a lot of food in a short space of time and feeling out of control)

- Purging the body (e.g. through vomiting, taking too many laxatives or over-exercising)

Binge eating disorder

- Worries about weight and shape

- Food restriction

- Bingeing

When you get into a pattern of eating difficulty it can become a vicious cycle, as illustrated below.

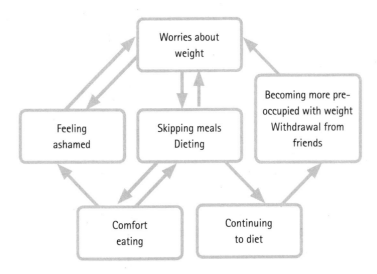

It's easy to get into a vicious cycle when you're worried about your weight and start to skip meals

How do eating disorders affect our physical and emotional health?

There are lots of different ways in which poor eating can affect our physical and emotional health. Remember we talked about the power-save mode earlier; your body needs to be charged up properly with energy in order to work well. If you are not eating sufficient fuel to charge your body, a number of things may happen.

Nutritional deficiencies

Reducing your food intake or avoiding certain foods can lead to nutritional deficiencies. We all need a healthy balanced diet so that we can function to our best ability. Food contains vitamins and minerals which are vital to our day-to-day functioning, contribute to growth and development, and boost our immune system to help us fight infection.

Impact on the body

Eating disorders can affect every organ in the body. When you are starving, your body begins to digest all your organs, taking energy from wherever it can to stay alive. Here are some of the physical problems that can occur.

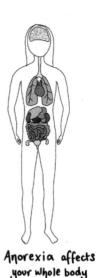

Anorexia affects your whole body

Heart If food intake is low, the heart struggles to pump the blood around the body effectively, which can lead to poor circulation, cold hands and feet, feeling dizzy or fainting and very serious heart problems. Repeated vomiting can also disrupt the functioning of the heart by causing low salts in your blood (like potassium).

Bones Healthy bone growth is impaired by low levels of calcium or lack of sex hormones. This means that your bones are more likely to break.

Skin We all need vitamins to keep our skin healthy; poor nutrition can cause dry skin and dry, thin hair.

Blood The blood cells don't develop properly, leading to anaemia, which can cause tiredness and poor concentration. You also might look paler than usual.

Gut When food intake is low the gut doesn't work as well and slows down, causing uncomfortable bloating and constipation.

Brain The brain needs lots of energy to carry out its normal tasks as well as making new neuronal connections. If there is not enough food, it is much harder to think and be creative. Scans of young people's brains show that the brain shrinks when they aren't eating enough food.

Energy levels Our bodies see food as fuel and we need fuel to do our many activities. Restricting your food can lead to a loss of energy. Purging the body can also lead to loss of energy as vital electrolytes like potassium and sodium, which are needed to keep your energy going, are lost when you vomit.

Physical symptoms can gradually creep up on you. Sometimes, young people notice that they are feeling the cold more than usual. Family or friends may notice that they are wrapping themselves up in thick jumpers and woolly socks. If you skip meals, you can feel faint or dizzy, particularly if it is a long time till your next meal. You may also experience loss of energy, poor concentration, dry skin, hair loss or low mood. If you are concerned about any of these symptoms, then it is important to see your family doctor.

Jen

> *Everything is starting to feel much harder. I get to the end of the school day and feel dizzy and exhausted. I can't concentrate on my homework and spend ages staring at my text book, but couldn't tell you what I have read or the answer to any of the questions that have been set. Mum and Dad ask if I am OK, but I just feel distant and cut off from them – like they are talking to me from far away.*
>
> *I find it really difficult to get to sleep at night, even though I am so tired. And when I do eventually get to sleep, I wake in the night and stay awake for hours.*

Our bodies need to be well nourished for us to sleep well. If we are not eating adequately, our sleep can become disrupted, and we may even find ourselves dreaming about food. Jen's disrupted sleep left her feeling very tired during the day and unable to concentrate on her schoolwork.

Young people who restrict their food intake or who have appetite loss may experience a vicious cycle which makes it hard to start eating normally again. This is partly because of the bloating that occurs when you are not eating well, which makes it uncomfortable to eat, and also the loss of appetite and low mood which make it hard to eat.

Impact on emotions

> *I notice that I am more irritable and snappy with my younger brother – I just can't stop myself but then feel really guilty afterwards. My friends have also noticed that I am quite down and really not myself at all. I am annoyed with myself for being like this, but find it really hard to change. It all came to a head when I had a huge row with my parents because I spend so much time alone in my room. I am beginning to feel really low, and nothing seems to help lift my mood.*

Not eating well can affect your mood, leading to irritability or even depression and anxiety. You may have noticed yourself that if you skip a meal it can make you irritable until you have eaten again.

Some teenagers may experience the urge to self-harm as a way of releasing unpleasant feelings. If this is happening to you, you may find it helpful to talk to an adult. Chapter 7 looks at managing stress and anxiety and there are other helpful books listed in the resource section.

The diagram on page 72 shows the vicious cycles you can get into. If you feel sad, anxious, angry or distressed, you may go off your food – and if you are not eating properly this can intensify those emotions. Some young people eat more when they have these feelings, then feel disgusted with themselves for eating so much, which can make them even more distressed.

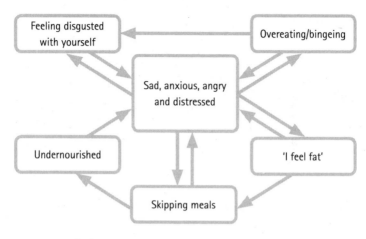

Eating or not eating can have a big effect on our feelings – and vice versa

Impact on social life

If you're feeling preoccupied by worries about eating or the need to exercise, you might find yourself withdrawing from your family and friends. Not eating enough can also leave you feeling too tired and exhausted to socialise. Going out for meals might also feel difficult, so it can be hard to join in with things that family and friends enjoy. Some people feel guilty or ashamed of their eating disorder behaviours, like bingeing and purging, which can make them want to hide away. All this can make the world feel like a very lonely place.

I can feel my energy levels dropping and I am so tired from lack of sleep. Each day is a struggle. When my friends invite me to hang out with them, I just say no. I think they are quite concerned. My best friend Zoe gets upset with me when I keep refusing to join in with anything she suggests. I think she knows there is something wrong and that I need help as she keeps trying to raise the issue with me. I just brush her off, but I know that she is just trying to help. I realise that my reaction is having an effect on our friendship, and I am beginning to think more about what she is saying.

Impact on learning

Poor eating can negatively affect the way your brain functions as well as your memory and concentration. This can make it much harder to cope with school or college.

I am beginning to notice that my school grades are starting to go down, which really upsets me. I just can't manage to get my homework done despite spending literally hours on it. I have even started to stay up late at night to try to revise for tests and have become really tired, which makes it even more difficult to concentrate during the day.

Who is at risk from eating disorders?

Check it out: Risk factors for eating disorders

- Family history of eating disorders
- Focus on eating, weight and shape in the family
- Family history of obesity
- Perfectionism
- Depression
- Being overweight
- Dieting
- Identifying as transgender or non-binary
- History of abuse

Eating disorders affect both males and females of all ages, socio-economic status and ethnic groups, whatever your body weight and shape or your sexual orientation. However, some people are more at risk than others.

Females are more likely to get eating disorders than males; significant numbers of males do develop eating disorders, but they may hide them and other people might not notice. There is an (incorrect) assumption that eating disorders are a female issue, which can create stigma and barriers to males in seeking help.

We know that eating disorders are partly genetic, so if any

relatives have had an eating disorder, it can be more likely that you will be affected. Also, living in a family where there is a lot of concern about eating, dieting and appearance can increase the chance that you will worry about these things too. It's important to say, though, that families are not to blame for disordered eating and in fact may be your best ally in getting well again.

Other factors are also significant. For example, young people who are perfectionists are vulnerable to developing eating disorders. Jen worried about her body not being perfect and so she set herself really strict standards about what she could and couldn't eat and tried hard to stick to them.

Teenagers who have low self-esteem may start to restrict their food intake to feel better about themselves, resulting in an unhealthy eating pattern. Having a history of being bullied or abused can also increase your risk.

Recent research has shown that there is a higher risk of developing an eating disorder in teenagers who identify as transgender or non-binary or those who identify as gay. Sam struggled with their gender identity and began to restrict their food as a way of dealing with the anxiety of dealing with sexual development in puberty. This is a really difficult struggle for many teenagers, because of the added difficulties around bullying, identity and self-esteem which need wider support over and above that around eating and body image.

Young people who are overweight are also at risk of developing eating problems, including binge eating or restricting their diet so that they lose weight rapidly.

A number of research studies have shown that teenagers who diet are much more likely to develop an eating disorder. Dieting is common in adolescence (about 50 per cent try dieting at some point), and most people who diet don't go on to develop an eating disorder. But if you have other risk factors, such as perfectionism or a family history of an eating disorder, then your dieting may put you at risk from developing an eating disorder.

How effective is dieting anyway?

Research shows that dieting is not an effective way of losing weight. Most people who diet tend to put the weight back on again. This cycle of losing and gaining weight can also have damaging effects on your body and emotional state.

How do eating disorders start?

Check it out: Triggers for an eating disorder

- Living in a society focused on body image
- Personal comments about weight/shape
- Stress
- Any weight loss
- Starting puberty early

As discussed earlier, in today's society we are bombarded with messages that to be happy or successful we need to have the perfect body. This can make us worry about how we look, and we can start to feel self-conscious about our eating. If you have any of the risk factors described above, you may be more likely to develop eating problems.

However, not everyone who has these risk factors develops a problem with eating. Sometimes there are specific triggers. A simple comment from a friend or relative that they have noticed some weight gain or change in shape may be enough to trigger the desire to lose weight. Alternatively, you may suffer a specific stress, such as the break-up of a relationship that makes it difficult to eat, or leads to eating more to comfort yourself.

When COVID-19 struck in early 2020 and we were in lockdown for long periods of time, lots of young people found it very difficult to cope. Some teenagers found that focusing on food and exercise helped them to feel in control during a really scary time, and helped fill the gaps where school and friends used to be. The problem was that it gave a chance for eating disorders to take hold. Research on the impact of COVID has shown that eating disorders in teenagers became more common during the pandemic and were often not detected until they had become very serious.

Something seemingly unrelated like having braces fitted on your teeth can disrupt eating for a short period and may lead to ongoing difficulties with eating.

Actually, weight loss from any cause can increase the risk of developing an eating disorder. In the 1950s an important research study (the Minnesota Starvation Experiment) was carried out in America. This involved restricting the diets of healthy male volunteers so that they lost weight, and then examining the outcome. There is no way this study would be allowed these days, but it gave lots of useful information about the effect of starvation on the body. The researchers found that the study's participants developed symptoms of eating disorders once their weight had dropped below a certain level, even though they didn't have an eating disorder to start with. These symptoms included worrying about food and weight, taking a long time to eat meals, cutting up food into small pieces, sleeping poorly and feeling bloated after meals. This shows us that weight loss can be a risk factor for developing an eating disorder.

Going into puberty early, like Chloe did, can trigger eating problems because you can feel very different from your peers.

What are the signs of an eating disorder?

There are different types of eating difficulty and they range in severity. Here are some of the thought patterns and behaviours that suggest you may be developing an eating disorder and need to take action to stop it taking hold and affecting your health and wellbeing. It is worth noting that many people with eating disorders can look healthy but actually may be extremely ill.

Thinking patterns

Negative thinking and negative mindsets
You may notice that you are preoccupied with negative thoughts about yourself and your body.

I just can't get these thoughts out of my mind. Thoughts such as 'I am fat and ugly', 'I am a failure' and 'No one likes me' seem to come out of the blue and I can't get rid of them. I wake up at night and the thoughts just go round and round my head. During the day it is hard to concentrate on school work, and my teacher keeps telling me that I seem to be daydreaming and not focusing on the lesson. I can't bring myself to tell anyone what is happening and I feel more and more isolated.

Negative thoughts are something that we all experience from time to time, but Jen was overwhelmed by them. For her it had become a mindset that was interfering with her life. It's a bit like when your internet freezes and you're stuck on the same webpage – it's difficult to think about anything else. She took a very important step in talking to her teacher about it and found it a great relief to finally share her anxieties with someone she trusted. She began to see that the thoughts she was having were making the problem worse. You can find out more about how Jen managed her negative thinking and mindset in Chapter 7.

Behaviours

In Chapter 2 we thought about how our behaviours are driven by our thoughts and feelings. When you have a worry about something, it's understandable that you might try and do something about it. Below are some of the behaviours that people do when they are worried about their weight, shape or eating patterns.

Restricting food Teenagers may start to eat less by eating smaller portions. Sometimes they may skip breakfast or lunch or cut out snacks, telling themselves that they don't have time and can eat more later. However, skipping meals can become a pattern and teenagers may try to hide that they are doing this so that others don't notice.

> *I have started to skip lunch break and just throw my packed lunch in the bin when no one is looking. I tell my friends that I am at tennis practice and going to eat later, so they don't know that I'm missing lunch.*

Excluding foods Sometimes teenagers avoid certain foods because they believe that they are bad for them or will make them put on weight. Foods containing fats and carbohydrates often get excluded. As we saw earlier, it is important to have a balanced diet including carbohydrates, fats and protein. We hear messages about healthy eating which encourage us to reduce fats or carbohydrates, but both these foods are crucial; we need the right balance in our daily intake. See Chapter 3 for more information on healthy eating.

Jen's parents

To start with, we thought that Jen was just trying to be healthy when she stopped eating crisps and chocolate. We know how important being good at tennis is to her, so thought she was just doing it to help improve her fitness. But we noticed that she started to refuse other foods containing fat, like milk, cheese and pastries. When we saw that she was losing weight, we tried to talk to her about it, but Jen became angry and told us she was just eating healthily like other top athletes do.

Strict rules around eating When teenagers worry about their eating, they sometimes develop rigid rules to help them feel more in control: setting calorie limits on their daily intake, eating food in a specific order or at a specific time of day, taking a long time to eat, or avoiding eating with their family and friends. Keeping to the rules can be time-consuming and cause conflict at home or with friends. Having to constantly think about the rules and make sure you follow them can also take up head space and can become obsessive.

I have downloaded this app that helps me to log the number of calories I'm eating. I only allow myself to have a certain number of calories at each meal and check the food packaging to make sure that I'm not going over the limit. I am starting to find it really difficult to eat the meals that my parents make because I don't know what is in them or how many calories there are. I am worrying about calories the whole time and I can't think of anything else.

Ask yourself:

- Do you have any rigid rules around eating?

- How do these rules affect your life?

- Do they make life easier or harder?

Hiding food Some young people may feel guilty about eating. They may try to pretend to their family or others that they are eating, to avoid being made to eat. This may lead them to hide food or throw it away when no one's looking. This may lead to family arguments when parents discover what is happening. Hiding food can be a sign that things are not going well. It can be stressful when it is discovered, but this may be an opportunity to talk to your parents about what is worrying you.

Eating secretly Some teenagers may avoid family meals or even snacks with friends and eat secretly or on their own as a way of hiding their difficulty. The problem is that they then miss out on social contact and begin to feel even more on their own.

Binge eating Teenagers who are restricting their food or skipping meals may start to binge eat and have a sense that their eating is going out of control.

Self-induced vomiting Sometimes when teenagers are binge eating, they try to get rid of the food after a binge by making themselves vomit. They can get caught in a cycle of over-eating, vomiting and bingeing, which can be hard to get out of.

Emotional eating As discussed earlier, eating habits can sometimes be a response to distress. When we are stressed, we may either eat too much or eat too little, as a way of trying to cope with the difficult feelings. Sometimes, it is hard to define exactly what the feelings are, and we can end up just 'feeling fat' as a way of describing our emotional state. The problem is that no matter whether you eat or don't eat, the emotions will still be present. Eating too much or too little to cope with stress and difficult emotions doesn't help in the long run.

Ask yourself:

- Do you over-eat or under-eat when you are stressed?
- What effect does this have on your mood?

Body checking People who worry about their body or eating often start to check their body regularly; for example, looking in the mirror many times during the day, measuring parts of their body to check that they haven't gained weight, or weighing themselves frequently. The problem is that these habits can make you feel worse about yourself, not better.

I spend ages in front of the mirror, turning from side to side to see if I have put on weight. I stare at my stomach, arms and thighs and could swear that they are getting bigger after each meal. I feel sick with disgust. I feel so fat and ugly.

Over-exercise Although exercise is a really important part of keeping healthy and is a great way to connect with others, over-exercising or exercising in a rigid way can develop when young people worry about their body image. Food gives us energy for exercise, but if we don't eat enough to fuel the activity we may lose weight and be at risk of developing an eating disorder. See Chapter 13 for more information on exercise.

Vicious cycles

We talked in Chapter 2 about how negative thoughts, feelings and behaviours can work together to produce a vicious cycle. The same sort of cycle occurs here. Negative thoughts are common in young people who have concerns about their body image. These thoughts can be overwhelming and lead to stress and low mood. Some young people may respond by restricting their food intake to try to feel better about themselves. The problem is that eating less can make you more preoccupied about your body image and lead to further negative thinking. The diagram below shows how this vicious cycle works.

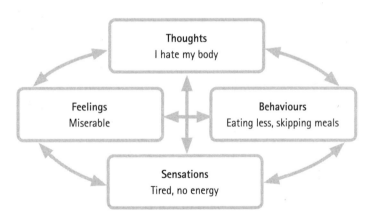

Our thoughts, feelings and behaviours can create a vicious cycle that can make us feel even worse about our bodies

Ask yourself:

- Are any of the above behaviours or thought patterns true for you?

- What impact are they having on your life?

- Is there any action you can take?

What can you do about it?

If you have developed any of these thought patterns or behaviours, there are lots of things you can do to get your life back on track. In Chapter 7, we will look at how teenagers can get out of the vicious cycles of poor eating and develop a positive relationship with food again. Chapter 10 gives some ideas on how to manage body image concerns and be more accepting of your body. Chapter 16 looks at what you can do if you get caught up in the cycles and develop an eating disorder. This is a crisis that can really disrupt your health and wellbeing. However, it is possible to make a full recovery from an eating disorder. The most important thing is to identify it and get help quickly before it takes hold.

Summary

- Eating difficulties can develop into eating disorders.

- The main eating disorders are anorexia nervosa, bulimia nervosa and binge eating disorder.

- Over- or under-eating can have serious effects on the body, emotional state and social life.

- Some young people are more at risk than others, particularly if they have a family history of eating disorders and/or are perfectionist and/or have low self-esteem.

Chapter 5

Worries About Body Image

Wes

I've just been to a gym session but ran out of energy and was way below my personal best. I looked at my muscles in the mirror in the gym and I'm sure they're not as big as they used to be. What will my followers think of me when they see that my performance has really gone down and I'm just a slob? I can't face my friends at the moment – maybe I should just stay in tonight instead of going out.

Next morning . . .

I didn't sleep at all well last night. I was worrying about how my body looks right now. I've just had a shower and had another good hard look at myself in the big mirror in the bathroom. I have checked my arm muscles, my leg muscles and my abs. I really look puny and weak. I'm never going to keep in the top rugby team at this rate. My friends will think I'm a loser.

What this chapter will cover:

- What is body image?

- How does it develop?

- What contributes to a positive body image?

- What leads to worries about body image?

- Body dysmorphic disorder.

- Visible difference.

- Assessing the level of the problem.

What is body image?

Body image is the way we think and feel about our body and how we imagine it comes across to others. Body image includes various aspects:

- Our perception of our body (what we see when we look at our body).

- Our thoughts and beliefs about our body.

- How we feel about our body (positive or negative feelings).

- What we do in relation to how we feel.

How you feel about your body and appearance is important as it contributes to self-esteem and to healthy attitudes to eating and exercise. If you have negative thoughts about your body, it can lead you to feeling worried or sad and you might stop taking part in activities, such as sport, or going out with friends. It can affect your behaviour in other ways too, such as leading you to diet, restrict your food intake or over-exercise, in an attempt to feel better about your body. Young people with poor body image are more likely to develop an eating disorder, as well as low mood, low self-esteem and feelings of isolation. In this chapter, we are going to discuss how body image develops, what builds a positive body image and what can lead to a poor body image.

Young people are the age group most likely to experience concerns about their body image. As we have seen earlier, the teenage years are when you begin to develop your own identity and self-esteem. How you feel about your body is an important part of this. At this stage of life, our bodies are changing rapidly and some young people can find it difficult to adjust to their new weight and shape as they go through puberty. Media pressure to conform to a certain image, to be, for example, slim, toned or muscular, or to have perfect skin and hair, and the right skin tone, certainly doesn't help.

Going through puberty can be particularly difficult for young people who are anxious or confused about their gender identity. They may feel that their body is changing in a way which is different from how they feel they want to be. This was particularly true for Sam.

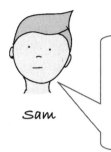

Sam

I really hate the way I look. My boobs are beginning to get bigger, my thighs are enormous and I'm putting on weight. My whole body is changing and it's gross.

How does body image develop?

Everyone's view of their own body develops from early in life, and is influenced by lots of different factors.

Our body image is influenced by lots of different factors

Family influences

Attitudes in our family can shape how we feel about our bodies. This isn't about blaming parents, but just acknowledging that they might have worries about their bodies too. Their beliefs and expectations about body shape or weight can affect how we view ourselves. Parents' opinions, whether they are expressed through comments or demonstrated through behaviours, have a strong influence on children as they grow up. For example, parents may be very conscious about their own physical appearance and may make frequent negative comments about their own bodies, or diet to change the way they look. This may make children more aware of and more critical of their own bodies.

On the other hand, parents who are accepting about their own and their child's appearance and emphasise other qualities rather than appearance can help their child develop a positive body image. Ella came from a family where her parents were very conscious about appearance and her mother went on regular diets. She learned from an early age that physical appearance is very important. Aisha's parents were overweight, and as a result she was determined not to put on weight.

The attitude and characteristics of siblings is also important. Having a sibling (of the same sex) who you feel is more attractive than you may contribute to feeling less good about yourself. Siblings can also commonly be involved in teasing about physical appearance or weight. Jen's brother, Ben, had noted that she had put on a bit of weight and teased her about it.

Peer influences

Friends are important in shaping beliefs and attitudes to body weight and personal appearance. Everyone wants to fit in, to be liked and admired. During adolescence this is probably more important than anything else. We are heavily influenced by the way our friends look, what clothes they wear, their hair style and make-up, etc.

Jen looked up to Ella and wanted to look like her. She compared herself unfavourably with Ella and began to feel very dissatisfied with her own appearance. Teasing by peers is common in the teenage years, and much of it relates to physical appearance. This can be experienced as very shaming, particularly if it is done in public or online, and can lead to intense dissatisfaction about your body. Chloe had experienced teasing when she was ten and started her periods early, leading to a rounder body shape. She felt very ashamed of herself at this age, and this led to ongoing concerns about how she looked.

Cultural influences

All cultures have an ideal body weight and shape for both men and women; indeed, some cultures value a wide range of body types. However, in Westernised cultures there is an unhelpful focus on women having a slim figure. Characters in children's books and movies, as well as dolls, can have a strong influence on what children think is an ideal body shape. Some dolls and action figures have body sizes and shapes that could be very unhealthy if translated into real life. Research suggests that playing with these can influence children's perceptions of ideal body shapes, leading them to think they need to look a certain way.

TV, the internet and magazines are full of images of models with very slim (often pre-pubertal) figures and perfect skin. The problem is that these images can be altered by technology to seem more 'perfect' than they really are. For example, the waist size can be made smaller, the body elongated to look slimmer and any imperfections in the skin airbrushed out. The result is an edited image that is far from real – nobody is so perfect in reality. These models appear to be successful and happy, and it is easy to develop the belief that to achieve success and happiness you need to be thin.

Physical characteristics and changes

The way we are physically and our attitude to this can have an impact on our body image. For example, our height, our body shape, the quality of our hair or skin, facial proportions, the presence of a scar or birth mark can all affect whether we feel good about ourselves. How comfortable or uncomfortable we feel about these characteristics is important in shaping our body image.

Bullying due to a visible difference from our peers can contribute to feeling bad about a physical characteristic.

How body image links with self-esteem and eating disorders

Teenagers who develop poor body image tend to have low self-esteem. Self-esteem is how we value and respect ourselves. If we have low self-esteem, we have a negative view of ourselves and don't value ourselves. It is as if we see ourselves through glasses that magnify our weak points and minimise our positives and strengths. This can extend to how we feel about our body, as self-esteem and body image are often linked.

As Chloe reached the teenage years, she began to feel uncomfortable about her body and focus on all the aspects she didn't like about it. The more she focused on the negatives the worse she felt and the lower her self-esteem became.

Young people who develop eating difficulties often have low self-esteem and poor body image. The problem is that by focusing excessively on their body and eating, they can feel even worse (when they hoped to feel better). This is because their focus can be very judgemental. Spending a long time being highly critical of how you look is guaranteed to make you feel bad about yourself.

See Chapter 9 for lots of ideas on how to improve your self-esteem and Chapter 10 for more discussion on how poor body image can get stuck – and what you can do about it.

What contributes to a positive body image?

As we have seen, body image starts to develop at an early age and is constantly developing in response to internal and external factors. When parents accept their child for who they are and praise their positive qualities rather than commenting on their physical appearance the child is more likely to grow up feeling good about themselves.

In the teenage years, spending time with friends who value you for who you are rather than how you look is equally important. Understanding the developmental changes in puberty, particularly the changes to the body, is important in accepting your body for what it is.

In order to feel good about your body, it is important to focus on things which make you feel good about yourself. Healthy balanced eating, regular exercise, contact with supportive friends and developing interests that you are passionate about, all contribute to you developing a positive body image. Chapter 10 has lots more ideas on how to feel good about your body.

What about teenagers with a visible difference?

It can be hard if you have a visible characteristic which makes you look different from others. For example, you may have been involved in an accident which has left you with scars, or have been born with a birth mark on your face or a genetic condition which results in facial difference. Alternatively, you may have severe acne or a skin inflammation which makes you very self-conscious. This situation can be made worse by the harmful influence of certain TV programmes or films that portray people with visible difference as villains.

You might have a physical disability such as difficulty in walking or using your muscles, which can make it harder to develop a positive body image. Whether the physical difference is temporary or permanent, this can be tough for a teenager. Other people may stare, or make comments or ask questions which may be because they don't understand your condition and are curious. There may be a small minority who are rude or tease you; usually, however, people just want to know more about what has happened to you.

Remember that your appearance doesn't define you; it is your personality that is important. Sometimes, it can be helpful to explain your condition to others or reassure them that you are OK. If you are in a situation where you are not able to explain or do not want to, such as shopping or having a meal out, you may find it helpful to distract yourself from the staring and focus instead on the activity you are doing. Having a positive attitude about yourself and your future makes a huge difference. It can be helpful to exchange ideas with other young people who experience similar conditions, sharing with each other how you cope.

There are helpful resources to support young people with visible difference – check out the resource section at the end of the book.

In fact, there isn't a direct strong relationship between the objective degree of visible difference and how someone feels about their appearance. A person with a visible difference may feel relaxed and happy about themselves, while a person who appears very attractive might feel very dissatisfied. What is important is your attitude towards your body and whether you behave in ways that make you feel worse about yourself (such as body checking or making comparisons).

Looking after your mental health and wellbeing is really important. This may involve learning strategies for managing anxiety, building up your self-esteem, developing a healthy lifestyle with regular exercise, healthy eating, making sure you get enough sleep and keeping close friendships (this is explored more in Chapter 6).

You may find you need support from your family, friends, and professionals. Sharing your feelings with those close to you can be helpful. Remember that it's not your fault if you find it hard to cope with a visible difference.

Body dysmorphic disorder

Some teenagers can become so over-focused on a part of their body that they don't like that it has a big impact on how they live their life. They may be preoccupied with tiny or even imaginary physical flaws that no one else notices. They may avoid going out or engaging in certain activities because of their worries. This is known as body dysmorphic disorder and can be a very distressing condition. It can be treated with CBT which may involve learning to stop checking your body or covering up your perceived flaws.

Assessing the level of body image problems

We all worry about our appearance from time to time, but it begins to become a problem when our worries take over and prevent us from enjoying normal activities or we spend enormous amounts of time checking ourselves, looking in the mirror or trying to change our appearance.

See if body image is a significant problem for you by answering these questions.

Ask yourself:

- Do you constantly worry about how you think you look?

- Do you keep looking at your body in the mirror to confirm how awful you look?

- Do you avoid going out because you worry about how you look to other people?

- Do you spend massive amounts of time trying to make yourself look perfect before you go out?

- Are you constantly comparing yourself with others regarding how you look?

If you answer yes to any of these questions you may be struggling with body-image concerns. See Chapter 10 for lots of ideas on how to improve your body image.

Summary

- Body image is the way we feel and think about our body.

- Body image develops throughout childhood and adolescence.

- Our families, friends and the culture we grow up in all influence how we feel about our body.

- Self-esteem is linked to how we feel about our body.

Chapter 6

Looking After Yourself

My eyes are really sore, and I have a headache. Just checked – it's almost midnight. I close my eyes to try to shut out the rubbish day I've just had. But it doesn't work. I forgot to take my PE kit to school (typical – why is it always me?) and the teacher called me 'lazy' in front of the class. Just when I've had my worst outbreak of spots. Everybody was looking at me and I could feel my cheeks burning and knew I was turning bright red. I was SO embarrassed.

At home, my parents are shouting at each other, and Mum can't stop crying.

I feel so ugly and horrible. Even worse – Mum was so upset I didn't dare ask her about dinner and I was so hungry I ate crisps and chocolate instead. I scroll through my feeds and see Ella sitting in front of a beautiful colourful salad with #healthy diet and #takingcareofme. I feel worse than ever. Why am I so useless compared with Ella?

Chloe

What this chapter will cover:

- Thoughts about day-to-day life as a teen.
- Ideas for looking after yourself.
- Sleep.
- Regular eating.
- Coping with feelings.
- Down time.
- Self-kindness.
- Social media.
- Exercise and activity.
- Friendships and family.

The teenage years can be tough at times. Adolescence is a time of change which can bring challenges as well as fun times, but it may all feel like a bit of a struggle. On the one hand you have more independence, but at the same time you are constantly being told what you should or shouldn't do by friends, teachers and parents. Parents are often struggling too. They may not know when it's appropriate to say something, or when it's better to keep their distance. Some adults can behave quite insensitively towards teenagers and forget how hard day-to-day life can be. Everyone's journey is different, and much of what happens is out of our control. Our genetics determine our height, weight, hair colour, eye colour, when and how we grow.

The good news is that there are some things we *can* control, and this is what we are going to think about in this chapter.

This is a time of life when it is common to worry about fitting in with others or embarrassing yourself. Most teenagers will do anything (sometimes even making unwise decisions) to avoid being laughed at or making a fool of themselves in front of others. It is a time when many things about you start to change – your friendships, taste in music, how you dress or do your hair, your hobbies, what you like at school (and expectations from teachers) and your experience of the world. All these are important and will help you work out who you are as you move towards adulthood and more independence.

In the midst of all this turmoil and change it is easy to forget to look after yourself. But taking care of yourself can help you feel more in control, and is an important part of maintaining both your mental and physical health.

How do we take care of ourselves? There is so much conflicting information online about skincare, what we should wear, what we should eat, how we should exercise and what we should do to relax. Some influencers have strong opinions on self-care but their recommendations can be expensive and complicated, which could just make you feel frustrated and bad about yourself.

Ideas for looking after yourself

Routines including sleep

Chloe

> *I'm scrolling through my phone – it's got really busy with everybody commenting on an argument between Zoe and Jen. I want to sleep but I don't want to miss out on the chat, and I'm scared that somehow if I'm not online they might all start talking about me. I also don't want to look like an idiot tomorrow morning if anybody asks what I think about it. My phone is just about dead but it's still pinging every few seconds and I don't want to miss out. I get a drink and keep reading, but am not sure whether to comment or whether I should take sides in the row.*

Sleep is really important to help us manage our feelings and our moods, as well as concentrate and learn at school. While we are sleeping, our brains and bodies grow and develop. Teenagers ideally should get about eight hours a night (and even more than this if you're very sporty).

Teenagers can really struggle to get to sleep. This is not your fault – we know that during the teenage years and up to the age of twenty, our brain clock resets and melatonin, the hormone that helps us fall asleep, is produced much later in the evening than when we are children (or over twenty)! This means that it is naturally harder to go to sleep at a decent time, and many teenagers find it hard to wake up in the morning and get out of bed. Life for teenagers might be better if school started later (for example, after 10 a.m.) but, unfortunately, school start times are one of those things we can't control.

In the evening you may be busy with homework, after-school activities, spending time with friends (in person or on social media), listening to music or scrolling through your messages, as well as trying to relax or spend time on your hobbies. This makes it hard to keep to a good routine and bedtimes can get later and later.

Worries and difficult feelings can also make it hard to sleep. Spending time on electronic devices can stop our brains from making melatonin because the blue light emitted tells our brains that it is daytime. It is also absorbing and prevents us from switching off and relaxing before we go to sleep.

What can you do to try and maximise your sleep?

Check it out: Top sleep tips for teens

- Try to get some time outdoors and be active earlier in the day.
- Finish homework and things that need a huge amount of concentration in time to allow a wind-down time before bed.
- Set a deadline for coming off your phone/ electronic device and social media.
- Avoid drinks containing caffeine from around mid-afternoon.

- Although alcohol can make you feel sleepy, it can really disrupt sleep.

- Exercise just before bedtime can make it harder to fall asleep.

- Try only to use your bed for sleeping.

- Do things to unwind before bedtime, for example, listening to music or reading a book or magazine.

- Avoid long naps during the day.

- Try to go to bed and get up at a similar time every day.

- If you have tried to fall asleep for 20 minutes and just can't, get out of bed, do something very quiet and boring for a bit and go back to bed when you feel sleepy.

- If worries are stopping you from sleeping, find somebody to talk to about these; writing them down in a notebook next to your bed to deal with the next day might help.

Healthy eating

Regular eating helps to give us energy, regulates our mood, improves sleep and ensures the healthy growth and development of our brain and body. However, it is quite common for teenagers to have erratic eating habits and it can be hard to prioritise food because of sports or other clubs at lunchtime and the need to spend time with friends. It's also easy to forget to take your packed lunch to school! Stress can also make it harder to eat. For example, Chloe has the additional stress of parents who are struggling with their own stuff and not always thinking about what she might need. Despite all these things going on, remembering to eat regularly can really make a difference to how you cope with challenges.

Sam had started reducing their food intake as they were concerned about stresses in their family as well as growing and developing. However, they noticed that they became very irritable when they didn't have enough to eat, found it hard to concentrate at school and ran out of energy very easily. So they now had extra problems to deal with and felt quite overwhelmed. When Sam got back to regular eating again they found they had more energy to deal with the other problems in their life.

Have a look at Chapter 3 for more details on regular eating and getting the right amount of nutrients to keep healthy.

Taking care of your feelings (emotions)

Feelings are an important part of the way we interact with the world around us. The way we feel tells us if things are going well or not so well.

Feelings are constantly there, and it is natural to try to avoid uncomfortable feelings – all humans tend to do this! It is also common to experience several feelings at the same time, from mild and hardly noticeable to super-strong and sometimes overpowering.

It can be tricky when dealing with more difficult feelings, but without the lows we don't get to experience the joys and the highs and live life to the full. What can make feelings difficult is when we don't understand quite what they are and why they are happening, and when we feel out of control.

For more about understanding and taking care of your feelings have a look at Chapter 7.

Down time

Everyone needs to have time to chill and relax. Life is busy for teenagers – with school, homework, helping out at home, trying to connect with friends, sports and hobbies. Relaxation can help you cope with everyday stress, boost your energy and help with sleeping. It is vital for your mental health and improves your memory and learning too. Relaxation allows your mind and body to recover.

Suggestions for how to relax include reading a good book, listening to music, going for a walk, talking to a friend, talking to your parents, having a relaxing bath or watching a film . . . you will also have your own ideas about things that help you relax.

Self-kindness

Self-kindness builds healthy brain pathways that can help reduce stress and enable us to manage when things are tough.

We aren't taught much about how to be kind and positive to ourselves. We think about giving kindness and support to others, but don't often think about applying that to ourselves. Often, we give ourselves a really hard time. How do you talk to yourself? Do you criticise yourself, or are you kind and encouraging? Do you put pressure on yourself to be perfect or are you able to forgive yourself for mistakes? Would you treat a friend the way you treat yourself?

We all have times when things don't work out the way we expect. Setbacks, mistakes and failures are a common part of life. Learning to be kind to ourselves and to learn from our mistakes helps us to move on.

Being kind to ourselves and learning to value ourselves can help to develop our self-esteem. This will be discussed in more detail in Chapter 9.

Ask yourself:

Think about a situation where you supported a friend who was struggling with something.

- How did you feel?
- What did you say to your friend?

Now think about a situation where you may have been struggling too.

- How did you talk to yourself?
- Is there a difference?
- Are you kinder to other people than to yourself?

Social media

Chloe uses her phone as a way of distracting herself from the upset that is happening at home and from a difficult time she had earlier during the day.

Teenagers connect with each other through social media, and it can help them feel supported and less alone. However, Chloe is negatively comparing herself to Ella online, which makes her feel even worse about herself.

It is easy to lose track of time on our phones and for this to interfere with other activities and sleep. Understanding how we use social media and keeping track of what we are following and posting, and how it makes us feel, is an important part of looking after ourselves.

Chloe might find that looking at memes that make her laugh, or having a chat with a friend online, might help her feel a bit better. See Chapter 12 for more information on social media and the internet.

Exercise and activity

Guidelines recommend teenagers should be spending at least an hour a day on physical activity in order to be mentally and physically healthy and to function at their best.

Physical activity boosts the growth of our nerve and brain cells, blood vessels and muscles. It fuels brain power and improves memory and attention span. It boosts our ability to multi-task and make decisions. Activity not only helps our bodies get stronger, it is also good for improving mood and busting stress.

Activity doesn't have to be a competitive or organised sport. Lots of things count: walking or cycling to and from school, dancing, playing outdoors (for example, football games on the school playground), walking to and from the park to hang out with friends, and even the sometimes-dreaded school PE.

Teenagers thrive on the fun and social aspect of an activity. Teenagers who regularly do physical activity with peers build positive friendships, feel more socially accepted, feel less isolated and learn ways to co-operate with others. What is important is that the activities we choose are things we find fun – if something isn't fun, we're not likely to keep doing it.

Remember – we all need a break from work and other challenges in life and it is important to take part in activities that make you feel good. Exercise is discussed in more detail in Chapter 13.

Friendships

Jake

I don't like big groups – I just don't know what to say and by the time I think of what I could say everybody has moved on to a different conversation. I'm sad my best friend from primary school is now part of the big group – I don't want to be on my own but I'm not comfortable with everybody. I like gaming but nobody else seems to talk about this.

Miss Smith talked to me and invited me to the coding club. I'll give it a go but I'm worried that I don't know enough about coding. Miss Smith said that finding people with the same interests will help me make friends and that I should give it a try. I'm not great with new things but I'll go for it and just see.

Friendships are especially important for teenagers. When we are younger, family is very important, but as we grow up and become more independent our friendships become increasingly significant. Because the teenage years are a time of growing and changing, friendships can change as well.

Friendships last longer when there are shared interests and values. Friends help us have a feeling of acceptance and belonging but also help us figure out who we are. Friends can be an important source of support and help us to develop our ability to care for others.

Teenagers with good friendship networks have higher self-esteem, fewer worries and anxiety, greater skills in managing emotions and improved performance at school. Friends help each other deal with stress. It is important to spend time with friends; it is quite natural to have different sets of friends. A healthy friendship is one where you both support each other and where you feel safe, and you trust the other person.

Sometimes things go wrong in friendships, which can be incredibly stressful; for example gossiping, spreading rumours, being left out or feeling under pressure to behave in a certain way in order to fit in. Earlier we mentioned the fall-out between Jen and her friend Zoe and how this was being discussed online. Lots of people were giving opinions and getting involved, which made it even harder for Jen and Zoe.

When friendships are difficult it can be hard to know whether we need to find out what might be causing the problem in order to talk about it and resolve it, or whether it is not possible to mend the friendship.

If you find yourself feeling bad about yourself when you spend time with particular friends, or if you feel put down and controlled, it is important to think about whether it is time to end the friendship. Having an adult who can listen and think through things calmly with you might help you decide what to do next.

Social media can be a way to make or maintain friendships but can also be a risk, for example, you don't always know who you are talking to, and difficult conversations can be misunderstood online.

Carers and family

Although in the teenage years friendships become more important, family, carers and parents are still needed for support. Every family is different – some teenagers may live with grandparents or other carers or with step-parents, and each home situation can have its own challenges.

Chloe is in a tough situation – her parents aren't getting on with each other and are preoccupied and maybe not noticing that she is struggling. It's also tough when parents are so upset that they aren't able to spend time together.

It is important that Chloe doesn't feel bad or guilty about asking her parents for help. She might want to wait for a quieter time and ask one of them if they can spend some time together away from the house. She might want to suggest whether they could have an evening meal cooked together, perhaps working out a rota of who could take responsibility for this. Of course, if things are really bad between Chloe's parents this might not be possible, and sometimes adult help is needed away from the family home.

Brothers and sisters can also be helpful and may understand how you are feeling better than anyone else. Sometimes it is easy to forget to make time for these important relationships.

Chloe's grandmother lives nearby, and when Chloe was younger she often stayed there after school. She decides to pop over to her grandmother's house at the weekend and ask if she can come over regularly. Her grandmother is thrilled, and Chloe realises how important this relationship is.

If Chloe didn't have a grandmother or family member nearby, spending time at a friend's house and building a relationship with their parents could be helpful.

It can be awkward to ask family for support, and many teenagers worry about their parents rushing in to 'fix' things and taking away their independence. Sometimes parents and other family members need guidance, and there is nobody better than you to tell them what you need. Chloe might want to suggest to her grandmother that sometimes she just needs to go for a walk with her or watch TV together or go for a drive – rather than feeling under pressure to talk about what is happening.

Making time to talk to your family can be a quick win if you need some support. Sometimes you might need to let your parents know how you are feeling or that you'd like to spend some time with them.

At other times you might want some space and privacy. It is OK to talk to your parents (at a time when everyone is calm) about the need to spend time alone in your bedroom, people knocking before they come in and how much responsibility you might want for taking care of your things. This will need to be renegotiated as you get older. It can be hard to have space and privacy if you share a room with a sibling, or if there isn't much space at home. You might find it helpful to speak to your sibling(s) or parents about how best to find space for yourself.

You shouldn't feel you have to face your stresses and difficulties on your own. If you are struggling and not sure who to turn to, think about talking to an adult that you trust from school.

*There are lots of tools you can use to look after
yourself when things feel tough*

Here are some possible ways in which you can make some
changes to look after yourself:

Take action!

- Have a think about your routines – the healthier
  ones, as well as the less helpful you might want to
  change.

- Think about which friends make you feel good
  about yourself and how you can grow the
  relationships that matter.

- Keep a diary (somewhere private) where you note
  your feelings and how they might be affected by
  sleep, social media use and activity.

- Spend time with friends, but also spend time with family.

- Maybe try a new sport or activity to see whether you like it or not.

Summary

- Self-care can be about caring for our skin, hair and body, but it is also about taking care of our routines which include trying to establish healthy sleep patterns and regular eating.

- Learning to name, talk about and express your feelings can help you feel less stressed and more in control.

- It is important to spend some time relaxing and doing things that make you happy.

- Ask yourself whether you would talk to friends in the way you talk about yourself.

- Making time for physical activity will boost your mood, your brain and can help manage stress.

- Spending time with friends, getting enough sleep and being mindful about how we use social media is part of taking care of ourselves.

Part 2

Overcoming Worries About Eating and Body Image

Chapter 7

Managing Stress and Anxiety

I'm in the middle of an exam at school, and I just can't work out the answer to a question. I slept badly last night and feel really tired. It's so hard to concentrate, and I am worried that yet again I'm going to get a low mark in the test. I can't stop myself looking out of the window and thinking what a complete failure I am.

My mind can't help wandering back to the situation at home. My parents have just had a massive argument and didn't even ask me how I was and wish me luck for the exam. So, I skipped breakfast just to get out of the house. I wish they would pay attention to me – but at the same time I'm not looking forward to going home later. I've promised myself that I'm not going to binge this evening, but I know I'm going to be so hungry that I probably won't be able to stop myself. I am just feeling more and more stressed. My heart is pounding and I feel hot and uncomfortable.

'Please put your pens down and get ready to hand in your paper.' That's it – the end of the test and I haven't even completed half the questions.

Chloe

What this chapter will cover:

- The role of stress and anxiety.

- What happens when you have too much stress?

- What is the difference between stress and anxiety?

- Different types of anxiety.

- What keeps anxiety going?

- The stress bucket.

- Tips for managing stress and anxiety.

Chloe was in a state of anxiety and tension in her exam which made it very difficult to concentrate. So, let's think about this state of mind, how it arises and what Chloe might be able to do to manage it.

The role of stress

Anxiety is a necessary emotion that helps us to manage danger, as discussed in Chapter 2. When we become anxious, we activate a system in the body known as the *sympathetic nervous system*. This causes our levels of adrenaline to rise: the heart beats fast and blood is diverted from the gut to our muscles. This is known as the stress response. It makes us ready to fight or run away, which is important if you are at risk of being chased by a menacing zombie! Another response is to freeze, which may be very helpful when you want to hide from the zombie.

Anxiety prepares our bodies to respond to danger

This alarm system is critical for our survival from threat or danger. It is unlikely that we will be chased by a zombie in everyday life, but we experience other events where a stress response is important. We actually need a certain amount of stress and alertness to perform well in exams and other tasks. This alertness helps to keep us motivated, concentrate on the task and keep going (rather than drift off in a day-dream). The Yerkes-Dodson Law (shown on the next page), which is based on research, describes how performance in a task is linked to arousal (i.e. alertness or stress levels). If we don't have enough stress, we may lose interest or go to sleep. If we have too much we can't function properly. We just need the right amount.

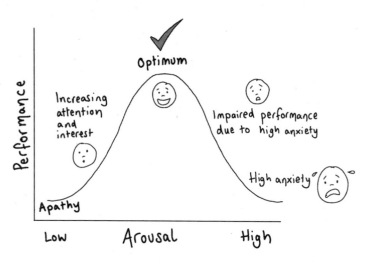

*Yerkes-Dodson Law: we need some anxiety,
but not too much!*

The stress response can also go into action in relatively harmless situations, like having to speak up in front of the class or going to a party when we don't know anyone. Our heart starts to beat fast, our muscles tense and our breathing becomes quicker, even though we are not going to fight or run away. Our mind might just go blank (freezes), and we experience the uncomfortable symptoms of anxiety.

Anxiety can get out of hand, creating vicious cycles of worry. It then ceases to be helpful, reduces enjoyment of life and can interfere with sleep, concentration, being able to enjoy yourself or socialising with your friends.

Stress triggers

All sorts of things can trigger a stress response. We don't have to confront zombies, but the sorts of stresses we do have are things like exams (especially if you don't think you have revised enough), having too many deadlines to meet, worries about the state of the world, climate change, wars . . . the list is endless. Relationships can also be a strong source of stress for young people. Break-ups with friends can be incredibly stressful, as can angry exchanges in families. What triggers your stress is unique to you, and it is helpful to be aware of what you find stressful. And, as we discussed in Chapter 2, situations can be more stressful or less stressful depending on the perspective we have of them.

Check it out: Common triggers for stress and anxiety – quotes from young people

Finding out that my friends are having a party and I haven't been invited.

Doing exams.

Breaking up with my boyfriend.

Getting a detention.

Giving a presentation in class and my mind going blank.

I have put on weight – it is really stressing me out.

What happens when you have too much stress?

When you are under immediate stress, your heart beats faster, your muscles tighten, your blood pressure rises, your breathing speeds up and your senses become sharp. These changes prepare you to fight or run away from the situation. Once you have taken action in the immediate situation, the body calms down and returns to normal.

However, if the stress becomes long term (and you are not able to do anything about it) physical symptoms start to appear, such as headaches, tiredness, muscle tension, chest pain, upset stomach or disrupted sleep. Some people lose their appetite; some people eat more. You can also feel irritable, restless, overwhelmed or lacking in motivation, which can lead to angry outbursts or keeping to yourself because everything becomes too much for you.

Sometimes teenagers use eating as a way of coping with the stresses in their lives – either eating too much or too little. The problem is that this doesn't help in the long term – in fact it can make you feel more stressed.

Jake

I am so anxious at school this week as we have to give a presentation on our project in front of the whole class. Whenever I think about it, my heart starts to beat fast, and I feel really hot and sweaty. I can't get the thoughts out of my mind that the others are all going to make fun of me, and it will be so embarrassing.

What is the difference between stress and anxiety?

Stress is the body's reaction to an external event or situation, like having an argument with a friend or having too much work to do. The way we respond and think about the stress is important.

Anxiety is our internal response to stressful situations and can persist, even when the stressful event is no longer there. Anxiety is generally focused on what might happen in the future or worrying about a previously experienced threat that might happen again. A tendency to be anxious often runs in families.

Anxiety tends to happen when we *overestimate* the likelihood that something threatening will occur and how awful it would be if it does, and at the same time *underestimate* our ability to cope with it, leaving us feeling anxious and overwhelmed. This can be demonstrated in an equation – see below.

$$\text{Anxiety} = \frac{\text{Likelihood X Awfulness}}{\text{Ability to cope}}$$

How we end up with anxiety – the anxiety equation

Different types of anxiety

Teenagers can experience many different sorts of anxiety.

- **Social anxiety** A common sort of anxiety where the teenager is very anxious in social groups. For example, Jake found it very hard to speak in front of his class.

- **Phobias** This is where there is anxiety about specific things, like dogs or spiders, and avoidance of situations where one might be faced with the feared object. This can make life very limiting, as dogs and spiders are everywhere.

- **Generalised anxiety** Young people experience anxiety which is not focused on anything in particular, but seeps into everyday life. They can worry uncontrollably about a range of different things. It can be hard to manage simple tasks if you are feeling anxious most of the time, and hard to sleep too.

- **Separation anxiety** Young people become very distressed about the idea of being away from their family, or something bad happening to a family member. This can make them very clingy and reluctant to do things away from their parents or other family members.

- **Panic attacks** Brief periods of intense fear with physical symptoms such as hyperventilation and tightness of the chest, even when there may be no clear danger or trigger.

Anxiety leads to similar symptoms as with stress; for example, headaches, tummy upsets, pounding heart, fast breathing or tight muscles. Anxiety can stick around if you don't do anything about it – but the good news is that there are lots of ways to get on top of it. Stress and anxiety can be managed in similar ways, as will be described later in the chapter. But first let's think about what keeps anxiety going.

What keeps anxiety going?

Thinking patterns that drive anxiety

 The thoughts we have when we are anxious can either help us cope or make it worse. Some unhelpful thoughts are called 'thinking traps' because we can become stuck in certain patterns of thinking that keep the anxiety going.

Check it out: Thinking traps that can make anxiety worse

- Catastrophic thinking – thinking that the worst-case scenario will happen.

- Black-and-white thinking – judging things as completely good or completely bad, and nothing in between.

- Overgeneralising – thinking that something is true in all situations, not just a specific situation.

- Blowing things up – thinking that something is far worse than it really is.

- Mind-reading – thinking that other people are thinking the worst of you.

Examples of thoughts that make anxiety worse:

- The anxiety is going to go on for ever (catastrophic thinking).

- I will never be able to manage this (black-and-white thinking).

- I gave the wrong answer in class so I must be a complete failure (overgeneralising).

- Everyone thinks I am stupid and a loser (mind-reading).

Behaviours that make the anxiety worse

Anxiety can increase depending on how you respond to it. For example, if you are anxious about going to school and decide to stay at home, then the anxiety grows, and it can become increasingly difficult to get back to school. A young person with separation anxiety may avoid going out anywhere on their own without their parents. This is known as an avoidance response. The same thing occurs if you are anxious about spiders or dogs and avoid them; you become more anxious over time, not less.

People who are anxious sometimes engage in rigid or obsessional behaviour patterns that they think will help them become less anxious. An example of this might be eating food in a particular order or repeatedly checking your body in the mirror.

Another response is to ask for lots of reassurance. This can (surprisingly) make you more anxious and can lead you to seek out more and more reassurance. Avoidance, reassurance seeking and obsessional habits are examples of 'safety behaviours' because we do them to keep ourselves safe (i.e. try to reduce anxiety). See also Chapter 2. In the short term these behaviours can make you feel slightly calmer, but over time you need to do more and more of these behaviours, and they work less and less well – and you end up feeling more anxious, rather than less.

Check it out: Examples of behaviours that can make anxiety worse

- Avoidance
- Obsessional rituals
- Asking for lots of reassurance

Physical sensations and responses

 Physical sensations such as a racing heart, breathing more quickly or feeling hot and sweaty are a big part of anxiety. These sensations can act as an alarm system to alert us to danger but can also make the danger seem more real in situations where there is no actual danger. When these symptoms persist in the night they can disrupt your sleep, making you even more on edge and anxious during the day.

The anxiety trap

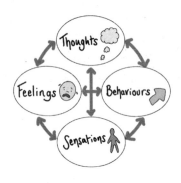

These anxious thinking patterns, behaviours and physical sensations can keep us stuck in an anxiety trap. Unhelpful thoughts can lead us to expect the worst to happen; but if we try to avoid or escape from scary situations, we don't get the chance to find out if the scary thing will really happen, or – importantly – if we can cope with it if it does. The scary thing remains scary in our minds because we don't give ourselves the opportunity to learn anything different about it, or about our ability to cope. In the same way, using safety behaviours, such as seeking reassurance or checking things excessively, can lull us into a false sense of security that reduces anxiety in the short term but keeps it going in the long term. We become reliant on these behaviours to feel OK.

Take Jake, for example, who had to give a presentation in front of his class. His anxious thoughts led him to expect that he wouldn't be able to get his words out and that his classmates would laugh and make fun of him. He felt anxious and miserable, and noticed that his heart would race and his palms would sweat every time he thought about the presentation. To try and cope with his anxiety, Jake tried to put off preparing for the presentation. He kept asking his dad if he thought it was going to be OK. On the day of the presentation, Jake felt so anxious and worried by the thought of making a fool of himself that he told his teacher he was unwell so that he didn't have to do it. But by avoiding the presentation, Jake didn't give himself the opportunity to learn that he could talk in front of his class or that others wouldn't make fun of him if he did.

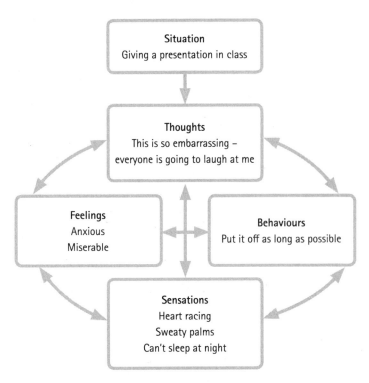

This is Jake's anxiety trap, showing the vicious cycles
that keep the anxiety going

We can also draw out the anxiety trap using the diagram below. We call this a vicious flower, with each petal representing the factors that keep the anxiety going. The good news is that you can learn strategies to deal with each petal, and the petals can be pulled off, one by one, as each issue is addressed. We'll have a look at some of the strategies for managing anxiety in the following sections.

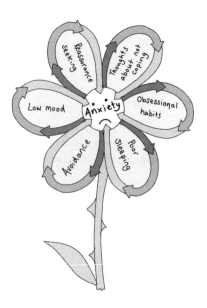

Anxious thoughts and behaviours work together to create a vicious flower that keeps anxiety going

Ask yourself:

• What makes your anxiety worse?

The stress bucket

Stress in our lives can be like carrying a bucket that fills up with stress and becomes heavier and heavier. If we have one or two stresses the bucket is lighter and easier to carry, but if there are lots of stresses it can be really hard. At the bottom of the bucket is a tap which can be turned on to reduce the stress load. There are all sorts of things we can do to lighten the load, such as doing things we enjoy, managing our time well and spending time with supportive friends. These are all described in the next section.

There are many things that make stress worse, but lots of things that can help relieve stress

Ask yourself:

- What's in your stress bucket?
- What might lighten the load?

Strategies for managing stress and anxiety

Check it out: Top tips for managing stress and anxiety

- Addressing your thought patterns:
    - Learn to manage negative thoughts
    - Address rumination and worries
    - Set aside worry time
- Doing things differently:
    - Take care of your physical health
    - Problem-solve
    - Stop avoiding
    - Drop your safety behaviours
    - Keep your relationships going
    - Learn to manage your time
    - Be aware of your triggers
    - Keep a diary

- Coping with feelings:
    - Handle difficult feelings step-by-step
    - Focus on positive experiences
    - Have fun!
- Dealing with the physical sensations of anxiety:
    - Calm your breathing
    - Relax
    - Be mindful

Most people experience stress and anxiety from time to time and it is helpful for all of us to develop the skills to manage anxiety.

The following is a list of strategies that have been found to be helpful in managing anxiety. Not all of them work for everyone – we are all unique! Try out the ones that appeal to you and work out which ones are the most effective.

Addressing your thought patterns

Negative thoughts have a habit of popping into your mind when you are least expecting them and can make you feel more stressed. These thoughts are very common, but learning how to get the better of them is a very important skill that you can use for the rest of your life.

Learn to manage negative thoughts

Jen

> *I couldn't get to sleep last night because of all the negative thoughts that were going round my head. Thoughts such as 'You are fat and ugly', 'No one likes you', 'You are going to fail your exams' and 'You are rubbish at tennis' just came into my head and wouldn't go away. I tried to push them away, but the more I did this, the more they came back, and I just couldn't get to sleep. I have been really tired today and just couldn't concentrate at school. I don't seem to have any motivation.*

Negative thinking can lead to low mood, poor sleeping and loss of motivation. This was certainly happening to Jen, who felt caught up in this vicious cycle. How was she going to get out of it? There are a number of different ways of managing negative/unhelpful thinking:

Check it out: How to manage negative and unhelpful thinking

- You can tell yourself that thoughts are thoughts, not facts.

- You can notice the thoughts and gently focus on something else.

- You can imagine that you are giving advice to your best friend who has a negative thought.

- You can imagine what your best friend might say to you.

- You can imagine that your thoughts are like leaves floating on a stream and just watch them drift away.

- You can try to answer back to your negative/unhelpful thought – what is the evidence for and against this thought? Weigh up the evidence and work out whether it is reasonable to have this thought.

- You can write down your thoughts to get some distance from them.

- You can substitute more positive/helpful thoughts:

    ◦ 'The anxiety will pass.'

    ◦ 'It is not the end of the world if I get a poor mark in the exam.'

    ◦ 'I can learn from what went wrong.'

    ◦ 'It is part of human nature to make mistakes, it does not mean I am a failure.'

    ◦ 'I can always ask for help.'

Take action!

- Try out one of the strategies above.

- Was the strategy helpful?

- Is there another strategy you could try?

- Try keeping a diary of how you have handled negative thoughts.

- Notice what works best for you.

I tried to answer back to my thoughts, but in the middle of the night I just couldn't think of any reasons why the thought might not be true, and this just made me feel worse. I tried other strategies and what worked best for me was to just notice the thoughts and then imagine they were leaves floating down the river. I watched them as they floated away getting smaller and smaller and then focused on my breathing going in and out. This helped to relax me and I eventually dropped off to sleep.

Let your worries and unhelpful thoughts float away

Ask yourself:

- What other advice would you give to Jen to help with her negative thinking?

Addressing rumination

It is very common when we are anxious to spend lots of time going over and over in our head unpleasant things that have happened to us, or could happen. These worries just seem to go round in circles and never get anywhere. This is known as rumination. It is worth asking yourself the question – does the rumination actually help? What are the pros and cons of rumination? Is this a problem I can do something about right now? If it is, you can try the problem-solving technique below. If it's not something you can deal with right now it might be more helpful to distract yourself.

It is useful to have a list of distraction activities to do when you are feeling overwhelmed. This can really help you break the cycle of rumination.

Check it out: Ideas for distracting yourself

- Going for a walk or other form of physical exercise (this can help boost mood as well).

- When you are out for a walk, have a look around: what do you notice in the surroundings?

- Reading a book.

- Watching a good film/TV programme.

- Listening to music or playing music.

- Activities that you have to focus on, such as doing a crossword or thinking of all the countries you can name starting with each letter of the alphabet.

- Trying self-soothing activities, such as having a relaxing bath.

- Doing some art/craft activities.

- Cuddling a pet.

Set aside worry time

Some young people find it helpful to set a worry time each day for a brief period such as 10 minutes. Then if a worry comes up during the day you can postpone thinking about it until the worry time, say 6 p.m. Practically, this means that you could say to yourself (aloud, or in your head): 'I acknowledge this worry, and I will give it a 10-minute appointment in my worry time at 6 p.m. this evening.' This means that you are not having to think about the worry all day long so you can get on with other things. It's helpful to plan what you could do afterwards to move on from the worry period, and best to avoid practising this strategy just before bedtime.

Doing things differently

Take care of your physical health

Anxiety can increase if we become run-down and unwell. Eating regularly, taking regular exercise and making sure we get enough sleep are all ways that we can stay as healthy as we can. As we discussed in Chapter 6, the benefits of a good night's sleep are huge. It is much easier to cope with stress if you are alert and energetic. Regular exercise (see Chapter 6 and Chapter 13) also has a big impact on mood and anxiety levels.

Take action!

- Check out your mood before and after you take some exercise.

- Has it changed?

Problem-solving

It is important to learn to tell the difference between worries that just go round in circles (rumination) and those that need to be addressed. If the worries are going round in circles and not getting anywhere, then distraction can be helpful. If the worries need to be dealt with, it can help to develop your problem-solving and planning skills. Problem-solving has a number of steps, and practising them can give you a system-atic way of addressing your problems and can make you feel more in control.

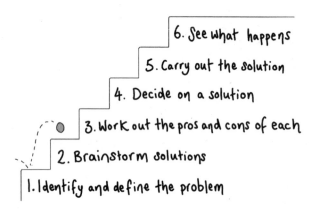

6. See what happens

5. Carry out the solution

4. Decide on a solution

3. Work out the pros and cons of each

2. Brainstorm solutions

1. Identify and define the problem

Steps for problem-solving

Stop avoiding

Avoiding things just makes the anxiety grow, so it can be helpful to work out small steps towards doing the things that you have been avoiding, for example giving a presentation in class. Jake really worried about this, so he worked out small steps to get to this point, starting with a discussion with the class teacher about his anxiety, working with others in small groups, putting his hand up in class and eventually doing a short presentation to the class (see Chapter 9 for more details). As well as managing his anxiety, Jake felt much better about himself when he had done this.

Recognise and drop your safety behaviours!

Reassurance-seeking and rituals develop as a way of reducing anxiety, but actually keep us stuck – and our anxiety grows. Reducing or stopping these behaviours can make a huge difference. It can be scary to start with, but over time it is possible to get on top of the anxiety so that we no longer need the safety behaviours. Aisha was checking herself in the mirror frequently during the day to manage her anxiety about how she looked. However, she had to keep doing this more and more, and she still felt anxious. She decided to reduce the number of times she looked in the mirror and this led her to feeling less preoccupied with her worries. As she reduced this even further, she gradually became less anxious.

Ask yourself:

- Do you have any safety behaviours?
- Do they make you feel better in the long run?
- What happens if you stop them?

Maintain friendships

Keeping contact with friends and sharing worries can really help when you are anxious. You may find that other people have similar worries to you and get stressed about the same things. If you are avoiding something that you are anxious about, for example, a social event, going together with a friend can increase your confidence.

Manage your time well

There are lots of things to fit in when you are a teenager – schoolwork, revision for exams, music practice, sports, reading, social media, going out with friends, spending time with family, etc. It can be stressful when you run out of time to do everything you need to. Learning how to manage your time well is a skill that, once mastered, is useful for your whole life. Managing your time is about working out your priorities, deadlines, how long a task will take and keeping to your timetable – ideally doing the difficult things first to get them out of the way.

Work out the triggers for your stress and anxiety

What are the things that regularly set off anxious feelings? Are they the same ones each time or do you have lots of different triggers? Is there anything that can be done about them? Try using your problem-solving skills to work out what you can do about the triggers.

Keep a diary

Some young people find it helpful to complete a diary at the end of the day. This helps them to think about what went well, and what didn't go so well, and why. What helped you to manage your anxiety? What made your anxiety grow? How can you build on the things that went well? What can you do to improve things? Worries can make us dismiss things that we are doing well, and we might focus only on what is going wrong. But if we try also to focus on our strengths, for example, being able to face a difficult challenge, over time this can help improve our self-esteem.

This reflection can make it easier to sleep as any worries are written down rather than whirling round your head at night.

Take action!

- Try keeping a diary.
- See what happens when you write down the events of the day and how you managed them.

Managing difficult feelings

 Difficult feelings very often contribute to eating difficulties and poor body image, so it is important to address how we feel. Some examples of feelings that we experience include sadness, distress, anxiety, anger, disappointment or shame. When we try to push feelings away, they have a habit of coming back. Our feelings affect our thoughts, our bodily sensations and our behaviours (see Chapter 2). Naming the feelings can help us build up a sense of control. It can also help to figure out how our feelings influence our thoughts and reactions.

Chloe

I've just had the most awful day. My best friend sat with someone else in class and I felt really ignored. Then the teacher was cross because I wasn't listening, I felt really embarrassed and knew everyone was looking at me. And now I've got home, and my parents are arguing again. It's late at night and I've just crept down to the kitchen to grab a packet of biscuits – and I've eaten the whole packet in my room. I feel really disgusted with myself.

Chloe has had a tough day with lots of difficult feelings: rejection, embarrassment, sadness and disgust. It is late at night and hard for her as she can't talk about it with her parents as they are having a row and are preoccupied with themselves. Noticing the things that are happening or what we are doing can help understand why these feelings are happening – and this is the first step in managing the feelings.

Steps for handling difficult feelings:

Step 1: Be aware of the feeling

Just notice the feeling and what is going on in your body right now. Has your heart started beating faster? Are you breathing quickly? What thoughts are going around your head?

Experience the feeling rather than trying to suppress it.

Name the feeling. Is it, for example, sadness, anxiety, anger or another emotion?

Step 2: Take a pause

Don't immediately react to feelings, for example by eating something or skipping a meal. Give yourself a pause. Remember that difficult feelings happen to everyone from time to time and they don't last. It can help to write your feelings down in a diary.

Step 3: What's gone well?

Remind yourself of the things that have gone well that day. When we are feeling bad, it is so easy to forget the positive things that have happened.

Step 4: What can you do right now?

Think about what might be helpful right now.

- Talk to someone (in person or on the phone).

- Text a friend.

- Go for a walk (if it's daytime!).

- Do some slow breathing.

- Write about your feelings in your diary.

- Be kind to yourself: take a relaxing bath, listen to your favourite music, watch a good film.

Step 5: Work out what might be causing the feelings

In the longer term, it can be helpful to work out what is behind the feelings. Is it something to do with problems with friends or family members? Is it due to particular stresses in your life? Is there something that you can do about the problem causing the difficult feelings? Is there someone you can talk to about the problems you are experiencing?

If you are in a situation where there is no immediate solution to the problems you are experiencing, it is helpful to get support from others in order to work out how you can get on with your life, despite the problems.

Chloe might find it helpful to write down her feelings and also remind herself that her friend came up to her after school and wanted to walk home with her (she had forgotten that!). She could distract herself by having a relaxing bath and then listening to her favourite music. Hopefully, she can get a good night's sleep and have a better day tomorrow and talk about it all with understanding friends or her grandmother.

Focus on positive experiences

There is evidence that if you write down things you are grateful for each day it can make you feel more optimistic and better about yourself. Noticing positive experiences can shift our attention from negative feelings.

Take action!

- Try coming up with three things you are grateful for right now.

Have fun!

Laughing is a great way to increase good feelings and discharge tension. Research has shown that even if we are just simulating laughter, our bodies interpret it as true rather than pretend, and we still get those benefits. So, smile and laugh to yourself (even if it seems silly)!

Ask yourself:

- What things make you laugh?
- Can you do more of them, e.g. watching comedies or funny videos, spending time with friends who make you laugh?

Check it out: Ideas for keeping your emotions in balance (emotional regulation)

- Write down how you feel in a private diary.

- Remind yourself of things that have gone well or things about you that you are proud of.

- If someone has really upset you or hurt your feelings, write a letter telling them how they made you feel – perhaps don't send it right away – read it again when you feel calmer, and maybe even tear it up and throw it away.

- Distract yourself with hobbies that you enjoy.

- Listen to music.

- Pamper yourself.

- Talk things over with a friend.

- Talk to a grown-up you can trust.

- Make sure you have enough to eat and drink: being hungry or dehydrated makes difficult feelings harder to manage.

- Think about what you would say to a friend who is struggling and try to treat yourself with the same kindness.

- Focus on positive experiences.

- Have fun.

Dealing with physical sensations of anxiety

Learn to slow your breathing

When a person is anxious their breathing often becomes fast and shallow, which can make anxiety worse and contribute to physical symptoms. Learning to breathe deeply and slowly takes practice but can make a huge difference to how you feel. Try it out and see if it works for you. As we discussed at the beginning of this chapter, when you are anxious, the sympathetic nervous system is activated, and your heart rate can go up and your breathing becomes more rapid. When your breathing is deep and slow, the opposite nervous system is activated – *the parasympathetic nervous system* – and your heart rate drops, and your body feels calmer. This is in contrast to the rapid deep breathing that can occur when you are in a panic and hyperventilate. This can make you feel dizzy and out of control and make other physical sensations worse.

Take action!

• Try practising deep breathing for a minute at a time whenever you are waiting for something, e.g. the kettle to boil or your computer to charge up. Practise breathing in and out to the count of 4. Notice your stomach rise as you breathe in

> and fall as you breathe out. If you practise this regularly throughout the day it will soon become a habit. You can search online for other breathing exercises.
>
> - When you find yourself experiencing anxiety, notice what is happening to your breathing and consciously slow your breathing down.

Specific relaxation techniques can be helpful, particularly if you have had a stressful or difficult day. Examples are box breathing, or finger breathing or relaxation apps that you can download on your mobile phone.

Breathing is one of the few body systems we are able to control (we can't tell our hearts to beat slower or change our body temperature at will). By focusing on breathing, it can give our brains a signal to slow down and relax.

It can be hard to practise breathing techniques when you're already upset, but doing these regularly – maybe when you are calmer – makes it easier to do when you are upset.

Check it out: Box or square breathing

Picture a square with four equal sides.

- Step 1: Breathe in through your nostrils, counting to four slowly (imagine travelling up one side of the square).

- Step 2: Hold your breath for four seconds (imagine moving across the top of the square).

- Step 3: Slowly exhale through your mouth for four seconds (imagine travelling down the other side of the square).

- Step 4: Hold your breath for four seconds (imagine moving across the bottom of the square).

- Step 5: Repeat until you feel calm.

Check it out: Five finger breathing

- Step 1: Sit comfortably with your back straight and place one hand out in front of you – palm open and fingers spread out wide.

- Step 2: Use the first (index) finger of your opposite hand and start at the base of your thumb, tracing up your thumb as you slowly breathe in.

- Step 3: Hold your breath briefly at the top of your thumb.

- Step 4: Slowly inhale as you trace from the tip of your thumb to the inside between thumb and first finger, pausing slightly.

- Step 5: Exhale slowly as you trace up towards the tip of your first finger, pausing again at the top.

- Step 6: Repeat the slow breathing and pause while you trace over all five fingers while slowly breathing. Notice the feel of your finger touching your other hand and notice the lines on the palm of your hand to engage your other senses while breathing.

Muscle relaxation

When a person is anxious their muscles typically become tense, which can contribute to physical discomfort and headaches.

Progressive muscle relaxation (PMR) can teach you to be aware of tension in your muscles and help you learn to relax them. The best way to do this is to find a comfortable quiet spot where you can sit or lie down, and progressively tense and relax the main muscle groups in your body. There are free audio recordings accessible online to make it easier. Just search for *progressive muscle relaxation.*

Check it out: Progressive muscle relaxation

- Step 1: Find a comfortable position (either sitting in a chair or lying on the floor).

- Step 2: Close your eyes (if you want to) and focus on your breath going in and out.

- Step 3: Scrunch up your toes as hard as you can, and breathe in; as you breathe out, relax the tension in your toes and notice the difference.

- Step 4: Clench your fists, breathe in, notice the tension and then as you breathe out let them relax.

- Step 5: Squeeze your buttocks, breathe in and then as you breathe out relax them and notice the difference.

- Step 6: Tense up your tummy, breathe in, then let it relax as you breathe out.

- Step 7: Squeeze your shoulders up to your ears, then let them relax as you breathe out.

- Step 8: Scrunch up your face, breathe in, then let your face relax as you breathe out.

- Step 9: Take a deep breath and, as you breathe out, notice how your whole body feels.

- Step 10: Continue to breathe gently in and out.

- Step 11: When you're ready, slowly wake up your body, wriggle your toes and stretch your arms and legs.

Mindful awareness

Mindfulness is about being fully in the present, with an attitude of friendly interest rather than judging what's going on. It takes practice to learn how to be mindful, but it can transform our lives. Worry takes us back to the past or into the future. Learning to be fully in the present can break the worry cycle and help us to get the most out of life. Try noticing what is going on in the present. What can you see, feel, hear and smell right now?

There are lots of different ways to be mindful, such as:

- Listening to music and really paying attention to it. What do you like about it? Try focusing on the different rhythms or melodies and the sounds of different instruments.

- Going for a walk and noticing the sounds of birds, the smell of flowers or the sun catching on the leaves. You might surprise yourself about what you notice!

- The breathing exercises described earlier can be done mindfully, just noticing the sensations with a friendly, curious attitude. How does it feel in your body when your breath goes in and out?

- Try pampering yourself in a mindful way, really paying attention to what's happening and the sensations you are experiencing.

- Even doing the washing up can be a mindful experience if you focus in on the bubbles or the textures of the different utensils you are washing, rather than rushing to get it finished!

There are lots of helpful websites about mindfulness out there – have a look in the resource section at the end of the book. Some are free, some need a subscription. You can also search mindfulness techniques.

So how did Chloe manage her anxiety and stress? One of the most important things for her was keeping contact with her friends, sharing how she was feeling and doing fun things with them. She also found that eating regularly with her mum helped with her energy levels and improved her sleep. She felt less fatigued during the day and more able to concentrate at school. When she was out walking, she tried to focus on what was in the world around her rather than what was going round and round inside her head. There were still tensions at home, but gradually she felt more able to cope.

Everyone has different ways of managing stress and anxiety. There are lots of ideas in this chapter – check out which works best for you.

Take action!

- Which stress management strategy might work for you?

- Try it out today when you are feeling stressed.

- If it doesn't work, try out another one.

- Check out how your friends/family members manage their stress.

Good luck on your journey to get the better of your anxiety!

Summary

- Stress and anxiety are a normal part of life.

- Too much stress can have a negative effect on our body and emotions.

- There are different ways to manage stress:

  ○ Work out your own triggers for stress.

  ○ Problem-solving and planning skills can help deal with worries.

  ○ Facing fears and stopping safety behaviours can help to decrease anxiety.

  ○ Make sure you look after yourself and find ways to manage your feelings.

  ○ Relaxation and slow breathing can help to manage the physical sensations of anxiety.

- Choose what works for you and keep practising them to build up your skills!

Chapter 8

Developing a Positive Relationship with Food and Eating

Aisha

I am determined to lose weight, so I have cut down on oils and other fatty food and decided to skip breakfast. I have begun to lose some weight, which was great to start with, but I have noticed that I am running out of energy and am exhausted by the end of the day. I have a great group of friends, but I just don't feel like doing anything with them. I just stay at home and have started to feel really miserable that I am missing out on all the fun things they are doing.

My friends keep asking me what's going on and I tell them to leave me alone, but inside I really want some help. I am going to pluck up the courage to talk to my best friend. I think I need to open up about what's going on and get some help.

What this chapter will cover:

- Noticing the problem.

- Deciding to change.

- Taking action.

  ◦ Developing more helpful eating behaviours.

  ◦ Managing negative thinking.

  ◦ Coping with difficult feelings.

  ◦ Engaging with friends and family.

  ◦ Building up other interests.

Noticing the problem

The first step in dealing with worries about eating is to accept that there is a problem. You may be aware that mealtimes have become more difficult, and you make excuses not to join the family for a meal; alternatively you realise that you can get through a whole packet of biscuits when you feel stressed, and then feel guilty. Sometimes, it is hard to notice these things in yourself, so someone close to you may point out what they see is happening. They may notice that you are staying in your room when it is time for dinner, or that you are regularly going on apps to check the calorie content of the food you are eating.

It is normal when somebody points such things out to you to react by becoming angry, irritated and wanting to defend your choices. None of us likes having someone else highlight a possible problem and you may deny that anything is wrong, especially if it feels like you are being criticised. However, your family members or a close friend might be doing this because they are concerned about you and want to help.

Try to listen to what they have to say and think about it when you are on your own, or when you're feeling calmer. Is it possible that you have developed a problem with your eating? Is this affecting your life in any way? Do you need to do something about it?

Deciding to change

Most people find it quite hard to make any changes in their life. It can be helpful to work out the pros and cons in order to decide whether you really do want to change.

Aisha made a list of the reasons to do something about her eating problems, and the reasons not to.

Reasons to change	Reasons not to change
• Feeling tired a lot of the time	• Feeling I have achieved something by losing weight
• Missing doing stuff with friends	• Pride in myself for skipping breakfast
• Low energy levels	• In control of one part of my life
• Not sleeping well	
• Not able to concentrate on schoolwork	
• Grades dropping	
• Lots of arguments at home	
• Running out of energy in sport at school	

Aisha's pros and cons of making changes

Thinking about the pros and cons of skipping meals and cutting down my food intake has made me realise that there are just too many downsides; nothing is going right and I am getting more and more unhappy. Something has to change. But I just don't know how to do it. I will talk to my mum; maybe she can help me at mealtimes and make sure I eat enough to give me enough energy for all my activities.

Ask yourself:

- What are the pros and cons of changing your relationship to food and eating?

- Who can you tell about it?

- Who can support you to make changes?

Once you have decided that you are going to change, the next stage is to take action! Telling someone about your plans really helps to firm up the resolve. Even better, asking someone to support you in your change is a great way of making sure it happens.

Developing a healthy relationship to eating requires taking a step back and starting to listen to your body and take care of yourself. Here are some ideas to help you feel differently about eating.

Taking action

Notice the hunger signals

Try to be aware of the hunger cues. The healthy body is very clever in helping you to understand your level of hunger. What do you notice in your body when you are hungry? Does your stomach gurgle? Does your stomach feel empty? Does your stomach hurt? Do you start to feel a bit faint, dizzy or even a bit sick? Do you get a headache? Do your energy levels drop? Do you find it hard to concentrate? Do you start to think of your next meal? Some young people, if they are worried about their weight and shape, can find hunger signals make them feel guilty. However, these signals are normal and a sign that your body is working normally.

When eating is erratic, it can be common to lose the physical signals of hunger. However, being preoccupied with food, looking at photos of food or cookery books, and talking about food, might all be signals that you need to feed yourself.

Take action!

- During the day notice the signs telling you that your body is hungry.
- Try to respond to these cues and make sure you eat something when you are hungry.

Getting back to regular eating

Eating balanced meals regularly helps us to maintain our energy levels, improves our mood, ensures our brain is functioning well and makes it more likely that we will sleep well at night. If you can't do this straight away, can you gradually work towards a more regular eating pattern?

I haven't been eating regularly, and I realise that it is affecting my mood and concentration. It has been so hard to focus on my lessons, and I have been getting behind. I know that I need to eat more regularly, but this is easier said than done! It is so hard to change the habits that I have got into. It has been very helpful talking it over with my mum. I have told her that I need help. She has agreed to sit down with me at each meal and help me finish it. She has also suggested that I talk to my friends at school, to make sure that I join them for lunch. Although this is hard, as I am used to eating on my own or skipping lunch, I am enjoying catching up with my friends.

Plan meals ahead

If you are struggling with eating, it can be helpful to plan meals ahead, ideally with a parent, so that you work out what you need to keep healthy and know what to expect at each meal.

Forget about good and bad food

It can be all too easy to get into a habit (just like Ella did) of labelling foods 'good' or 'bad'. But remember: there are no good and bad foods, and what is important is the balance of foods that we eat (as discussed in Chapter 3).

Ditch the diet

If you have been thinking of going on a diet, try to think for yourself about the pros and cons of dieting. Remember that diets don't seem to work in the long term and can lead to eating disorders or becoming overweight.

Taste and enjoy your food

When you have your next meal, try to eat mindfully, really noticing what you are eating. What is the smell, flavour, appearance and texture really like? Focus on each mouthful and work out whether you are enjoying the food or not. If you have been in the habit of eating 'on the run' while doing something else, experiment with eating more calmly while sitting down at a table. Explore the most relaxing context for eating. However, it is also important to be flexible – sometimes we may need to eat in the middle of doing something else.

Eat mechanically and distract yourself

Sometimes it can be challenging to eat mindfully. If you are finding it difficult to eat, perhaps because you are feeling guilty, you can manage this by eating in a mechanical way, just opening and closing your mouth on the food rather than focusing on it. You may find it helpful to distract yourself at the same time, for example by listening to music or having a conversation. Once you have got used to eating, then it is more possible to enjoy your food.

Notice the signals for when you have had enough food (satiety)

Try to notice when your body is telling you that you have had enough. What are the signs? Does your stomach feel full? Has the feeling of hunger reduced?

Research has shown that, when we are full, a hormone called leptin is released by the body which reduces the craving for food. If we are under-eating or have lost weight, the levels of leptin are reduced and so we crave more food. However, the gut also works more slowly so you may feel full for longer after a meal. This usually changes when you get back to normal eating again.

If you have no cues of hunger or satiety (which can happen when eating is erratic) you may need to work out appropriate portion sizes for each meal (your parent/carer may be able to help you with this) and stick to this until your normal hunger signals return.

Get rid of the rules

Having rigid rules around eating can make us feel more anxious, not less. Rules might include setting calorie limits on daily intake, eating food in a specific order or at a specific time of day, taking a long time to eat, avoiding eating with your family and friends, stopping yourself from having seconds or dessert.

Ella had lots of rules about which foods she could or couldn't eat. She was worried that if she dropped these her eating would go completely out of control. She was also concerned that her 'followers' on social media would feel let down.

Ask yourself:

- Do you have rigid rules for eating?
- What are they?
- Where do the rules come from?
- Do you have any concerns about what will happen if you break the rules?

Take action!

- Take one rule at a time.
- Try dropping it – and see what happens.

Stop counting calories

Sometimes, young people may start to count calories as a way of taking control of their eating. Almost every packaged food displays calorie levels of the contents, so it is very easy to become preoccupied with this. Nutrition labels show this information so as to help us make 'healthier choices', but we can become preoccupied with checking how many calories are in various foods. This can lead to increased anxiety. In addition, the calorie counts specified tend to be inaccurate, as they are based on averages and don't account for individual differences in the way people digest their food.

If you are counting calories, you may want to try other ways to manage your food, such as thinking about the balance of nutrients that you need (see Chapter 3) or the energy that you need that day to fuel your activity. As you gradually focus less on calories you may be anxious to start with, but you will eventually experience a sense of relief that you don't have to do it.

Eating with others

Some young people who develop eating difficulties may find it hard to eat with friends and family. Not only is there a sense of embarrassment, but it can also be anxiety-provoking being amongst people who are eating normally. The problem is that when you start to eat on your own, you lose a sense of connection to others and the enjoyment of eating socially.

I used to meet regularly with a group of my friends at the weekend and really enjoyed doing stuff together and talking about what was going on in our lives. But as my eating difficulties got worse, I made excuses and just stayed at home. But I missed hanging out with my friends. In the end I managed to talk to my best friend about it all. She had noticed that I was keeping to myself and had been worried about me. She was really supportive and suggested that we met up, just the two of us, in the local park.

I didn't want to go to start with, but she managed to persuade me. It is a relief to be able to talk to her about what was bothering me, and it's good to be out rather than stuck in my own room at home.

Plan an activity after eating

If you are beginning to develop eating difficulties the time immediately after the meal can be quite stressful. You may be thinking, have I eaten the right food, have I eaten too much, have I eaten enough? It is helpful to plan an activity after each meal that takes your mind away from food. This might be doing a puzzle, listening to music or watching TV. It is surprising how helpful distraction can be. You may have particular activities that distract you.

I am starting to eat more normally, but I'm really anxious after meals, so I have decided to watch my favourite TV series with my sister, Rashmi. This is helping to distract me and by the time the programme has finished I feel a bit less anxious and I'm able to go to my room and do my homework.

Take action!

If you notice thoughts creeping in after a meal such as *'I shouldn't have eaten that much'* or *'Better skip the next meal'*, try out different activities to distract yourself and see what works for you best. Here are some suggestions:

- Listening to music
- Playing a board game
- Watching TV
- Doing your homework
- Chatting with your siblings

Addressing exercise

Regular, enjoyable exercise is good for all of us. It helps to regulate our emotional state and keeps our bodies, brains and bones healthy. However, it can be easy to get into the trap of doing too much or too little. Often young people with eating problems can end up over-exercising to try to control their weight. But they can get into unhealthy cycles of setting rules of over-exercising which can leave them more exhausted and unable to manage their eating.

See Chapter 13 for ideas on how to develop a healthy relationship with exercise and activity.

Addressing negative thinking

Negative thoughts can contribute to unhelpful eating habits as a way of trying to feel better about yourself. See Chapter 7 for ideas on how to deal with negative thoughts and Chapter 9 for managing thoughts to improve your self-esteem.

Managing feelings

Difficult feelings, such as sadness, distress, anxiety, anger or disappointment, often contribute to eating difficulties, so it is important to address these feelings. See Chapter 7 for some steps to take in dealing with difficult feelings.

If you are in a situation where there is no immediate solution to the problems you are experiencing, it is helpful to get support from others. This may help you to work out how you can get on with your life despite the problems. Chloe can't control the rows between her parents, but figuring out how it makes her feel might help her understand herself more and feel more in control of her life.

Chloe

I feel very upset at home, especially when my parents are arguing. It is at times like this that I creep down to the kitchen to find a packet of biscuits and then eat the whole lot. Afterwards I feel disgusted with myself.

I have spoken to a counsellor at school about what is happening, and she has given me some ideas to try out to manage my feelings. When I feel all churned up inside, I start by just noticing how I feel and what is happening in my body. Then I try to work out what the emotion is. Often, it is sadness about what is happening at home, but sometimes I feel really angry. Instead of reaching out for the biscuits, I have learned to give myself a break, telling myself that these feelings won't last for ever. I then call a friend and have a chat, or arrange to meet up to get out of the house.

Making time to be with friends and family

It can be hard to make time with your friends and family when you are feeling awful about yourself. But spending time with people who care about you can be so helpful when times are tough. If you are feeling supported, it is easier to get back on track with eating.

I have been more and more distant from my family, particularly because of all the rows my parents are having. I end up spending lots of time in my room, bingeing on biscuits and chocolate which makes me feel even more unhappy and stressed. I've realised that this isn't doing me any good and I have been getting quite lonely. I have begun to go for regular walks with my mum, which is a time when we can focus on each other and just enjoy the surroundings (our favourite walk is along the river just close to our home). Although there are lots of problems in the family, this is a time when we can both have some relaxing time outdoors, and it has helped us to feel closer again.

Building up interests

If you are preoccupied with eating difficulties, it can be all too easy to lose sight of other interests. However, your interests can help give your life a sense of meaning and purpose, and it's helpful for your mental health to try and put time into them. If other parts of your life are feeling really difficult, going back to things you enjoy can give you the motivation to keep going. Dealing with eating difficulties is a lot easier if there are other things in your life that you are passionate about and give you pleasure.

Although I was still going to tennis, I had stopped going out with my friends and was less interested in watching movies and listening to music. My mind was taken up with thinking about the next meal and how I was going to get through it. I began to realise that my life had become very boring and full of stress. I decided to talk to my friend, Zoe, who turned out to be very supportive. Zoe suggested that we go out to watch a film together. I used to really love going to the cinema, so it was great to do this with Zoe.

Jen

Take action!

- Think about one thing that you would like to do today to build a more positive relationship with eating.

- Work out what you are going to do.

- Tell your friend or a parent what you are going to do.

- Do it!

- Write down how it went.

Summary

- It is easy to slip down the route into an eating disorder, but hard to get out of it again.

- Taking action to change involves weighing up the pros and cons and making a decision to change.

- Getting back to regular eating can help.

- Friends and family can be an important support.

Chapter 9

Improving Self-Esteem

Jake

I hate school. The lessons are so hard. Everyone else gets what the teacher is saying, but to me it's like they're talking another language. It's really hard to concentrate and I keep getting distracted by other things going on in the classroom. I feel so stupid when everyone else puts their hand up because I haven't got a clue what the answer is. The other kids laugh at me because I can't sit still, and I get angry when I can't do the work. I might as well not bother 'cos I'm only going to get it wrong. I'm such a loser.

What this chapter will cover:

- What is self-esteem?

- What does low self-esteem look like?

- Thoughts, feelings and behaviour and the low self-esteem trap.

- How to improve your self-esteem.

- Questioning unhelpful thoughts.

- Changing unhelpful behaviours.

- Building a healthy self-esteem – learning you're OK as you are!

What is self-esteem?

Your self-esteem is made up of the thoughts and feelings you have about yourself. These thoughts tend to be about how good or bad you feel about yourself. If you are accepting of yourself and can think positively about your skills, talents, attributes and qualities, then your self-esteem is probably quite good. However, if you think negatively about yourself, have self-critical thoughts, or struggle to identify any positive qualities, your self-esteem might be quite low.

Ask yourself:

- How do you describe yourself?

- Do you use mainly positive or negative words?

- What are they?

In adolescence, your self-esteem is influenced by a number of factors which relate to the physical and social changes that you are going through, and all the demands and expectations that you face at this stage of life. Because this is a time of change, and when you are working out who you are or want to be, it's quite common for self-esteem to be lower during the teenage years. Factors that influence self-esteem include:

Physical appearance For Chloe, starting puberty early adversely impacted on her self-esteem. She felt very self-conscious and different from her friends, and was teased for wearing a bra in primary school. Sam also feels uncomfortable about their body and worries about it changing. Ella's appearance is also a large part of her self-esteem: getting positive comments from others helps her to feel good about herself, but she feels a pressure to look good all the time and worries about what people will think of her if she doesn't. Ella spends a lot of time on social media looking at models with 'perfect' bodies and really wants to look like them.

Academic skills Jen sets high standards for her academic performance, and always wants to get top marks in school. This has become more important now that she is studying for her exams. Getting high grades helps Jen to feel good about herself, but she worries about failing and this makes her very anxious. Jake also finds that school affects his self-esteem. He really struggles with learning because of his ADHD and ASC and this can make him feel really bad about himself.

Feeling socially accepted Aisha often feels different from her peers because few of them come from the same cultural background as her. She feels bigger than her friends, having gained weight during puberty. Aisha worries that others won't like her, so tries to lose weight to fit in more. When her pictures are liked on social media, she feels more accepted and better about herself. Sam also feels different from their peers because they are unsure about their gender identity, and don't know many people who feel like this. Sam worries that people might be judgemental or misunderstanding about how they are feeling.

Sport It's not just schoolwork that affects Jen's self-esteem – being successful at tennis influences it too. However, Jen worries about not living up to the expectations set by her coach and her dad, and not being good enough. Wesley also worries about not being muscular enough or performing well enough in rugby, and so he spends a lot of time in the gym trying to improve his personal bests.

Behaviour Jake can often struggle to follow the rules; he finds it difficult to understand other people's points of view and can sometimes act impulsively. This can get him into trouble at school and can make him feel bad about himself.

We can think about our self-esteem as slices on a pie chart. If our self-esteem pie is split into a number of different equal slices, it can act as a buffer against difficulties. This is because if something goes wrong in one slice or we feel badly about ourselves in one area there are still several other slices that we can feel good about. However, if our self-esteem pie only has a few slices, or one slice is much bigger than the others, this can make us more vulnerable to experiencing low self-esteem: because if something goes wrong in one of the big slices, there are fewer positive influences to balance it out.

We are more vulnerable to low self-esteem when our self-esteem is concentrated in a small number of areas.

Ask yourself: What does my self-esteem pie chart look like?

- Make a list of the different areas of your life that are important to you and that contribute to your self-esteem. This might include things like academic ability, friendships, physical appearance, sport or other hobbies (playing a musical instrument, drama, or being creative and making things). It can also include personal qualities like being kind, thoughtful, creative, practical or having a good sense of humour.

- Put the list in order of what is the most and least important to your self-esteem. To help you do this, you can ask yourself *'If I was having difficulties in this area, how much would it affect me?'* It's likely that the more important something is, the more effect it would have if something went wrong.

- Next, turn each of these areas into slices on a pie chart: the more important an area is, the bigger the slice.

- Have a look at your pie chart. How many slices are there? Are any slices much bigger than the others? Is this how you would like your self-esteem to look?

Our self-esteem can also suffer if we think there is a big difference between how we currently see ourselves, and how we would ideally like to be. The problem is that when we have low self-esteem, we often underestimate our positive qualities, and overestimate the qualities that we think others have, which makes the gap seem even bigger than it actually is.

Take Chloe, for example:

Chloe

There's a girl in the year above me, Ella, who everybody likes. She's always got this big group of people around her, whereas no one really wants to hang out with me. Ella's tiny, but she's got this personality that kinda stands out. I'm the total opposite – I stand out for all the wrong reasons, and no one would think I'm interesting or cool. Ella's super-disciplined – she eats really healthily and works out every day. I try to eat less, but just end up pigging out on junk food, and I can't afford to go to the gym. I wish I was more like Ella.

It's normal to doubt your abilities or lack confidence from time to time, but if you tend to think negatively about *all* aspects of yourself *all* the time, you may have low self-esteem.

What does low self-esteem look like?

Throughout this book, we've been exploring the relationships between thoughts, feelings and behaviours. When you have low self-esteem, you might notice that there are particular thoughts, feelings and behaviours that you experience. We've listed examples of these in the table on the next page. Are any of these familiar to you?

Thoughts	Feelings	Behaviours	Sensations
• Thinking you are useless or not good enough	• Sad	• Avoid doing things that feel challenging in case you fail	• Tense
• Putting yourself down	• Anxious	• Give up when things feel difficult	• Restless
• Doubting yourself and your abilities	• Guilty	• Work really hard or over-prepare to try and prevent failure	• Tired
• Thinking negatively about yourself or your appearance	• Ashamed	• Try to make sure that your work is perfect with no mistakes	• Heavy
• Disliking yourself	• Disgusted	• Avoid being around people in case you are rejected	• Hot
• Comparing yourself to others who you think are better than you	• Embarrassed	• Hide your true self or pretend to be someone else (wear make-up, don't talk, put on an act)	• Cold
• Setting very high standards for yourself	• Frustrated		• Heart beats quicker
• Wanting to be perfect	• Angry		• Breathing increases
	• Jealous		• Headache
	• Hopeless		• Stomach-ache
	• Lonely		• Feel sick

- Focusing on your
  weaknesses/the
  negatives/things that
  go wrong

- Dismissing or
  discounting positive
  achievements, or
  putting these down
  to luck

- Expecting things to go
  badly

- Expecting to fail

- Blaming yourself if
  things go wrong

- Worrying about
  letting others down

- Worrying that no one
  will like you

- Try and do what
  others want, to please
  them

- Try and change
  yourself (appearance,
  interests) to fit in with
  others

- Apologise even when
  you've done nothing
  wrong

- Ignore your own needs
  and wishes

- Seek reassurance or
  compliments from
  others to feel better
  about yourself

- Act aggressively
  towards yourself and
  others

Thoughts, feelings, behaviours and physical sensations associated with low self-esteem

Thoughts

When you have low self-esteem, it's a bit like having an invisible bully who constantly whispers in your ear and tells you that you are not good enough. Sometimes it might even shout at you. It's hard to ignore the bully because it feels that everything they tell you is true! The bully notices everything that doesn't go quite right, or if you've made a mistake. It also likes to tell you all the bad things that it thinks other people think about you. If things have gone well, the bully twists it to make you think that you've been lucky, or that others are just being kind. It likes to make predictions about what is going to happen; for example, telling you that you will fail a test because you're not smart enough, or that you won't be invited to a party because no one likes you. The more you listen to the bully, the stronger the thoughts get and the more powerful the bully becomes.

A self-esteem bully constantly puts you down, criticises you and tells you you're no good. Instead, can you talk to yourself like a friend

Feelings

If you've got a self-esteem bully constantly telling you that you're no good, then it's no wonder that you might feel sad, disgusted or ashamed about yourself. The self-esteem bully is also good at making you feel worried and anxious about things that are going to happen, like exams or social activities, because it makes predictions about how badly they will go. People with low self-esteem can feel sad and anxious most of the time.

Behaviours

As humans, we're programmed to avoid danger and distress, and so it follows that we behave in certain ways to cope with our self-esteem bully. This might mean that you *avoid* doing things that feel really challenging or where there is a risk that you might fail or be rejected. Or perhaps you *escape* from situations that feel overwhelming. At other times you might try really hard to make up for your shortcomings by engaging in *safety behaviours*, like overpreparing for a test or trying to make your homework perfect (have a look at Chapter 2 for more information). In social situations this might mean putting on an act or changing your appearance (for example wearing lots of make-up or losing weight) to try and fit in. In other words, you try to prevent the self-esteem bully's predictions from coming true.

Physical sensations

Our thoughts, feelings and behaviours can affect our bodies too. The sensations we experience will depend on what we are thinking, how we are feeling and what we do. So if you feel anxious or worried, you might notice that your heart rate increases and that you feel tense and restless. If you feel sad, your body might feel heavy and tired.

The low self-esteem trap

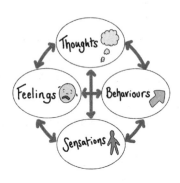

The problem is that the safety behaviours that we do to protect ourselves from our self-esteem bully often back-fire and make the situation worse. This ends up confirming what the self-esteem bully says because it's more likely that the negative predictions come true. This in turn triggers negative feelings. Even if the safety behaviours don't make things worse, they stop you from learning that the self-esteem bully's predictions might not actually be true, because you don't give yourself a chance to find out what happens without the safety behaviours. Having low self-esteem can have an impact on many areas of our lives; for example, school performance, family, friendships, hobbies, body image and wellbeing.

For example, Jen's self-esteem bully constantly told her that she was no good at school and useless at tennis. It always predicted that she would fail and let everyone down. This made Jen feel anxious and sad. To try and prevent the predictions coming true, Jen would study every evening until very late and all weekend. She stopped seeing friends to focus on schoolwork, and put all her effort into trying to make her work perfect. To try and improve her tennis performance, Jen began to eat less to lose weight as she thought this would make her quicker on the court. The result: Jen felt so exhausted and lacking in energy that both her school and tennis performance reduced, which confirmed the self-esteem bully's predictions and made Jen feel even worse. The self-esteem bully told her she wasn't trying hard enough, but the more she tried to study harder and lose weight, the worse things became. Jen was trapped.

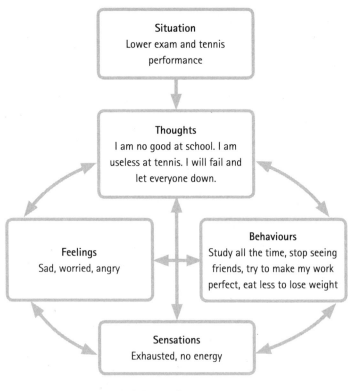

Jen's low self-esteem trap

Jake's self-esteem bully always told him how rubbish he was at school. It told him he was stupid and that everyone else was better than him. When his teacher introduced a new topic that Jake didn't understand, he felt anxious and embarrassed. He started to mess around to avoid doing the classwork. If he didn't do it, then he wouldn't get it wrong and the self-esteem bully's predictions couldn't come true. When his teacher confronted him about his behaviour, Jake felt angry and left the classroom, and felt even worse about himself for being told off.

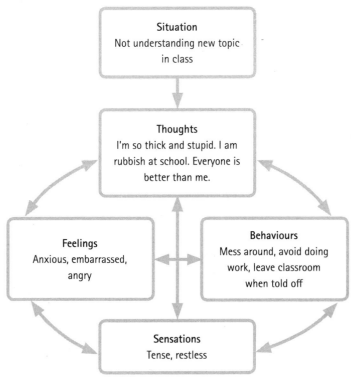

Jake's low self-esteem trap

Aisha's self-esteem bully tells her that no one likes her because she is weird and ugly compared with her peers. Aisha really wants to be liked and fit in, so she copies the other girls' interests, wears lots of make-up to try and improve her appearance and tries to lose weight. When she's with her peers, she either keeps quiet or agrees with what everyone is saying even though she often has different opinions. But rather than increase her confidence, Aisha continues to feel bad as she's constantly worried that she will be 'found out' and that her peers would reject her if they knew the 'real' her.

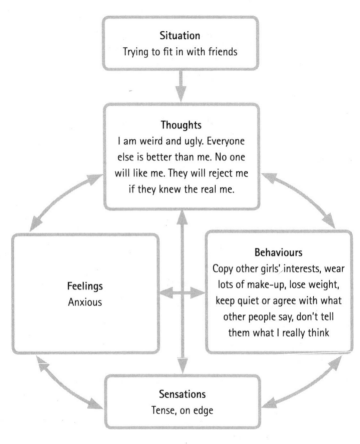

Aisha's low self-esteem trap

Ask yourself:

- What does your self-esteem bully tell you?

- How does this make you feel?

- What do you do to prevent the self-esteem bully's predictions coming true?

- Do your behaviours make the situation better or worse, or just keep you stuck?

- What effect does this have on your self-esteem?

How to improve your self-esteem

If you think that you are suffering from low self-esteem there are lots of things that you can do to build your confidence and feel better about yourself. Imagine a balance scale which is heavily weighted down on one side with your low self-esteem. Improving your self-esteem means questioning and changing the unhelpful thoughts and behaviours that weigh your self-esteem down, and adding positive thoughts and experiences to the other side to create a more balanced perspective. Remember, having healthy self-esteem is not about thinking that you are brilliant all the time: it's about having a balanced perspective that recognises both your strengths and weaknesses and allows you to accept yourself just the way you are.

You can create a more balanced self-esteem by questioning and changing unhelpful thoughts and behaviours, and adding positive thoughts and experiences

Questioning unhelpful thoughts

Stand up to your self-esteem bully When your self-esteem bully criticises you, tells you that bad things are going to happen or that no one will like you, you don't have to listen to it or believe what it says! We're often taught to stand up to bullies or ignore what they say, and that's exactly what you can do when your self-esteem bully is giving you a hard time. Remember, the things the self-esteem bully tells you are not facts, they are just unhelpful, biased and inaccurate opinions designed to make you feel bad (check out Chapter 2 for more information on facts and opinions). Here are some ways you can stand up to your self-esteem bully:

Try to ignore it and concentrate on something else Sam noticed that their self-esteem bully tended to be loudest when they were on their own and not doing much. Once they recognised this, they were able to tell themselves *'It's just my self-esteem bully talking, I don't have to listen to it'*, and they went and found something to do. Try not to suppress or push away the thought as this can make it bounce back. Instead, notice when it is there and then distract yourself with something else so that you don't have to listen to it. When does your self-esteem bully tend to bully you? What can you do at these times to help you to ignore it?

Use your imagination to make it less powerful Jake felt so small when his self-esteem bully started to criticise him. He found it difficult to ignore because the bully seemed so huge and powerful. Jake could picture his self-esteem bully towering over him and giving him a hard time. However, he realised that he could change the image in his mind. The next time the bully had a go at him, Jake imagined it getting smaller and smaller. As it got smaller, the bully's voice got squeakier and squeakier until Jake could no longer hear what it was saying. By using his imagination to shrink the image of his self-esteem bully, Jake no longer felt power-less and was able to laugh at his bully. You could use your imagination to change the image of your self-esteem bully so that it no longer feels so threatening to you.

Hit it with the facts Jen found it really helpful to remind herself that the things her self-esteem bully told her were not true. When her self-esteem bully criticised her or told her she was no good, Jen would remind herself of the facts: *'What evidence is there that the things the self-esteem bully says are not true?'* So, when the self-esteem bully told her she was a failure, Jen created a list of all the evidence that showed this wasn't true, such as getting good marks for her homework, being made sports captain at school, having a good end-of-year report and being picked for the county tennis tournament. She found it helpful to write down evidence of her strengths and achievements in a notebook. What evidence do you have that your self-esteem bully is not telling the truth?

Ask yourself:

- What can you do to help you to ignore your self-esteem bully?

- How can you change the image of your self-esteem bully to make it less threatening?

- What evidence is there that the self-esteem bully is not telling the truth? How could you start collecting more evidence each day?

Stop expecting the worst

Is it possible to predict the future or read someone else's mind? If you could, you probably would have won the lottery by now! So why should you believe your self-esteem bully when it predicts the worst will happen? We can only ever guess what will happen in the future, or what another person is thinking. It's a bit like guessing lottery numbers – it's not at all accurate or reliable. It's important to keep an open mind about what might happen in a situation, or what others might be thinking, because you can never know for sure. We need to look for the facts and find out what really happens when we stop avoiding situations or drop our safety behaviours (see below).

Stop focusing on the negative

If your self-esteem bully is in charge, you may find yourself being on the lookout for any sign that what it tells you is true. It's a bit like wearing a pair of glasses that are programmed to allow you only to see the negative things the self-esteem bully tells you. For example, Aisha was constantly on the lookout for any sign that her friends didn't like her. She was so focused on this that she didn't notice anything that didn't fit with this negative view. Aisha needed to re-programme the glasses so that she could also see the positive to help her to develop a more balanced perspective. So, although Aisha saw that one of her friends would sometimes partner another girl in class, she also noticed that at other times she would be chosen instead. When Jen re-programmed her self-esteem glasses, she learned to focus on the points she had won in tennis, rather than focusing on the points she had lost – and added these to her notebook of achievements too!

Ask yourself:

• What new information do you notice when you re-programme your self-esteem glasses?

Stop jumping to conclusions

We can also fall into the low self-esteem trap when we jump to conclusions about a situation without really knowing what is happening. When Sam noticed their classmates talking and laughing across the school canteen, Sam instantly thought that they must be laughing at them. Sam reminded themself that there could be lots of reasons why their classmates were laughing, so they decided to ask them what they were finding funny. Sam found out that they were laughing about something that had happened in their geography lesson, and not about them at all.

Stop making comparisons

When you have low self-esteem, it's common to compare yourself with others who you think are so much better than you. Jake constantly compared himself against the students who always got top marks in class, which increased his belief that he was stupid. But then his teacher helped him to realise that comparing himself against students without learning difficulties was not a fair measure. This helped Jake to focus on the things *he* could do, regardless of how others in his class were doing. When he stopped comparing himself with others, Jake began to feel better about himself.

Change unreasonable standards

Jen

My self-esteem bully is always telling me that I <u>should</u> get top marks for my school work, or that I <u>must</u> win all my tennis matches. It's so demanding and exhausting! If I don't live up to its expectations, then I think I am a failure.

Does your self-esteem bully have very high standards, or expect you to be perfect all the time? Does it use words like *'You must . . .'* or *'You should . . .'* and demand that you follow the rules that it sets? These standards and rules are another part of the low self-esteem trap: they are often unfair and set you up to fail because they are impossible to stick to or achieve all the time – no one could! When you don't reach the self-esteem bully's high standards (and it's pretty likely that you won't) or you break the rules that it sets (which tends to happen because they are too strict), the self-esteem bully makes you believe that it's because you are not good enough. But the problem is not you – the problem is that the rules and standards are unreasonable and unfair!

Changing the rules and standards so that they are realistic and fair can help to improve your self-esteem. It's helpful to think about what you would reasonably expect someone else to do. Would you expect them to be perfect, or always be the best? Flexible guidelines are more helpful than rigid rules, because they can be adapted to fit the situation you are in. If you find that you're always trying to live up to the self-esteem bully's high standards, you might find it helpful to have a look at Chapter 11, which talks more about perfectionism and how to overcome it.

My self-esteem bully's unreasonable standards and rigid rules	My reasonable and realistic standards and flexible guidelines
• You should always get top marks for your schoolwork. • You must win all your tennis matches.	• Try your best – it doesn't have to be perfect. • You don't need to win all the time – it's just as important to have fun!

Jen's flexible guidelines

Ask yourself:

- What are your self-esteem bully's unreasonable standards and rigid rules?

- Would you expect a friend or family member to live up to these rules?

- What reasonable and realistic standards and flexible guidelines might be more helpful?

Changing unhelpful behaviours

By now, you may have realised that you don't have to listen to your self-esteem bully or believe everything it tells you. We've shown that it's very likely that the things it says have been twisted or are not true at all. As well as challenging the things the self-esteem bully tells you, it's important not to give in and do what it says. You can stop the self-esteem bully from controlling your behaviour by *doing* things a bit differently too.

Stop avoiding

Now that you know the self-esteem bully can't predict the future or mindread, it's time to stop avoiding situations and to give things a go. Approaching, rather than avoiding, situations can be really useful because it helps us to gather more evidence so that we can hit the self-esteem bully with the facts. For example, instead of avoiding doing his mathematics because it seemed too difficult, Jake asked his teacher for help and found out he was able to complete the questions. Jake learned that he was actually able to do mathematics and that it was good to ask for help. He was able to hit his self-esteem bully with the facts and feel proud of himself.

It might feel a bit scary to stop avoiding and give things a go. It can help to do this step-by-step, starting with smaller challenges and building this up. Jake's teacher helped him to identify several steps he could take to stop avoiding situations where he was worried about getting things wrong or appearing stupid. The list below represents the different steps on a ladder. The items at the bottom of the list/ladder are easier to achieve; as you climb the ladder it gets progressively harder until you reach your goal at the top.

Do a short presentation to my class

Put my hand up to answer a question

Put my hand up to ask a question

Work in a pair to complete a mathematics problem

Work with a teaching assistant to complete a maths problem

Complete a worksheet on something I have read

Jake's challenges to feel more confident in the classroom

Drop your safety behaviours

Remember that safety behaviours are things that we do to help us to cope with difficult situations, but which actually tend to keep us stuck. Jen's safety behaviours were to overwork without taking any breaks to try and prevent failure at school or tennis, while Aisha would wear lots of make-up and agree with her peer group to try to fit in and be liked. The problem with safety behaviours is that they make us believe that they are the only reason that things go well, and that we must keep doing them to cover up our flaws. Safety behaviours can often make things worse and lock us into a low self-esteem trap. One way to break free of the trap is to drop your safety behaviours. It's likely that the self-esteem bully will tell you that this is a bad idea, but remember, you don't have to listen to it! In fact, dropping your safety behaviours can be another way of gathering more evidence so that you can hit the self-esteem bully with the facts.

For example, Aisha decided that constantly putting on an act to try and fit in with her friends was exhausting. She worried that she might slip up and be found out and that her friends wouldn't like the 'real her'. However, Aisha realised that she wasn't giving them a chance to like her because they didn't really know her. Aisha decided to drop her safety behaviours to find out how her friends would respond if she didn't wear make-up all the time or if she shared her opinions. Aisha's self-esteem bully predicted that they would think that she was weird and ugly and that they would stop hanging out with her. However, when Aisha didn't wear make-up one day, she was surprised to find out that her friends all commented on what lovely skin she had. On another occasion, when one of her friends was talking about a film they had enjoyed, Aisha shared that she actually hadn't liked it much, and found out that several of her friends felt the same way. Aisha learned that the predictions made by her self-esteem bully had not come true, and that her friends did not reject her when she was being true to herself. Aisha began to feel more confident about herself.

It can feel a bit scary to drop safety behaviours, but learning what happens without them can really help improve your self-esteem.

Take action! My safety behaviour experiment

- What safety behaviour would you like to drop?

- What does your self-esteem bully predict will happen if you don't do your safety behaviour?

- What do you need to do to drop your safety behaviour? When will you do it?

- What happened when you dropped your safety behaviour? Did the self-esteem bully's prediction come true?

- Have you learned anything different about yourself?

Building a healthy self-esteem – learning that you are OK as you are!

We've looked at how you can challenge and change some of the unhelpful thoughts and behaviours that keep low self-esteem in place, but remember that it's important to add positive thoughts and experiences to build a more balanced perspective. Why not try some of the ideas below?

Invest in different areas of your life

Take a look at the pie chart you made on page 183. How many slices are there? Are any of the slices significantly bigger than the rest? If your pie chart has very few slices, or there is one dominant slice, you might find it helpful to try and make your pie chart more balanced. This might mean investing more time and attention to some of the smaller slices so that they begin to take up more space. You can also introduce new slices by trying out new hobbies and activities. For example, Ella realised that she only had a few slices on her pie chart, and that her appearance was a really dominant slice. To help create a more balanced pie chart, Ella decided to spend more time with her friends and started a part-time job. The more Ella invested in other parts of her life, the less important her appearance felt to her.

*By investing in other areas of her life, Ella's self-esteem improved.
Healthy self-esteem is spread across lots of different areas of
our lives with no dominant slices.*

Do things for fun rather than for achievement

During adolescence, there can often feel like a lot of pressure to achieve, to pass exams or get the right grades for college or university, or to apply for a job. But not everything you do has to be about being the best you can be, and focusing on achievement all the time can suck the fun out of things. It's important to do things just for fun – it doesn't matter whether you're good at it or not, as long as you are enjoying it! What things do you enjoy doing? How can you make more time to do them more regularly?

Take action! Invest in different areas of your life and doing things for fun

- What types of hobbies and activities do your friends do? Can you go along and try them out?

- What clubs or activities are advertised at your school, local library or community noticeboard, newsletter or website?

- What do you notice other people enjoying?

- What hobbies or activities have you done in the past that you enjoyed?

- Are there things that you've always liked the idea of doing, but never tried?

- What activities could you do on your own? With friends? With your family?

- What could you do that might fill a day? What might you do in spare moments here and there?

- What activities could you do in your own home or garden?

- What activities or hobbies can you think of that might not cost anything? Are there others that you might have to pay for?

- What activities can you think of that use your mind? That get you physically active? That are about self-care?

(adapted from Melanie Fennell, 2021)

Notice your positive qualities

Chloe really struggled to think of herself as having any positive qualities because she was so preoccupied with how negatively she felt about her body. When Chloe was encouraged to think about how she would describe the qualities she valued in her closest friends, she was surprised to notice that her friends' physical appearance didn't matter to her at all! Instead, she thought about how caring, loyal and funny they were. Chloe asked her friends and family what words they would use to describe her, and learned that they valued her for being kind, a good listener and having a great sense of humour. Chloe started to pay attention to times where she helped others or made them laugh, which helped her to see herself in a different way. She realised that she had lots of positive qualities and that how she looked didn't matter to other people at all.

It can feel hard to notice your positive qualities if you experience low self-esteem, but it's very likely that there are several things that are good about you! To help you to identify them, you could try asking your family and friends what they like about you and keep a diary of the times and situations where you show these qualities. Gathering evidence of your positive qualities is another way of hitting the low self-esteem bully with the facts and creating a more balanced view of yourself.

Listen to compliments and take credit for successes

Do you find yourself ignoring or dismissing compliments and positive feedback (*'They're only saying it because they are being kind'*)? Do you tend to put your successes down to 'good luck' or something about the situation rather than your ability (*'I only did well because it was an easy test'*)? To combat low self-esteem, it's important to recognise your talents, strengths, achievements and qualities as things that belong to you rather than some fluke. If someone compliments you, try saying 'Thank you' instead of dismissing it. If you've done well in something, accept the praise. This might take a bit of practice, but it is an important step in improving your self-esteem.

Spend time with people who make you feel good about yourself

Sometimes the people around us can really influence how we feel about ourselves. It can be helpful to spend time with people who make you feel good about yourself, who you enjoy spending time with and have fun with. This might also mean spending less time with people who might knock your confidence or criticise you.

Treat yourself like a friend

Would you speak to your best friend in the way the self-esteem bully talks to you? Most people are horrified to imagine criticising or putting down someone they care about. To help build your self-esteem, try talking to yourself in the way that you would speak to a friend. This might mean being positive, encouraging and non-judgemental, noticing and praising the things that go well, and being supportive and kind when things don't go to plan. It's also important to treat yourself kindly and take care of yourself. What actions can you take to look after yourself (see Chapter 6 for some ideas)?

A word on coping

It is important to remember that situations don't always go to plan, and sometimes things happen that can knock our self-esteem. At these times it's important not to take things to heart or allow your self-esteem bully to take control. Use the strategies in this chapter to try and keep a balanced perspective – and don't forget the coping strategies discussed in Chapter 7.

Summary

- Self-esteem refers to how good or bad you feel about yourself. Self-esteem can feel lower in adolescence because of all the changes, demands and expectations that you are experiencing.

- Having low self-esteem can affect your thoughts, feelings and behaviour. Some of the things you do to cope with your low self-esteem can lock you into a low self-esteem trap.

- Building a healthier self-esteem involves changing unhelpful ways of thinking and behaving and developing more balanced thoughts and positive experiences.

Chapter 10

How to Feel Good About Your Body

On Saturday, I went to meet my friends in town. We were standing together in a circle talking about a TV series that everyone is watching, but I found it so difficult to focus on what they were saying. I just couldn't stop thinking about how much bigger and taller I am compared with everyone else. They looked tiny in their skinny jeans and tight-fitting T-shirts, and even though I had tried to hide my body under a baggy jumper and loose-fitting trousers, I just felt ginormous. As we stood there, I was aware of slouching down to try and make myself look smaller and less noticeable. I could feel myself getting hot and sweaty in my big jumper. I couldn't help looking at other girls as they walked past — they were all so much smaller and prettier than me. When I got home, I went straight to my room, and I couldn't stop myself going on social media and looking at influencers with perfect bodies and pictures of girls I know, like Ella in the year above, who always looks amazing. By this time, I was feeling really bad about my body, so searched for 'how to get the perfect body' and read about dieting and weight loss regimes. When I went to bed that night, I spent ages standing in front of the full-length mirror in my bedroom staring at my body from different angles and pinching my hips, thighs and stomach. I wish I wasn't such a big, fat, ugly giant.

Chloe

What this chapter will cover:

- What keeps body image worries going?
- How to improve body image.
    - Strategies for challenging unhelpful behaviours.
    - Strategies for improving body acceptance.

In the last chapter, we looked at self-esteem, and thought about the different factors that can influence it, like your academic skills, sporting ability, behaviour, social acceptance and physical appearance. Teenagers experience huge changes in their physical appearance during puberty (see Chapter 1). They are also exposed to lots of messages and images on social media about what the 'perfect' body should look like, at a time of their life when it feels important to fit in. All this can really affect a young person's body image and self-esteem.

In Chapter 5, we talked about some of the factors that influence the development of body image concerns. This chapter thinks about what keeps them going, and looks at how to overcome body dissatisfaction and improve body acceptance.

What keeps body image worries going?

It's understandable that when you have a big worry, you might want to take action to try and fix it, or to make yourself feel better. Remember, we learned in Chapter 2 that our behaviours are connected to our thoughts and feelings, and are usually our best attempts to cope with the worries that we have. But do these behaviours help you to manage body image concerns, or can they make things worse?

Check it out: Behaviours that can increase body image concerns

- Mirror checking

- Body checking

- Weight checking

- Making comparisons

- Avoiding your body

- Restricting food

- Exercise

- Body blaming

Now let's look at each in turn.

Mirror checking

Most people use mirrors on a daily basis to check their outfit, brush their teeth or do their hair. But when you have a body image concern, you might have an urge to keep looking in the mirror because you are worried about your body shape or size.

Aisha

As soon as I wake up, the first thing I think about is whether my body has changed overnight. I have this ritual where I stand in front of the mirror to check whether anything has changed. I spend ages staring at my stomach, hips and thighs to see if they have become bigger and questioning whether they look different from the day before. I check myself in the mirror after I've eaten too, because I feel so bloated and fat. I turn this way and that to check my body out from different angles, but the more I look, the harder it is to know whether what I'm seeing has changed. Sometimes I swear it has – and it makes me feel really anxious.

I notice that I also check my reflection every time I pass a mirror or window to see if it looks big. I look at my body before I go to bed too and repeat the checks I do in the morning. I don't like looking in the mirror, but I just feel so scared about my body changing that I can't help it.

Have a look at the table below and think about which mirror-checking behaviours you find yourself doing. We've highlighted the behaviours that are pretty typical and part of everyday life, versus those that are unhelpful and tend to maintain body image concerns.

Typical behaviours	Unhelpful behaviours
Using the mirror to brush/style hair	Returning to look at yourself in mirrors several times throughout the day
Using the mirror to clean teeth	Spending long periods of time checking yourself, or feeling 'stuck' in front of the mirror
Using the mirror to put make-up on or to shave	Scrutinising particular parts of your body (e.g. stomach, thighs, legs) while ignoring other parts
Using the mirror to check an outfit	Examining your body from different angles or positions
Using the mirror at particular times of the day (e.g. when getting ready in the morning or going to bed at night)	Needing to change your outfit several times in front of the mirror before you are ready to leave the house in the morning or during the day
Glancing at your reflection in windows and mirrors when out and about	Checking your reflection repeatedly in mirrors and windows when out and about

Typical and unhelpful behaviours relating to the use of mirrors

But why is mirror checking so unhelpful, and how does it keep body image difficulties going? Mirror checking is unhelpful because what you see in the mirror is never a truly accurate reflection of your appearance. There are several reasons for this:

- Mirrors are often slightly curved, which can make you appear either taller and slimmer, or shorter and fatter, depending on how the mirror is made.

- Have you ever had a spot on your face that seems absolutely ginormous when you look in the mirror, yet your parents and friends tell you they can barely see it? Scrutinising parts of your body for long periods of time can have a *magnifying* effect and make things appear bigger than they actually are. This is because when we stare at one part of ourselves, we lose all perspective. We don't see how big the spot is compared to the size of our nose, our whole face or the rest of the body; we only see the spot. It's similar when you stare at your stomach or thighs: you lose all sense of scale.

- When you only focus on the parts of your body that you are dissatisfied with, you tend to ignore and not notice other parts that you might feel neutral about or even quite like. This can give a very unbalanced perspective of ourselves. When Aisha looked at herself in the mirror, she only paid attention to her stomach, hips and thighs and completely ignored the parts of herself that she felt OK about, like her hair, teeth and skin tone.

- What you see when you look in the mirror can also be affected by your thoughts and feelings. Have you noticed that you sometimes feel better about looking in the mirror on days when you're feeling more happy or positive, while on those 'down' days everything seems bad?

Body checking

I use a tape measure to check whether my body has got bigger, and I'm constantly running my hands around my waist to check my stomach is flat and that I'm straight up and down.

There are many ways of body checking, like pinching the flesh on your stomach or thighs, measuring parts of your body, checking clothes for tightness, or looking at the way your thighs spread or your stomach bulges when you sit down. Just like mirror checking, these behaviours are unhelpful and not an accurate way of checking your size and shape because they focus on the negative and magnify perceived flaws. Everyone's thighs spread when they sit down because of the effect of gravity – you're just unlikely to notice this in other people because you don't look at their legs from the same angle as you see your own when you are seated. Most people will notice some rolls of flesh when they sit down, but these stretch out when they stand up straight.

Weight checking Frequent weight checking is another behaviour that keeps body image concerns going. The problem is that your weight changes up to 2 kg over the course of a day depending on what you have eaten and drunk, whether you have been to the toilet, how hot and sweaty you are and (for girls and women) where you are in your menstrual cycle. Weighing yourself several times a day means that you notice these small and normal changes and think they are more significant than they actually are.

It's important to remember that during adolescence you are growing, so your weight will continue to increase into your early twenties. This is a normal and healthy part of growth and development, rather than a sign that you are getting fat. If your clothes feel too small, it's likely that you've grown out of them because you are getting older, rather than it being a sign that you are overweight.

Making comparisons When you compare your size and shape to other people, does it make you feel good about yourself? We tend to be drawn to making comparisons with people we think are better than us in some way. This makes us feel bad because we're focusing on what we like about them and what we dislike about ourselves, so the difference between us and them can feel huge. We don't often pay attention to people we think are similar to us or worse off than us. This means that the comparisons that we make are biased and unfair. When Chloe thought about the people she compared herself with, she realised she always focused on the girls she thought were smaller than her, which reinforced her image of herself as being a 'big fat ugly giant'. She barely noticed girls with different-shaped bodies because she was so focused on a particular body type.

The way we compare ourselves to others can create difficulties too: we might spend a lot of time scrutinising our own bodies but make decisions about what other people's bodies look like on the basis of a quick glance. We also never really know what other people's bodies are like under their clothes. It's quite possible that they might not be as 'perfect' as you think they are.

Comparing yourself with images on the internet or on social media can be even more problematic. Not everybody posts pictures of themselves on the internet, and those who do are not always representative of the wide range of body types that exists in the world. These idealised bodies are also very likely to be edited, or at least presented from the best angle or against the best backdrop, for maximum effect.

In cases where prominent online influencers are close to us in age, or we relate to them in some other way, such as having similar hair colour or height, it is all too easy to compare ourselves with them. It can be helpful to view images of people online with a cautious eye – the photo is likely to be just a snapshot into someone's life and might not be reflective of who they are or what they really look like and how they really feel. When we start to compare ourselves with people online (who we know or don't know) we can set ourselves an unattainable standard of 'perfection' against which we always perceive ourselves to fail.

It's also not fair to compare your teenage body with the body of a model who spends all day, every day, trying to look that way because it is their job. As a teenager, you have lots of other things going on, which means that you can't (and shouldn't) invest so much time controlling your weight and shape.

Avoiding your body It's not unusual for people with body image concerns to avoid looking at their body (and stop others looking at their body) by wearing baggy clothes, not looking in the mirror, avoiding getting changed in public places like changing rooms or avoiding drawing attention to themselves by slouching down. Sometimes people flip from body checking to body avoidance to cope with the distressing thoughts and feelings that body checking creates. The problem is that the image we have of ourselves in our mind may not be how we actually look. It tends to be distorted by the negative thoughts and feelings we have about ourselves. Avoiding or hiding your body prevents you from finding out that your body might not be as bad as you think, and prevents opportunities for learning something new about yourself. Some avoidance behaviours, such as slouching or wearing big baggy clothes, can even make us appear bigger than we actually are.

Restricting food We know from Chapters 1 and 3 that our body shape, size and height are largely determined by our genetics. Limiting your food intake to change your body is not only extremely unhealthy, but can also take a considerable effort which is hard to keep going over several weeks and months. Constantly trying to control your weight and shape will lock you into a continuous cycle of worry. This is how Aisha felt when she went on a strict diet.

Exercise Regular exercise is an important part of our physical and emotional wellbeing. However, if you feel like you *have to* exercise, you feel guilty about not exercising, or if exercising is getting in the way of other things like going to bed at a reasonable time or seeing friends, it may have become another way of managing body image concerns. The problem is that excessive exercise (particularly if you are underweight) can increase your risk of physical health problems, like stress fractures in your bones (see Chapter 13 for more details). Excessive exercise can also keep the spotlight on body image concerns by locking you into a cycle whereby you feel you *have* to exercise in order to manage your weight.

Body blaming

> *I'm sitting at my desk trying to get through a mountain of homework, but I can't concentrate because I just feel so fat. I always feel this way after meals or when I'm sitting down doing schoolwork. It's there when I have a bad training session too. It's really confusing because the scales say my weight is the same, but I keep feeling fat.*

Jen

Sometimes we can 'feel' fat even when we know our weight hasn't changed. Jen often experienced 'feeling' fat at particular times of the day, such as after meals or when she's trying to do her homework, even though she knows her weight hasn't changed.

So what's going on? *Feeling* fat does not mean *being* fat. We can show this by the two lines on the graph below: the 'feeling fat' line changes, despite the weight line staying pretty stable. It's likely that Jen was mislabelling physical or emotional states and blaming her body for things that felt difficult. For example, Jen tended to mislabel the bloatedness she experienced after meals or the anxiety she felt about her homework as 'feeling fat'. She also blamed her body when she felt frustrated with her tennis performance.

Feeling fat doesn't mean being fat

The body image trap

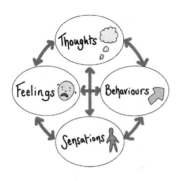

If you feel concerned about how you look, then you might notice that you do some of these behaviours too. The problem, as with many of the other difficulties we have been discussing in other chapters, is that the behaviours we do to manage our body image worries often keep us stuck with the worry, or can make the worry worse. This is the body image trap.

For example, Chloe had a worry that she was so much bigger than all the other girls in her year group. This led to lots of self-critical thoughts about being 'fat and ugly'. She felt upset and unhappy, and noticed her body becoming hot and sweaty. She went out of her way to make herself less noticeable when she was with her friends, but when she tried to hide her body by wearing oversized clothes and slouching down, she noticed she felt no better, and felt as big as ever. When Chloe compared herself with other people, or checked her body in the mirror and pinched her flesh, she didn't feel any better about her body; in fact, it made her pay more attention to the parts she didn't like, which made her feel even worse. The behaviours Chloe did to try and cope with her body image kept her stuck in the body image trap.

Behaviour	Consequence
• Wearing baggy clothes.	• Makes me feel even more gigantic than I really am.
• Slouching down.	
• Looking at models on social media.	• Makes me look really big and awkward.
• Comparing myself with other girls at school.	• Makes me feel awful! I know I can never look like that.
• Looking in the mirror and pinching my stomach and thighs.	• Makes it really difficult to concentrate on other things because I'm always checking out how other people look.
	• Makes me focus on the parts of my body that I don't like.

The negative consequences of Chloe's body-checking behaviour

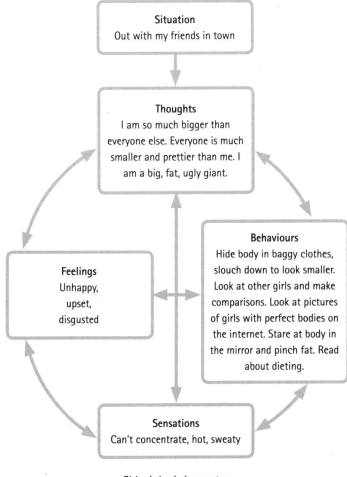

Chloe's body image trap

Aisha also felt intensely uncomfortable in her body and experienced lots of worrying thoughts about her body changing and becoming bigger. This caused her a lot of anxiety, and she would often feel sick, tense and restless. Aisha felt compelled to keep checking her body for any sign that it was changing, including measuring herself with a tape measure or scrutinising herself in the mirror several times a day. But rather than reassuring Aisha, these behaviours had the opposite effect of constantly reminding her of how much she disliked her body.

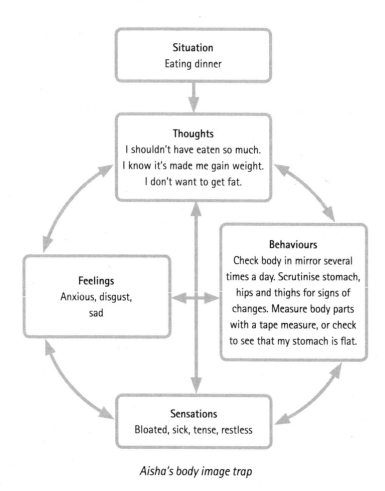

Aisha's body image trap

Ask yourself:

- What behaviours do you do when you feel worried about your body image?

- What effect do they have on your body image concerns?

We can draw out the body image trap using the diagram below. We call this a 'vicious flower', with your thoughts about your body image in the middle and each petal showing a behaviour that is done in response to the worry. Although you are trying to feel better, these behaviours tend to keep the focus on the worry, or make the worry worse. Some of your petals might be similar to Chloe's but you might have other ones too, like doing more exercise, frequently checking your weight, or avoiding looking at your body at all.

Chloe's vicious body image flower

Ask yourself: My vicious body image flower

- What might your own vicious body image flower look like?

- Try mapping it out: put your worry thought in the middle, and all the behaviours you do in response on each petal.

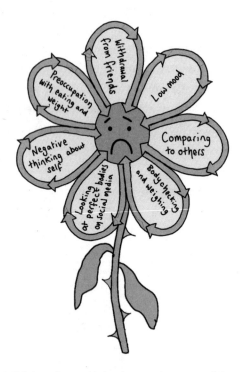

Unhelpful thoughts and behaviours can create a vicious cycle that keeps body image concerns going

How to improve body image

We've identified that many of the behaviours that we do when we have body image concerns can actually make our concerns worse and can have a negative impact on other aspects of our lives. But how can you improve your body image? One thing you can do is to change unhelpful thoughts and behaviours. The other is to learn to accept and appreciate your body as it is. These strategies are not about changing your body but reducing the level of distress you might experience.

Strategies for changing unhelpful thoughts and behaviours

Once you have identified the behaviours you do in response to your body image concerns, the next step is to try and change them. Some might require a bit of modifying (for example, how often you look in the mirror), while others are better to stop completely (for example, measuring or checking your body). As you change your behaviours, imagine pulling the petals off your vicious flower. The more petals you pull off, the more your worries about your body will reduce.

Reduce mirror checking We all need to look in the mirror as part of our daily routine, so trying to completely stop using mirrors is unrealistic and probably unhelpful (see the section on body avoidance on page 235). So, if you know that scrutinising your body in the mirror is unhelpful and inaccurate, how do you change it? It can be helpful to try and limit mirror checking to those listed in the 'Typical behaviours' column of the table above. This might mean setting limits on when you stand in front of the mirror and for how long. When you see your reflection, look at it in relation to other features in the room (for example, the window or furniture) to help give a sense of perspective and scale. If you notice that the urge to mirror check is driven by worry about your body, try to resist doing it by moving away from the mirror and distracting yourself with an absorbing activity. Rather than going straight to the mirror when she woke up, Aisha made sure that she got dressed first, which helped her to focus on what she was wearing, rather than on what her body looked like. Instead of mirror checking after she'd eaten, Aisha distracted herself by spending time with her sisters until the bloated sensation had gone away. This was hard at first, as checking herself in the mirror had become a habit, but slowly it got easier over time and she noticed that the distress about her body reduced.

Stop body checking Body checking tends to be quite secretive and doesn't serve any helpful function, so it's best to stop doing it all together. The first step is to notice when you're most likely to do it (for example, after a meal, during lessons, when you're in the shower), and try to distract yourself or use some coping skills to resist the urge (see Chapter 7). Rather than focus inwards on your body, you could try and turn your attention outwards and use your five senses to notice things going on around you. When you stop body checking, it's not unusual to feel more preoccupied with body image concerns for a short while, but this soon reduces if you keep resisting the urge to check.

Check it out: Ideas for turning your attention outwards

- **See** Look at a picture or the objects around you and describe what you see in as much detail as you can.

- **Hear** Listen closely to the sounds around you or choose some music and tune into the different instruments you can hear.

- **Touch** Pick up an object and describe how it feels.

- **Smell** Go outside and focus on the smells around you.

- **Taste** Prepare yourself a snack and pay attention to different tastes.

Stop weight checking Weighing yourself several times a day or week is unhelpful, so if you are feeling preoccupied with this you might want to consider getting rid of your scales. If someone else at home uses the scales, try and let them know that you don't want to weigh yourself and that if they want to continue doing it ask them to do it out of your sight. Remember that changes in weight are unlikely to mean that you are eating too much or you need to control your diet.

There are lots of reasons why weight changes on a daily basis (for example, how much you have drunk, sweated or been to the toilet) and in the longer term (for example, because you are growing), and it doesn't mean that you need to take action to fix it. It's also important to remind yourself that your weight or clothes size is just a number and does not give a measure of your qualities, talents, strengths and all the other important factors that make you YOU!

Ask yourself:

- Does the number on the weighing scale measure the type of person you are? You might want to take a look at Chapter 9 to think more about self-esteem.

Stop making comparisons Making comparisons is not an accurate way of evaluating our bodies because of biases in the way we compare ourselves to others, and who we compare ourselves with. It can be helpful to try and look at a wider range of body shapes when you are out and about, rather than focusing on people you think are smaller than you. Chloe tried to do this the next time she was in town. This helped her to realise that people come in lots of different shapes and sizes, and helped to reduce her focus on her own body.

Check it out: Take a look at other people's body shapes

- Go to a shopping centre and look at the body shape of every fifth person you pass.

- What do you notice?

- Is every person thin?

You might also find it helpful to reduce the time you spend on social media or unhelpful internet sites, particularly when you're feeling anxious about your body. It can be a good idea to clear your browser history so that you're not constantly bombarded with adverts or links showing triggering images.

Stop avoiding your body If avoiding your body keeps you stuck in the body image trap, it can be helpful to try and get to know your body a bit better. Remember, lots of people switch from body checking to body avoidance because of how upset the checking behaviours make them feel. But this means that you can get stuck with a distorted image of what your body looks like. Getting to know what your body is really like can help you to feel better about yourself, and also give you confidence to do things that your body image worries made you avoid, like swimming or going into public changing rooms.

The activities below might help you to become more confident with your body. When Chloe started to wear clothes that fitted her shape better, instead of baggy sweatshirts and jogging bottoms, she was surprised to find that she actually felt more confident in her body.

Take action! Get to know your body

- Get used to touching your body by washing or applying body lotion. Start with the parts you feel more neutral about and work towards touching areas that feel more challenging.

- Get used to looking at yourself in the mirror without mirror checking. Pay attention to the parts of your body that you feel neutral about and keep a sense of scale by focusing out on other objects in the room rather than focusing in on your body parts.

- Get dressed in soft lighting instead of getting dressed in the dark.

- Experiment with gradually wearing less baggy clothes and try clothes that fit your shape.

- Allow yourself to be hugged by people you feel comfortable with.

- Practise getting changed in public changing rooms. You might want to start at times when shops and swimming pools are quieter and build up confidence to go at times when they are busier.

Don't restrict food Our bodies are happiest and healthiest when they have enough food to maintain our physical health and fuel our growth and activities. Eating regularly, including three main meals and snacks in between, is important for both our physical and mental wellbeing. Jen noticed that when she started eating regularly again, she felt much happier and far less preoccupied with her body. Check out Chapters 3 and 8 to find out more about healthy eating.

Exercise for fun If exercise has become something that you feel you have to do, it's important that you set limits on the amount you do to avoid injury and prevent it from fuelling body image concerns. Changing the meaning of exercise from something that is done to manage your weight and shape to something that is done for fun, to socialise or relax can also be helpful. Instead of completing gruelling workouts or gym sessions by yourself, try joining a class or team sport, or giving yoga or Pilates a go (which have benefits for emotional as well as physical wellbeing).

Stop body blaming If, like Jen, you 'feel fat' when you experience uncomfortable physical or emotional states, when you're faced with a challenge or something doesn't go to plan, it may be that you are blaming your body rather than the real cause of the problem. Remember 'feeling fat' does not mean 'being fat', so it's helpful to try and work out what's really driving these uncomfortable feelings. When Jen realised that she was blaming her body, she started paying attention to her feelings and tried to label them more accurately by asking herself *'What is really going on right now?'* Once Jen identified that the problem was really something other than being fat she was able to deal with the trigger more effectively, like reminding herself that bloating after a meal is normal and will pass, or trying problem solving and anxiety management to cope with her worries around homework and tennis (see Chapter 7).

Some teenagers may be told that they are overweight, but it is the way we *feel* about ourselves that matters. We may be over-weight but feel good about ourselves because we recognise all our values and attributes. Alternatively, we may be aver-age weight but 'feel fat' because we are stressed or anxious.

Ask yourself:

- *Feeling* fat doesn't equal *being* fat. What might really be going on for you when you 'feel' fat?

Strategies for improving body acceptance

Having a positive body image is not about liking every aspect of your body all the time: it's about having a balanced perspective and accepting and appreciating our bodies as they are. There are lots of things that you can do to feel better about your body.

Notice the positive In the section above, we looked at how focusing on the things we dislike about our body can have a magnifying effect and lock us into having a negative body image. To change the record, it's important to start pay-ing attention to the parts of your body that you find more neutral or might even like. This might feel really hard to start with, but the more you do it, the easier it gets. For example, when Aisha allowed herself to look at her body for positive features, she was surprised to realise that she actually quite liked her eyes, hair and smooth skin tone. This helped her to have a more balanced view of herself when she looked in the mirror.

Celebrate your body for what it can do, not what it looks like Rather than focusing just on what your body looks like, focus on what your body enables you to do. It can be helpful to write a list of all the things your body has allowed you to do over your lifetime, like being able to think, hug, run, dance, play sport or an instrument. Instead of worrying about being a giant, Chloe thought about how her height was actually an advantage so that she could see over people's heads when she went to music concerts; Jen realised that her muscular thighs and arms gave her strength and speed as a tennis player.

Take action!

- Write a letter to your incredible body to thank it for what it enables you to do.

Take care of your body Once you have noticed all the amazing things your body can do, it's time to look after it – after all, it's the only one you're ever going to get. What can you do to look after your body? The list below might help.

Take action! Looking after my amazing body

- Eat well – give your body nutritious food to fuel activity, and treats.

- Sleep well – allow your body to rest and repair.

- Take a bath and fill it with bubbles.

- Use moisturiser to look after your skin.

- Treat your body to a massage, facial or manicure.

- Get moving! Dance, run, swim to make your body feel alive.

Wear clothes that help you to feel good about yourself
Embrace your own style, rather than copying the latest trends if this is not something that you want to do. Different clothes suit different body shapes. It can be helpful (and fun!) to go shopping with a trusted friend and experiment with trying on different styles.

Choose friends who help you to feel good about yourself
It's not helpful to be surrounded by people who constantly make comments about weight, shape and appearance. If you find that your friends discuss these things all the time, it might be helpful to talk to them about the impact they are having and suggest that they focus on other things. Sometimes it might be necessary to turn your attention to people who help you to feel good about yourself. Jen found that spending time with her friend Zoe and sharing their

love of scary movies made her feel far happier than trying to fit in with Ella.

Change your role models We know that social media, TV, magazines and advertising are full of people who are celebrated for their looks. We can't change those images, but we *can* change what we pay attention to, and which role models we choose. There are lots of really inspiring young people out there who are doing amazing things, including athletes, artists, scientists, environmentalists and human rights activists, to name a few! Rather than looking at role models who are famous for what they look like, you might find it empowering to choose role models who are celebrated for what they do.

Invest in other areas of your life If you experience body image concerns, you might find that this gets in the way of other aspects of your life, and you stop doing things that you used to enjoy. Putting too much importance on your body image, particularly if you don't feel good about it, can lower your self-esteem. While physical appearance may be an important part of someone's self-worth, remember that it is only one dimension. It's important to invest in other areas of your life, like friendships, family, school and hobbies, to have a balanced sense of self-worth. If self-esteem is something that you struggle with, you might find it helpful to read Chapter 9.

Nurture your body image

Summary

- When we feel worried about something, it makes sense that we want to do something about it; however, some of the things we try to do to manage body image concerns, like mirror and body checking or comparing ourselves with others, can make it worse.

- It can be helpful to identify all the behaviours that you do when you feel worried about your body, and try to change them or stop them altogether.

- There are lots of thing you can do to feel better about your body, like noticing the positive and celebrating what your body can do, taking care of your body, investing in other areas of your life and changing your role models.

Chapter 11

Dealing with Perfectionism

Jen

It's Saturday night and I'm sitting at the desk in my bedroom trying to do my homework, but I'm finding it really hard to get started. I could have been at a sleepover at Zoe's, but instead I'm trying to find the perfect opening sentence for my English essay, and I can't find the right words. I type out a few lines, then delete them, jabbing at the delete button on my keyboard in frustration. I've been sitting here doing this for nearly an hour and still can't come up with anything that's any good. If I don't get a top grade it will be awful and I will probably fail my exams. I think about the evening ahead. I need to do an extra workout to keep on track with my training schedule, finish my homework and revise for the mathematics test on Monday on top of this stupid essay. It just feels so overwhelming. If I do the extra workout, then there won't be enough time to revise, and I'll fail the test. But if I revise, then how will I ever lose weight and win my next tennis match? It's going to be another late night. I feel sick, tense and restless, and the thought of failing just keeps going round and round in my mind.

What this chapter will cover:

- What is perfectionism?
- How is perfectionism different from having high personal standards?
- What influences perfectionism?
- What makes perfectionism problematic?
- How to overcome problematic perfectionism.

What is perfectionism?

In Chapter 10, we looked at the relationship between body image and self-esteem. This chapter explores perfectionism, which can also influence how you feel about yourself. Perfectionism is about setting extremely high standards and trying to achieve them *perfectly*, all the time. Most people have personal standards which help to guide their behaviour, but perfectionism can be a problem because it can have a negative impact on your life.

Personal standards v. problematic perfectionism

Check it out: Pluses and minuses

Personal standards	Problematic perfectionism
• are motivating	• is relentless and demanding
• help you to reach your goals	• is about trying to prevent failure
• help you to learn new skills	• takes a lot of time and effort
• help you to overcome challenges	• gets in the way of enjoying life
• don't get in the way of your life	• can make you feel bad about yourself
• help you to feel good about yourself	• negatively affects self-esteem
• don't negatively affect your self-esteem	

Having high standards and wanting to do well in areas of our lives that are important to us can be positive, and helps to motivate us to work towards our goals. Having standards helps us to learn new skills, rise to challenges and can feel great when we're successful. For some people, however, the drive to achieve can start to take over and have an impact on mood and other aspects of their life. This is because the need for achievement is driven by a fear of failure rather than a healthy pursuit of their goals. It's another example of the self-esteem bully trying to make you feel bad about yourself.

Perfectionism is about trying to escape from failure rather than working towards your goals

Just like people with body image concerns – whose self-esteem is hugely influenced by the importance they place on their appearance – people who struggle with perfectionism tend to base their self-esteem on achievement and success. It's likely that their self-esteem pie chart would have a large achievement slice, and fewer and smaller slices for other aspects of their lives. This type of problematic perfectionism has been shown to put people at risk of developing eating disorders and other mental health problems.

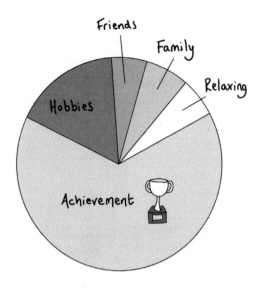

*Jen's self-esteem pie chart had a very
large achievement slice*

What influences perfectionism?

In adolescence, it's hard not to feel a pressure to achieve. It's a time when there's likely to be a strong emphasis on doing well in exams at school or college so that you can progress towards further education or getting a job. Perfectionism doesn't just have to be about academic achievement, though: it can also include trying to be the best in sport, being popular or having extremely high standards about the way you look or what you eat. You might be perfectionistic in some areas of your life, but not in others. For Ella, always looking her best, exercising and only eating low-calorie meals gave her a sense of achievement, especially when people liked or commented on her social media feed.

> *It feels so good when my phone pings with people's likes and comments on my pictures. I love to scroll back over my posts and read what they've put. It makes me feel great. I wonder what I should post about next? It must be better than the last one or I'll lose followers. Maybe I should do a photo of me going for a run, or I could make a super-healthy fruit smoothie and post about that? I will need to work out what I'll wear, how my hair and make-up will look, and calculate how many calories will be in the smoothie so that I can create the perfect post.*

Ella

Our society tends to reward people who do well and gives negative feedback when we're not successful. For example, doing well in school tends to be rewarded by praise and approval from parents and teachers, enables you to get into a good college or university and secure a better-paid job. Athletes who are successful in their sport may be rewarded with medals or sponsorship deals. Social media is full of images of people displaying 'perfect' bodies, exercise regimes or healthy meals, which are rewarded by thousands of likes and shares. It's hard not to feel the pressure to be perfect as a teen!

Problematic perfectionism

So what can make perfectionism problematic? Firstly, we need to look at the standards and expectations that drive it. Then we will consider the thoughts and behaviours that keep perfectionism going.

Rigid rules and extreme expectations

In Chapter 2 we talked about how we all have an internal rule book that tells us what we 'should' think and how we 'must' act. People with problematic perfectionism tend to have extremely demanding and rigid standards in their rule book that are all about preventing failure. The rules tell us that we 'must' achieve a certain standard . . . *or else* we are not good enough. Jen's rule book was all about being the best, always getting things right and never making mistakes . . . *or else* she would be a failure. Ella's rules told her that she must always look perfect and eat the perfect diet . . . *or else* no one would like her. People with this sort of perfectionism try to stick to their rules all the time, despite this having negative consequences on their lives. They might expect others to live up to their extreme expectations too.

But there are several problems with having such rigid rules and extreme expectations.

Firstly, the standards that drive perfectionism tend to be set at such a high level that they are *unrealistic*, so it can feel like you're constantly failing because the standards are impossible to reach. Is it realistic for Jen to expect herself always to be the best? It's likely that there are lots of factors that could prevent her from being the best in tennis, and that many of these might be beyond her control, like being drawn against a more experienced tennis player at a tournament. Having unrealistic standards, or extreme expectations, increases the likelihood of failing at the things we set out to achieve.

Another problem is that the standards that perfectionists set are often very *rigid*, which means they stay the same, even if the situation changes and the rule might not be appropriate anymore. Jen's rigid rule about 'being the best' becomes even more unhelpful when she's ill or injured, because it still demands success even when circumstances prevent it.

These rigid rules and extreme expectations may also be based on information that is *inaccurate* and *unhelpful*. For example, Ella's rules about the 'perfect diet' were based on information she found on an online influencer's website, rather than on scientific findings about the nutritional needs of teenage girls.

Ask yourself:

- What rigid rules and extreme expectations are in your rule book? Have a look at the examples below. Make a note of the ones that are true for you and add any others that you think might be in your rule book:

    ○ I must always be top of the class
    ○ I must always get things right
    ○ I must never make mistakes
    ○ I must never fail
    ○ I must always win
    ○ I must always be the best
    ○ I must always work hard
    ○ I must always be liked
    ○ I must always look perfect
    ○ I must be thin

- ○   I must always eat healthily
- ○   I must never eat junk food
- ○   I must exercise every day
- ○   I must always be tidy
- ○   I must show I am a good friend
- ○   I must be liked by everyone

Unhelpful thinking patterns

Having such a strict rulebook in place can really influence the way we think about things:

Being on the lookout for failure Our extreme expectations influence what we pay attention to. Because perfectionists are often afraid of getting things wrong, they are always looking for signs of failure. Rather than focusing on the 78 per cent Jen got right in her mathematics test, she agonised over the 22 per cent she got wrong. Paying attention to her mistakes meant that Jen was constantly getting feedback that she was a failure.

All-or-nothing thinking Rigid rules and extreme expectations also influence the way we make sense of our experiences. They trip us into thinking about things in an 'all-or-nothing' way. This is because the rules only allow for two options: anything that is not a complete success is experienced by perfectionists as a complete failure. Jen's rule that she 'must' win every tennis match trips her into all-or-nothing thinking. If she doesn't win, she thinks she has failed, no matter how well she played or how many points she scored.

Self-criticism Perfectionists are also very critical about themselves and blame themselves when they don't live up to their extreme expectations. This was Jen's response when she got her mathematics test result. Because she had broken one of the rules in her rule book – 'I must not make mistakes', this triggered a whole load of self-critical thoughts, such as *'I am so stupid'*, *'I am lazy'*, and *'I'm such a failure'* – even though she had actually done really well!

Discounting successes Even if success is experienced, perfectionists are rarely satisfied by their achievements. They may ignore or discount their successes and see them as 'lucky' or insignificant. When Jen got a good mark for some homework, she told herself it was because the assignment was easy or the teacher was being nice, rather than her mark being due to her abilities. Experiencing success can also lead perfectionists to reset their standards at an even higher level, fuelling the relentless pursuit of achievement. Getting positive comments and likes on her social media account didn't make Ella relax her standards: it made her want to post even more 'perfect' pictures.

Ask yourself:

- How do your rigid rules and extreme expectations influence the way you think?

Unhelpful behaviours

Another problem with having extremely demanding and rigid standards is that they drive us to behave in ways that can keep perfectionism going. There are two types of behaviour that perfectionism tends to drive: *trying too hard*, and *putting off or avoiding* situations when there's a chance the rigid rules might be broken, or the extreme expectations might not be met.

Trying too hard If, like Jen, you have a rule that you 'must always be the best' *or else* you are a failure, you'll probably work excessively hard to try and live up to the standard. You might spend all your time studying or training, take great care over your work and find yourself repeatedly checking it to make sure you're not making any mistakes. Or maybe you're like Ella, whose rule that she 'must always look perfect' *or else* no one will like her, means that she spends a long time choosing clothes and doing her hair and make-up, and posting 'perfect' pictures on her social media accounts to get the approval of others. The problem is that these behaviours tend to be time-consuming and exhausting because all your time, energy and effort are focused on following the rules. They can stop you from doing things you enjoy and make your life very narrow. They can also be self-defeating because they actually make it more likely that you won't achieve the standards that you set. Trying too hard to be successful meant that Jen felt exhausted, which affected her performance in tennis and at school.

Putting off or avoiding things Because perfectionists are trying to avoid failure, they can find it difficult to make decisions or get started with work in case they get it wrong. They can procrastinate and put things off, like Jen who couldn't seem to find the 'perfect' opening sentence for her English essay. Sometimes, they can avoid tasks all together if they are worried that they are going to fail. These behaviours tend to be unhelpful as they get in the way of completing work and therefore reduce the likelihood of being successful.

Ask yourself:

- Which behaviours do you do to try and manage your rigid rules and extreme expectations?

Trying too hard:

- Study or work all the time.
- Check over work several times.
- Question yourself all the time.
- Spend lots of time making lists.
- Check your appearance several times before you go out.
- Change your outfit several times before you go out.
- Take photos of yourself over and over again until you look just right.
- Only eat certain foods.
- Spend a lot of time tidying and cleaning.
- Doing tasks yourself because you don't trust others to do them correctly.
- Seeking reassurance from others.

Putting off or avoiding things:

- Have difficulty making decisions.

- Avoid making decisions.

- Avoid things in case they go wrong.

- Delay starting work until you can do it right.

- Give up if you can't meet your standards.

The perfectionism trap

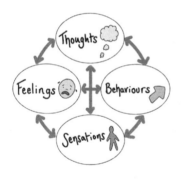

Just like the other traps we've discussed in this book, the rigid rules, thinking patterns and unhelpful behaviours work together to create a perfectionism trap. The rigid rules and extreme expectations make us think and behave in ways that have a negative impact on our lives and keep us stuck in a relentless cycle of trying to live up to our self-imposed yet unrealistic standards.

For example, Jen's rules about always being the best and never failing or making mistakes filled her with anxiety. To try and live up to these expectations, she spent every evening and weekend revising and stopped spending time with her best friend Zoe. Working so hard meant that Jen's life became very

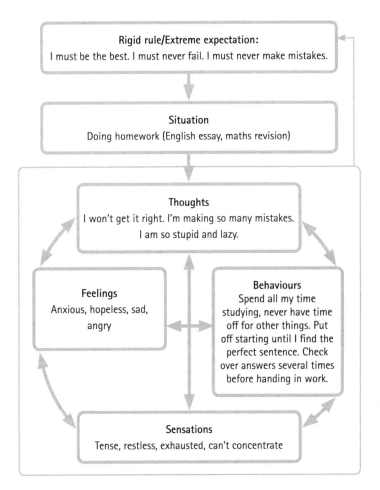

Jen's perfectionism trap

narrow and even more focused on achieving at school and in tennis. She dismissed any activity that didn't contribute to her meeting her goals as a waste of time. By continuously working late and pushing herself, Jen felt exhausted and unable to concentrate on her work. She would often put off getting started on assignments because she was worried that she would get it wrong. As a result, she was less successful in her schoolwork and tennis performance. But rather than seeing the rigid rules and extreme expectations as the problem, Jen blamed herself for being stupid and lazy, which pushed her to work even harder to try and follow the rules. This kept Jen's rigid rules and extreme expectations firmly in place.

Ella's rules about always looking perfect meant that she was constantly checking her appearance, smoothing her hair and reapplying her make-up. She would change her outfit several times a day to make sure she looked her best. Ella's social media account was full of 'perfect' pictures, but she would often have to take them several times to make sure they looked right before posting them online. Ella's attempts to follow what she thought was the 'perfect' diet led her to eat a really narrow range of low-calorie foods and avoid anything that didn't match her extreme (and inaccurate) expectations of 'healthy' food. Trying to live up to such high standards took a lot of Ella's time and focus, and made her miss out on things, like joining in with her brother's birthday takeaway – much to the annoyance of her parents. Ella was so stuck in her rigid rules and extreme expectations that she expected others to follow them too and would make comments about her friends' food choices if they didn't match her standards. But despite all Ella's efforts, she never felt satisfied, which pushed her to try and reach even higher standards of perfection, where she thought she might find happiness. She became more and more caught up in the perfectionism trap.

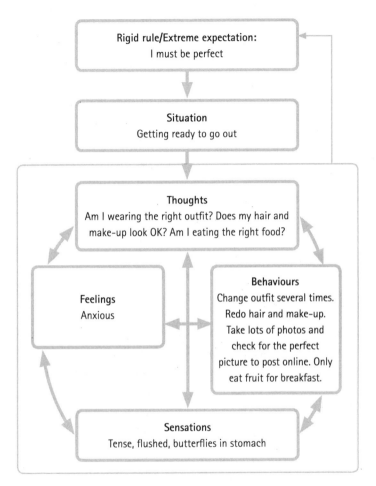

Ella's perfectionism trap

Both Ella and Jen are stuck in a perfectionism trap. What about you? Do your rigid rules and extreme expectations make you think and behave in ways that trip you into a perfectionism trap and keep you stuck there?

Ask yourself:

- Are you stuck in a perfectionism trap?

- Do your rigid rules and extreme expectations keep you stuck in an unhelpful cycle of thoughts, feelings, sensations and behaviours?

- Try mapping out your perfectionism trap, like the examples above.

Overcoming problematic perfectionism

If you think perfectionism is getting in the way of your life, you might find some of the ideas below helpful. When perfectionism has been in your life for a long time it can certainly feel like part of your identity. Overcoming perfectionism is not about losing the part of yourself that cares about the things you do and what you achieve, but it is about finding ways to achieve your goals without them having a negative impact on your life. Some of these ideas are similar to strategies we discussed in Chapter 9 on self-esteem, so you might find it helpful to have a look at those too.

Take action!

- Strategies to help you overcome problematic perfectionism:

   ○ Review your rules and evaluate your expectations.

   ○ Fact-check your rules and expectations.

   ○ Question all-or-nothing thinking.

   ○ Edit your expectations and generate good-enough guidelines.

   ○ Put your good-enough guidelines into practice.

   ○ Practise being imperfect.

   ○ Do things for enjoyment, not achievement.

   ○ Stop putting off or avoiding things.

   ○ Learn from your mistakes.

   ○ Tune into your achievements.

   ○ Stop self-criticism.

Review your rules and evaluate your expectations

Take a look at the rigid rules and extreme expectations that you have listed. Try to step back and look at them from a different point of view. What are the pros and cons of having these standards? Jen made a list of the pros and cons of her rule about always being the best.

Pros	Cons
• It feels good when I am successful.	• It's a lot of hard work.
• It helps me to feel in control.	• It takes up a lot of time.
• It keeps me focused.	• I feel stressed all the time.
• It helps me to be successful at tennis and in school.	• It's exhausting.
• Other people respect me.	• It's hard to keep it up all the time.
• It might help me be successful in the future (e.g. university, work).	• I miss out on seeing my friends.
	• My friends get annoyed with me.
	• I have no time for other hobbies.

Jen's list of pros and cons

It's likely that you've identified quite a few pros that feel important, like the feeling you get when you achieve something or receive praise from others. But what about the cons? Have you thought much about them before? Jen realised that there were lots of cons in sticking to her rigid rules: they made her feel exhausted, stressed and unhappy, took up all her time and were affecting her friendships because they didn't leave her any time for fun.

Looking at the cons you have listed may help you to realise that there are many costs of perfectionism, such as the
amount of time and effort it takes, and how it interferes with
other aspects of your life, like hobbies and friendships. The
effort you put in to being the best is likely only to be helpful to a point, before perfectionism starts to have a negative
impact on your success and wellbeing, as shown in the diagram below.

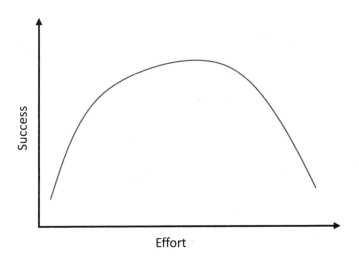

*Putting lots of effort in is only helpful to a point: too much effort can be
exhausting and reduce the chances of achieving success*

Ask yourself:

- What are the cons of perfectionism?

- Are there any negative consequences of trying to follow the rules all the time?

- What impact do they have on you, your life and other people?

- Is it possible to keep these standards going in the long term?

- Would you expect your friends and family members to stick to the rules all the time?

Fact-check your rules and expectations

It's also important to question whether your rules and expectations are based on accurate information. You may find that they are made up from selective or biased data sources and so might not be based on fact. This was a really important lesson for Ella, who realised through a discussion with her family doctor that her version of a 'healthy' diet wasn't healthy at all. Ella learned that the diet advice she had been reading online was pretty limited and left out a lot of important information about balanced nutrition.

> **Ask yourself:**
>
> • What information are your rules and expectations based on?
>
> • Are they accurate and based on reliable sources?

Question all-or-nothing thinking

As mentioned above, our rigid rules and extreme expectations can trip us into all-or-nothing thinking where our actions are either viewed as 'good' or 'bad'. For example, Jen's rules about not making mistakes led her to view her performance in school as either a 'success' or a 'failure'. According to her rule book, she must be 100 per cent successful in every subject; anything less would be experienced as a failure. Jen's rule only gave her two options:

FAILURE	SUCCESS

But is this a realistic or helpful way of thinking about our actions? Can performance (or achievement, or food, or weight) be neatly divided into two opposite categories, one 'good' and one 'bad'? Instead of looking at things in an all-or-nothing way, try thinking about where they fall on a scale, with the extreme categories at opposite ends. This can help us to see that things are very rarely as 'all or nothing' as they might first appear and are much more likely to be somewhere in between.

When Jen didn't get the grade she wanted for her English essay, she instantly thought she was a total failure. However, when she questioned her all-or-nothing thinking using a scale like the one below, she realised that although she might not have been a 'total success', she was a long way from being a 'total failure'. Jen thought back to her pros and cons list and realised that 'total success' wasn't as great as she first thought as it required so much effort and gave her no time for other things.

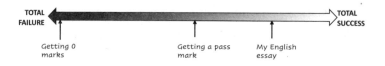

Jen's failure/success scale

Ella used a similar scale to question her all-or-nothing thoughts about 'good' and 'bad' foods. Having fact-checked her rules about nutrition, Ella was able to see that only eating fruit and veg wasn't very 'good' or healthy at all as she wasn't getting the nutrients her body needed to grow and repair. At the other end of the scale, she realised that treats and snacks are only problematic when they are eaten in huge quantities *all* the time but aren't 'bad' in themselves. In fact, she learned that they are an important part of enjoying food and socialising with others. Fact-checking her rules and questioning her all-or-nothing thinking helped Ella to realise that no food is 100 per cent healthy or unhealthy, that eating something is better than eating nothing, and that having a variety of foods is a much more healthy way of meeting her body's nutritional needs as well as her social and emotional needs.

Ella's 'bad' food/ 'good' food scale

Ask yourself: Questioning all-or-nothing thinking

- What are your all-or-nothing thoughts?

- Try mapping them out on your own scale with the extreme categories at either end

- Do your actions and behaviours lie at the extremes, or somewhere in the middle?

- What impact do the extreme ends of thinking have on how you behave?

Edit your expectations and generate 'good-enough' guidelines

If you've read this far, you'll have seen that it's impossible to live up to the rigid rules and extreme expectations of perfectionism because they are unrealistic, inaccurate and unhelpful and make you feel like you're never good enough. But it's not *you* that needs to change – it's the rules!

Editing your expectations is about making your standards more realistic and less demanding. Instead of having a strict rule book, try developing some flexible guidelines. Guidelines help to provide a bit of direction, but are also supportive, encouraging and help us to cope when things don't go to plan. Guidelines help us to work towards the things we value, but don't give us a hard time when we don't quite reach them. Guidelines are not about being perfect, they are about being good enough. To help you to generate your own good-enough guidelines, it can be helpful to think about what you would expect of a friend.

Rigid rules and extreme expectations	Good-enough guidelines
I must always win my tennis matches I must always get top marks I must always work hard	It's good to try my best at tennis, but that doesn't mean that I'm going to win all the time. Not winning doesn't mean I am a failure. As long as I've tried my best, it doesn't matter if I don't get top marks. It's important to take breaks, spend time with friends and do things for fun. Taking time to recharge will help me to work more effectively.

Jen's flexible guidelines

Put your good-enough guidelines into practice!

Once you've developed your flexible guidelines, it's important that you put them into practice. For Jen, this meant limiting the amount of time she spent doing homework to one hour a day and making sure she had rest days from tennis training. It can feel like hard work to stop following our old rules, but remember, changing behaviour is a really powerful way of helping us to change our beliefs. To start with, Jen worried that reducing the time she studied, and taking breaks, would have a negative effect on her work, but she actually found that following her new guidelines had little effect on her marks or tennis performance. She noticed that she felt happier and less stressed too.

Practise being imperfect!

As well as following your new guidelines, you can rip up the old rule book by deliberately breaking the rules! That's right – make a few mistakes in your homework! Skip a training session! Go out without any make-up! Eat junk food! Whatever your old rule tells you to do, do the opposite! You don't have to do this forever, but it can be a good way of showing yourself that you don't *have* to follow the rules.

Try doing a behaviour experiment to test out what happens when you break the rules and drop your safety behaviours. What do you learn about yourself when you do this? Does dropping your standards and safety behaviours mean that you achieve less, are less popular, become fat or lazy? It's really unlikely that breaking your old rules and dropping your safety behaviours will result in anything terrible happening; and it can help you learn that the old rules aren't as important or as helpful as you might have thought. There is more information about using behaviour experiments to drop safety behaviours in Chapter 9.

Take action! Conduct a behaviour experiment

- What is the rule that you would like to test out?
- What safety behaviours do you need to drop to test the rule out?
- What do you think will happen if you drop your safety behaviour?
- What happened when you dropped your safety behaviour? Was it as bad as you thought?
- What does this tell you about the rule? What have you learned about yourself?

If it feels too hard to completely break the rule in one go, you can try doing it in a gradual way. To help her to feel confident about going out without any make-up, Ella started by gradually wearing less make-up. As she realised that no one noticed, she soon felt confident enough not to wear any make-up at all, which helped her to realise how unhelpful her old rule had been.

Old rule	How can I break the old rule?	What do I think will happen?	What actually happened?	What did I learn?
Make sure my make-up is perfect before I go out	Go out without make-up	People will ignore me because they think I am ugly	No one treated me any differently from how they usually do	I don't need to look a certain way for people to like me
Only post perfect pictures of myself online (keep taking pictures until I get the right shot)	Post the first picture I take of myself	People will make nasty comments about how I look and I'll get fewer likes	I still got lots of really nice comments and likes	I don't have to look perfect for other people to like me
Don't wear the same outfit twice	Wear yesterday's clothes	People will notice and comment on it	No one noticed!	People don't pay that much attention to what I wear
Post a picture of myself working out every day	Post a picture of myself watching TV in my pyjamas	People will comment that I am lazy	People commented about the programme I was watching, not about me being lazy	Relaxing and watching TV doesn't mean people think I'm lazy: other people watch TV too!

Ella's behaviour experiments

Enjoyment – not achievement!

Another way to reduce the power of perfectionism is to choose activities that are about enjoyment, and not achievement. Are there any hobbies that you used to enjoy, or interests that you'd like to develop, where it doesn't matter how good you are at them? For Jen, going for bike rides, reading and watching scary movies with her friend Zoe helped to take the focus off achieving all the time. This helped to reduce the achievement slice of her self-esteem pie chart because she was investing time in activities that she enjoyed. Jen learned that she didn't have to be productive all the time. You might find it helpful to have a go at the activity on page 208 to help you to identify things that you can do for fun!

Stop putting things off or avoiding them

Having extremely demanding standards can often make it difficult to get started with tasks because of the worry of not being successful. If you've been able to edit your expectations, you might now find it easier to give things a go without being held back by the worry of getting things wrong or not being perfect. Having a go and doing something imperfectly is always better than avoiding things and doing nothing at all. You can use behaviour experiments here too. What happens when you stop putting things off and give things a go? You might actually surprise yourself and do better than you predicted!

Learn from mistakes

Remember, making mistakes or getting things wrong is not a bad thing. Everyone does it! It's impossible to be 100 per cent perfect 100 per cent of the time. Rather than seeing mistakes as a personal weakness, try looking at them as opportunities to do something differently or learn something new. This can sometimes mean asking for help with things that you are finding difficult or doing some problem solving to work out a different way of doing things (see Chapter 8). Most successful people say that making mistakes is a really important part of their success.

Ask yourself:

*   Are there things you might not have learned if you never made any mistakes?

Tune into your achievements

Remember how perfectionism made Jen focus on the 22 per cent she missed in her mathematics test, and ignore the 78 per cent she achieved? Rather than focusing on the negative, it's important to tune into your achievements, and focus on what you *have* accomplished, and not what you haven't. Even when things don't go as well as you would like, it doesn't mean that you haven't achieved anything at all. It can also be helpful to widen your perspective and look for other examples of things you have done well in. Jen might not have won the tennis tournament, but she won three of the matches that got her to the final.

Stop self-criticism

It's easy to slip into criticising yourself when things don't go quite as well as you want them to. But criticism never helps make the situation better; it just makes *you* feel worse. If you notice that you're giving yourself a hard time, stop, and try the activity below.

Ask yourself:

- What do your self-critical thoughts say about you?
- How do your self-critical thoughts affect your feelings and behaviour?
- Are these thoughts fair or accurate? What facts are you missing that show that they aren't true?
- How can you be more kind and encouraging to yourself? What would you say to a friend if they were in this situation?
- What's a more balanced way of looking at this situation?

When Jen kept missing shots during her tennis practice, she noticed that she started to criticise herself and tell herself she was useless and lazy. She felt herself getting more and more stressed and this made it harder to play. Jen realised that talking to herself negatively was only making the situation worse. Instead, she tried to be kind and more encouraging – *'Don't worry, you can do it!'*, *'It's only a practice'*, *'Take a break and try again when you've had a rest'*. She also reminded herself of the evidence that showed she wasn't useless or lazy: *'You train hard, so you're not lazy'*, *'Doing well in the tournament last week shows that you're not useless at tennis'*. Questioning her self-critical thinking helped Jen to create a more balanced, helpful thought: *'Just because you're missing a few shots doesn't mean you're useless or lazy, you're just having an off day. Take a break, relax and try again in a bit.'* This helped Jen to relax and refocus her attention on her game rather than on her performance, and her playing improved.

Having a balanced pie chart is healthy and will protect you from perfectionism

Summary

- Perfectionism is about setting extremely high standards and trying to achieve them *perfectly*, all the time. But trying to be perfect can take over your life, get in the way of doing the things that you enjoy and have a negative effect on your self-esteem.

- Perfectionism is driven by rigid rules and extreme expectations which tell us what we 'should' think and how we 'must' behave, but these standards can be unrealistic, inaccurate and unhelpful, and often set us up to fail.

- To overcome perfectionism, it's helpful to change your rules and expectations so that they are more flexible and realistic.

- Remember: no one is perfect, and everyone makes mistakes! Making mistakes can help us to learn new things!

Chapter 12

Social Media and the Internet

I scroll through my social media. There are videos of dancers, showing what they are eating and how they are working out. There are at least ten different workouts for dancers and I'm not sure which one to choose. I swear I didn't follow all of them – I'm not sure who they are and how they came up on my feed. The dancer in this video looks amazing – just the way I'd love to look. I'll do her workout and post it.

My make-up has stayed pretty perfect during my workout. I change the lighting, camera angle and background and check it again – yes, that looks good. I wonder if there is anything else I could change or edit before I post this.

I feel a knot in my stomach – I hope everybody likes this, and no one finds any flaws.

I quickly shower, do my hair and make-up again and go down to dinner to take some more pictures of what I'm going to eat. I serve up my salad,

Ella

making sure to tidy the kitchen surfaces around where my plate is sitting and try photographing it from different angles. Once I've found the perfect picture, I post this to my account.

When I go back to my workout video that I posted earlier, only seven people have seen it and there is only one like so far. I check the video again, trying to decide whether to leave it or delete it.

Ella

My feeds are full of influencers showing the perfect foods to eat. Did I choose the best dinner? Will this be the right food to make me toned? It's so hard to know what to choose. I wonder if I should have had a green shake with my dinner or not.

Mum interrupts, yelling at me for being on my phone and telling me I'm selfish. She doesn't understand me. I'm obviously using my phone for something important. I don't feel like eating right now and fight back the tears.

What this chapter will cover:

- Our online world.
- Social media – the positives and the negatives.
- Online bullying.
- Questioning the media.
- Internet addiction.

- Cookies, algorithms and adverts.
- Online influencers and body image.
- Fitness, healthy eating and weight loss websites.
- Strategies to stay safe.

Our online world

More and more of our time is spent online. From checking the bus timetable to arranging to meet our friends on the way to school, from taking photos or checking out the latest celebrity gossip with our friends to handing in homework, listening to music or chatting with friends – we are all into it. Outside school, we might watch films, scroll through our social media feeds, or watch funny videos that our friends send us, or we send on to them.

In this chapter we look at our online world and how this has become such a big part of our lives. We think about the positive side to social media as well as some of the risks, particularly regarding how we feel about ourselves. We will think more specifically about some of the risks around eating and body image later in the chapter.

What is social media?

The dictionary definition describes social media as 'websites and applications that allow us to create and share content and network with each other'.

It's unlikely that your parents will have grown up with a smartphone or social media, so they may find it hard to understand how, despite spending all day with them, you still want to get in touch with your friends after school.

Being involved with social media is important for young people, but it is all too easy to spend time scrolling through and not particularly engaging with what we're looking at. Passing the time in this way may not help us feel happy or relaxed. Studies show that different parts of our brain light up depending on whether we are doing purposeful online activity (with reward or alert brain networks lighting up) compared to when we are randomly scrolling through online media while other things are going through our mind. Scrolling online can feel helpful in the short term as a distraction to worries, but ultimately it may not be useful in tackling difficult feelings.

The positive side of social media

Social media is somewhere we can build connections, learn many new things, have fun, be creative and join other communities based on shared interests. It is a great place for learning skills, from editing videos to painting, from learning a new language to finding out about a different culture or exploring music online.

The teenage years are a crucial time for discovering who you are or who you want to be, and what is important to you. Social media can influence your values, interests and relationships. It offers a chance to meet other people who share similar interests.

Some teenagers find it easier to talk to their friends online than in person. You might want to share something embarrassing and upsetting, for example. Texting can feel less scary than talking, and using emojis can help show, at the touch of a button, complicated feelings that you might be experiencing. For some teenagers who find it hard to make friends, gaming online can offer a way to connect with others of a similar age.

Social media can give you a sense of control over how you present yourself to others, which can be helpful if you are feeling self-conscious. Teenagers who find social contact difficult can practise interacting with others in a way that is anonymous and allows them to build up confidence in real-life situations.

Many teenagers say social media helps them think about bigger issues in the world as well as breaking down stigma and becoming more aware of social justice. Social media has a positive side, and many teenagers say it helps them feel connected with friends and provides a way of supporting them. Some young people use it to do homework together or to talk about things that have happened during the day. It keeps you feeling connected and can also be motivating – especially when the homework feels really boring!

Chloe

> My class group chat has gone mad with a huge number of new messages. Jen and Zoe have had a massive fallout, and everybody is talking about it online.
>
> Some are saying that 'Zoe is being a control freak' or that 'Jen is being attention seeking'. Jen and Zoe aren't saying anything, but the thread is getting longer and longer with everybody's comments about what did, or didn't, happen.
>
> I don't want to post anything here but it's hard to put my phone down in case I miss something and look really stupid tomorrow at school. It's going to be really awkward again! I really worry that one day I'll say or do something that makes everybody start talking about me. Don't people remember that Zoe and Jen will be reading this too?

What could be the downside?

Mental health and misunderstandings

Research shows that teenagers who spend six or more hours per day on social media (regardless of why or what they are looking at) are more likely to be lonely and struggling with their mood or feelings.

Social media can be a place where teenagers can misunderstand each other and where a fallout can be public, with everyone knowing what is happening and giving an opinion.

It can be hard to understand people's intentions when they say things on social media, for example whether they are joking or being deliberately nasty.

When something like the argument between Jen and Zoe happens, what might have been a private disagreement between friends has suddenly become very public and everybody seems to have an opinion. How might Jen or Zoe be feeling? Do we sometimes say things online that we might regret?

Sometimes you might write something in the heat of the moment. Even if you delete it or if it is sent privately to only one friend, it can be embarrassing to find that it's been screenshot and shared with everybody. There are risks around being embarrassed or upset by what your friends share about you, especially personal information without your consent, including photos.

The pressure to show a perfect life

People viewing Ella and her 'perfect life', 'perfect workouts' and 'perfect food' can compare themselves negatively with Ella and this can lead to feeling bad. Should everybody at school be trying to be like Ella? What do Ella's posts say about her? Does Ella feel connected to her friends, and do they become closer to her through her posts? Because social media feeds portray just a snapshot of people's lives, almost like a reel of highlights, it can seem as if there is a perfect life we should all aspire to.

People who know Ella might be afraid to post about things that feel 'imperfect', like the more difficult parts of life, or even the more ordinary things that your friends might relate to and laugh with you about. Ella's life as presented online might seem 'perfect', but there is no such thing. In fact, we know that she has her own difficulties. We know she feels she has an image to maintain, and this can feel like a lot of pressure. By trying to reach perfection online, Ella might feel more and more disconnected from her followers and friends.

Research shows that while having positive acceptance from friends can help teenagers to feel better, an over-reliance on likes and follows can have a negative impact on self-esteem (see Chapter 9).

Online bullying/cyber-bullying

Research shows that at least one in five teenagers experiences online bullying every year, and that more than half have at least one experience of online bullying. Research also shows that most teenagers being bullied at school are likely to be bullied online as well. Much of the bullying will be from other students and may go unreported. Schools may be reluctant to get involved in bullying that takes place after school hours. Only about half of those who report bullying feel that school deal with it well.

Bullying between teenagers is nothing new: but what cyber-bullying can do is follow you home and continue long after school has finished. It can snowball, ending up involving many bystanders, including people from other year groups or classes who might not have been aware of what was going on if it was just happening at school. Depending on what media the bullying has taken place on, it can be easy to hide it and therefore hard to prove that it has happened.

More than half of all teenagers who play video games report using or hearing abusive language when playing games online. One in five admit they will bully others during an online game, although most of them say they would never say those things to another person in real life.

Check it out: Terms used by researchers to describe different types of online bullying

- **Outing** Sharing private information about another person to many others.

- **Masquerading** Pretending to be somebody else and sharing information to damage somebody else's reputation.

- **Flaming** Writing rude and angry messages.

- **Cyber-stalking** Making threats to find and harm another person.

- **Denigration** Spreading rumours about another person to put them down.

- **Exclusion** Excluding a person from an online group chat (sometimes in order to talk about them behind their back).

- **Ganging up** A group gathering to criticise a person.

- **Trolling** Posting online to deliberately provoke others (which can involve many of the types of bullying on this list).

286 Overcoming Worries About Body Image and Eating

Internet addiction

Being online is easy and can be exciting, but can also become a habit. How do you know if your time online is too much or becoming a problem? Internet addiction is when somebody needs to spend so much time on the internet that relationships, health and work start to suffer.

Here are some questions to ask yourself if you think that your time online might be a problem.

- Are you missing out on food or sleep or school because of being online?

- Feeling unhappy and bored or upset when you're not online?

- Staying online and scrolling through things even when they're not that interesting, often losing track of time and finding long periods of time have passed without you noticing?

- Spending time online instead of spending time with friends or doing hobbies that you enjoy?

- Trying hard to reduce your time online, but not being able to?

If you feel that your internet use is getting out of control, you may need support from family and other adults you trust. Although it might initially feel boring and less fun than being online, what can help is spending more time with family and friends, getting back to hobbies and sports that you used to enjoy and maybe charging your mobile devices outside your bedroom.

Ask yourself:

- How much time am I spending online?

- What am I doing when I am online?

- Do I feel connected with my friends or am I becoming isolated?

- Is this making me feel happy?

- Am I losing out on certain things by being online? Are these things important to me?

Cookies, algorithms and adverts

What keeps the internet (and many social media sites) going is selling adverts and content to make money for businesses. Social media sites experiment with personalised adverts to attract and keep people looking at them. Algorithms latch onto what content we look at and feed us lots of similar content. This might be endless cute dog videos, or things that trigger anxiety or upset us. What you see online can be different from what your friends see, and this can have an impact on how you feel about yourself.

Ella has looked at workouts showing how to have a perfect dancer's body, and now all her social media feeds are full of workouts. Ella is becoming overwhelmed about which to choose, and rather than spending time with friends is trying many different workouts and different foods, and

288 Overcoming Worries About Body Image and Eating

photographing these. She is also spending less time (online and in real life) interacting with and seeing her friends.

What you choose to look at can contribute to poor body image

You can now see more pictures of friends, celebrities, online influencers and fashion models online than ever before. It is so easy to look at an image of someone else and focus on unhelpful comparisons. Ella compares herself with famous dancers and online influencers and tries to mimic them to feel proud of herself. She relates to these people as they share her love of dance, or have other factors in common. Finding things in common with others can be a wonderful point of connection, but it also makes comparison online so much easier. Ella found that when she saw dancers posting dance shots in scenic locations, or workouts in rooms with perfect lighting, she desperately wanted to be able to do the same thing. She could never get the posts to be exactly the same as her idols (of course, because she was a different person!), and this made her miserable.

Her school friends (and other younger pupils) like and admire Ella and want to be like her and look like her. Chloe feels bad about how she looks compared with her friends, and scrolling through their social media feeds gives so many more opportunities to compare herself with others.

Studies show that looking at images online, particularly at people who seem to have the perfect body, can lead to negatively comparing yourself with others. This can make appearance become very important, often at the expense of other parts of yourself. Studies talk a lot about the 'internalised thin ideal' (more common in girls) or an 'internalised muscular ideal' (more common in boys) which describes an unrealistic thin or muscular 'ideal perfect' body which very few people have. This can shape our view of what we think is attractive or how we should look.

Some images on websites are captioned so that you know if they have been altered; however, they may still have a negative impact on how you feel about yourself.

Comparing yourself with the 'ideal body' can lead to frequent body checking, negative thinking and dissatisfaction about your appearance. In reality, the 'ideal body' changes all the time (in a similar way to how fashion trends change). When you feel negatively about your appearance compared with the 'ideal', you are more likely to buy products from influencers. Unfortunately, businesses profit from how beauty standards make us feel negatively about ourselves.

To read more about managing poor body image have a look at Chapter 10.

Fitness, 'healthy eating' and weight loss websites

There are many unregulated websites around the topics of fitness, healthy eating and weight loss. Some of them encourage us to eat in a particular way (which might not be

290 Overcoming Worries About Body Image and Eating

healthy), to follow fitness programmes to get a particular body shape (which might be unrealistic or even harmful) or to lose unhealthy amounts of weight to look underweight.

These websites can have chat forums which may be helpful and supportive, but may also have potential dangers, with people pretending to care and making you feel like you belong while, at the same time, encouraging you to eat or exercise in a way that is harmful.

If you have worries about this yourself, or about a friend, you may find it helpful to talk to somebody. You might wish to report or block unhelpful content, which would not only help you but is likely to help other teenagers as well.

To read more about healthy eating, have a look at Chapter 3.

Strategies to keep you safe and healthy online

Think before you post

It can be helpful to THINK before you write online, to stop situations like the row between Jen and Zoe.

Ask yourself: Before posting online, THINK

- T – is this information **True**?

- H – is this information **Helpful** (for me and others)?

- I – is this information **Important** for me to share? Is it informative or interesting?

- N – is it **Necessary** to share this?

- K – is it **Kind** to share this information (about me and others)?

It's important to THINK before posting online

Separating fiction from fact

Ella

I look at the stunning dancer online. She is promoting a health tea which she says has helped her fitness and helped her tone her body. She has a tiny waist and very long legs. I bet she has altered her pictures, but I still feel bad about myself when I look at her. I try the same pose and feel ugly compared with her. I take a few pictures – no way will I look like her. I experiment a bit – make my eyes bigger, neck and legs longer and I try to change the lighting and filters. I worry that others will know what I've done but relax more when the likes and comments flood in – 'You're so beautiful – wish I had your body'. I beg Mum to buy me this tea as I really want to look like the stunning dancer – and feel so irritated that she doesn't understand and won't do it.

It can be hard for you (and even many adults) to know what is true/real online and what might be fake. Examples of this include:

Information that calls itself 'scientific information' It can be easy to write something quite persuasive that seems real and looks like it has been studied and is true. Some examples that can be important for teenagers include advice on how to look after your skin, what a healthy diet looks like or how to change your body shape with workouts. People sometimes include photographs which seem to confirm the text and it can be hard to spot whether what you are reading is true. You may need to talk to an adult (for example parent, school nurse, science teacher) when you are not sure.

News News is readily available online and there are many new news outlets. It can be hard to know what is real, what could be a conspiracy or what might be manipulating you.

Digital alteration of images It is now easier than ever to digitally alter photographs, especially of people, with everything from filters to software editing. Products are advertised showing beautiful people with perfect bodies and perfect skin. Some studies say that up to 75 per cent of teenagers alter pictures of themselves before posting online, but that fewer than 25 per cent realise that their friends are doing the same thing.

Sometimes it becomes clear that the reason this information is posted is to get more followers or to sell a product or to build up the profile of an influencer.

Ask yourself:

- **Who** has posted and written this information? (Do they tell you their qualifications and where they work?)

- **What** is the purpose of this website? Is it selling things or to persuade you about something that might not be true?

- **When** was this information posted? Is the website updated regularly?

- **Where** does the information come from? Is this published scientific research or just somebody's opinion?

- **Why** is this information being posted? Is this information useful?

Five Ws to ask yourself when looking at information online

Keeping your personal information safe

Ella's accounts are public, which means that anybody can follow her or read her posts. It can be easy for strangers to figure out where she lives, where her dance school is or whether she goes to school. Because people online can sometimes pretend to be someone else, this can put Ella at risk.

You might want to check whether people can work out where you live, what school you go to and other bits of personal information. Also, be careful about letting other people use your devices.

It's a good idea to check whether your passwords are a bit too easy for others to guess. Try not to have the same password for everything.

Deleting your cookies and browsing history on a regular basis

We can clear browsing history and cookies and reset our browsers to avoid seeing more of the same content. We can also think about who we follow and what we look at to change the content in our feeds.

Consider how much you post online and who you follow

Ella and her friends might want to talk about this and maybe commit to each other to try and post less online. They might wish to unfollow unhelpful accounts online. One of Ella's friends might want to talk to Ella about how it makes her feel. As a group, maybe they could think not only about who they follow but also about what they post and how they support each other with making changes.

Summary

- Social media and the internet can have a strong influence on people's lives – especially teenagers and young adults.

- There are many positives such as staying in touch with friends, managing shyness, reducing stigma and being aware of things happening in the world, as well as finding information for school and completing homework and projects.

- Excessive use of the internet is shown to be associated with poor mental health and can also increase the risks of bullying, getting incorrect information, developing poor body image and people gaining access to information about you.

- Think before you post things online – not only about your safety but also whether or not you would say this in a face-to-face situation with another person.

- It is important to question information you read online as it might not only be incorrect but also harmful.

- Algorithms and cookies can lead to you being shown unhelpful or biased content, so it is important to delete these if this is happening to you.

Chapter 13

Worries Around Exercise

Wow, that workout was painful. How come that dancer makes it look so easy? I'm watching what I eat and doing the online workouts perfectly. I just don't understand why I don't look like the ballet dancers I follow online. I think I need to try harder. Maybe I should get some other workouts from other professional dancers to add to my routine. I will look at the photos I've taken during my workout and choose the best one and post it to my profile: #balletworkouts; #livingmybestlife; #dancerbody.

The hot water from the shower warms me and feels good on my aching muscles and joints. I hope I'm not too stiff tomorrow at dancing. I wonder when my dance teacher is going to notice just how hard I am working. As I get out of the shower, I have a huge head rush. I must prove how hard I have worked and how strong I will be getting.

Ella

What this chapter will cover:

- The benefits and importance of physical activity.

- Strategies to be more active.

- What does healthy activity look like?

- What does unhealthy exercise look like?

- Challenges for the teenage competitive athlete.

- Relative Energy Deficiency in Sport (REDS).

Athletes are celebrated by society. They are seen as people to aspire to – physically in great shape, strong, fast, flexible, disciplined, talented and motivated. Videos of their workouts are accessible on social media and – especially for teenagers – it can be hard to know whether it's a good idea to follow these workouts.

Ella is suffering from the workouts she is doing. She is dizzy afterwards and experiences muscle pain which is likely to be affecting her dancing and blocking her progress. She knows that other students at school will be looking at her social media profile and comparing themselves to her.

What do we know about exercise and activity?

Physical activity is described as any movement that works your muscles and requires more energy than resting. This can include walking to and from school, walking to the park with your friends, gardening, games and sport.

Exercise is described as a physical activity that is carried out for a specific purpose, such as improving health or fitness. This can be walking, running, yoga, going to the gym or taking gym classes.

Sport is described as a specific physical activity or game, played either as an individual or as part of a team, involving practice, pushing oneself to develop specific abilities either for entertainment or competition. Examples include swimming, athletics, rugby, tennis, netball, football and many others.

Benefits of physical activity, exercise and sport

Exercise has a number of physical benefits which help people of all ages, but are particularly important for growing teenagers. These include improved heart health in the longer term, stronger muscles and bones, more energy, greater physical endurance and keeping weight within a healthy range for growth and development.

There are also many psychological benefits. Teenagers who are regularly active have lower levels of anxiety (including social anxiety), lower levels of depression and are less likely to self-harm. There are also social benefits including more social acceptance, better problem-solving and leadership skills and less risk-taking behaviour.

It is medically recommended that teenagers up to the age of 18 need at least an hour of moderate physical activity per day to grow and develop in a healthy way.

As well as organised sport, there are many casual ways to get regular physical activity, such as walking or biking to and from school, walking to friends' houses or to the park. However, many teenagers don't get enough physical activity, which can have a negative effect on mood, sleep and wellbeing.

Teenagers who come from a physically active family are more likely to be active. Many families enjoy doing activities together such as walking, swimming or cycling. However, it can be harder to motivate yourself if your family is not so interested in physical activity.

What if sport is something you hate and feel you're not good at?

Many children stop doing sport from the age of eleven or when they reach puberty or move on to secondary school and they can become much less active. Research shows that this also happens because they become worried about not being good enough or being laughed at by others. What research also tells us is that teenagers thrive doing something they enjoy alongside friends. Many teenagers don't want to do competitive sport and prefer something less organised by adults. Doing something that you enjoy, that is fun and gives you a chance to be with friends means you are more likely to stick to the activity.

During a growth spurt, teenagers can temporarily become clumsier and might find they struggle with sports skills that they found easier in the past. It is helpful when coaches and adults around you understand this.

Sometimes young people, such as Jake, who don't like organised sport, find other hobbies that result in an increase in activity. Even hobbies like photography or fishing involve activity without you even realising it. Physical activity does not need to be competitive, but it must be enjoyable.

Jake

I hate sport so much! I hate being smaller than the other boys in my class. Nobody ever passes the ball to me, so I just hang around looking stupid. And when the ball accidentally comes towards me it hits me in the face and my glasses fall off and everybody laughs. I don't like everybody shouting all the time during a football game.

I'm so good at computers. Who wants to bother about stupid sport anyway?

Harry has asked me to try taekwondo with him and I've been a few times. That's much better – nobody is shouting at anybody, and everybody is focused on themselves. I find it hard but the teacher has given me some stuff to do at home to get stronger, so I'll keep trying it to see whether I get any better. I'm glad nobody from school except Harry comes here.

Strategies to be more active

If you're planning to become more active, try out several different activities with friends to see what you might enjoy – some gyms and sports clubs have taster days or social activities that you might be able to try over a school holiday. Research tells us you are more likely to stick to something new if you try it with a friend and if it has some fun element. It is normal for teenagers to be put off activities which are very competitive and they don't feel confident about joining.

To begin with, activity might not feel that rewarding. It can feel tiring and can make your muscles ache. If you can persist and if you are around people who make you laugh and feel good, your brain will begin to produce more dopamine over time. Dopamine is a chemical that helps our brains feel rewarded.

What does healthy exercise look like?

Healthy exercise has huge benefits for our physical and mental wellbeing. Teenagers who are active tend to have positive mental health and are less depressed or anxious.

The sort of activity undertaken will vary for different people. There is no right form of exercise, but healthy exercise is enjoyable, makes you feel good afterwards and often has a social and fun element. You are more likely to stick to something that you enjoy.

Exercise can be a great stress buster and a way of managing difficult feelings after a bad day. However, a note of caution – if exercise is the only way to manage very difficult feelings it can become unhealthy, so it is important that you develop other ways of managing stress too.

Doing activity with friends or family can bring people closer together and help them feel less isolated. Activity outdoors – especially in nature – can help recharge your energy.

What does unhealthy exercise look like?

Exercising because you don't like, or want to change, your appearance can become unhealthy and even harmful. Ella is desperate to have a 'perfect dancer's body' and is doing painful workouts to try and look a certain way.

When exercise becomes the only way of dealing with upsetting feelings, this can be unhealthy because there will be times when you need to use other ways of coping with stress, for example when you are ill, or very busy and unable to exercise.

Exercise can become a rigid rule – Ella is forcing herself to do workouts she isn't actually enjoying and feels bad if she is too tired to complete one. This can be a sign that exercise is becoming unhealthy.

Compulsive exercise/over-exercise is when you feel you have to do it whether or not you enjoy it, and feel guilty if you don't do it. If you exercise when feeling tired or ill, or when you're no longer enjoying yourself and you're doing more than you should, it is becoming unhealthy and you are putting yourself at risk of injuries. Your body generates stress hormones which can break down muscle rather than building up muscle. Teenagers who exercise too much can become socially isolated and lose friends. It can cause sleeping problems and difficulties concentrating at school. Some teenagers who are struggling with too much exercise might feel restless and on edge all the time and can struggle to rest or relax, even when they are exhausted.

Unhealthy exercise
A rule that you have to, painful, helps avoid difficult feelings, done to earn food or change appearance

Healthy exercise
Social and fun, makes you feel good, celebrates you, helps you feel strong

Healthy exercise is very different from unhealthy exercise

What might healthy and unhealthy exercise look like?

Healthy exercise	Unhealthy exercise
Enjoyable, makes you feel good afterwards	Exercising because you don't like, or want to change, your appearance
You want to do it, rather than must or should do it	You feel you have to exercise whether or not you enjoy it
Feels like a stress buster (amongst other stress-busting strategies like sharing worries with people you trust)	Exercise that is rigid and can feel forced
Doesn't have to be a specific team sport (although it can), but can include individual activities like yoga	Exercise is the only way of dealing with stress, and becomes a cause of stress

Ask yourself:

- Do I exercise even when I'm not feeling well?
- Do I exercise no matter how bad the weather is?
- Do I exercise even when I have exams and stressful deadlines coming up?
- Is the first thing I think about every day what workouts I need to do?
- If I miss an exercise session, do I feel irritable and down in mood?
- If I can't exercise, do I start to worry that I'll gain weight?

If you recognise this might be a problem, it is important to talk to your parents or a school counsellor or your doctor. You might need some blood tests and a physical examination to check whether your exercise regimes are starting to damage your body. Your doctor might pick up a slightly slow heart rate, or low blood pressure.

Take action!

- Make sure you have one to two rest days every week. If rest days make you feel stressed, try to have family or a friend with you and find some things that might distract you (e.g. going to a movie, going on a slow walk with friends, getting involved in a board game or watching something on TV with a friend).

- Try to do exercise that has a beginning and an end, for example, a sports class at school or a gym class. It is better to do this with a friend.

- Avoid exercising on your own or doing workouts that you have set up for yourself. Activity in a group which has a social and fun element can help break patterns of unhealthy exercise.

What about the teenage competitive athlete?

Zoe stops in the corridor and grabs me before we go into our next lesson. 'Jen – any chance you can come to my birthday party next weekend?'

I feel awful inside – I have another tennis tournament next week. I really wish I didn't have to go – I'm tired all the time and it feels like I'm either training, playing matches or trying to catch up on schoolwork. At this rate I'm not going to have any friends soon.

I can't believe how badly I lost last weekend. The new girl was taller and thinner than I am. She looked so pretty. Dad and my coach were really irritated with me and told me off for not trying hard enough.

I just feel miserable. Mum and Dad have sacrificed so much for my tennis over the years. I really don't enjoy it anymore, but I feel so guilty about the money they have spent on me. It feels like it's my duty to keep going and to keep trying to improve. My coach would go straight to my dad if I mentioned anything. Perhaps Zoe would understand, if I talked to her, but I don't see her much these days.

Sometimes I wish I'd do so badly that I'd get chucked off the development squad. I'd also feel bad though about how let down Dad would feel.

Jen

Teenagers who are competitive sports players may love their sport and really enjoy hard training and competition and look forward to continuing to compete, perhaps as a career. They may have played their sport for a long time and their parents may have invested a lot of time and money into helping them achieve at the highest level. However, sometimes they may change their mind about what they enjoy and might no longer want to spend all their time training and competing.

It can be very tough for teenage athletes. From the outside it looks like they are really successful and popular, and that people can look up to them and see them as better than everybody else. However, in reality, most athletes (and teenage athletes too) are working, focusing and training really hard and can feel quite tired a lot of the time. Athletes are often praised for their discipline – how they eat in a particular way, don't go out, work hard at their sport and spend all their free time studying or sleeping. They can be expected to put their sport first, and everything else (schoolwork, relaxation, friendships) comes second.

Very often they are not quite certain how it started or when it became serious, or even who decided they should train like a professional athlete. Sometimes it doesn't feel fun; they may not be allowed to take a break because of a belief that hard work will pay off, and very often they have few opportunities to develop other interests or spend time with friends. Some teenagers feel that the only thing worthwhile about themselves is how well they do at sport and so will be driven to work and achieve because they base all their self-worth and self-esteem on that belief.

Jen feels trapped and starts to believe her only value as a person is by performing in tennis, rather than being able to get to know herself as a whole person with lots of other qualities and interests. Sometimes friends stop hanging out or even inviting her out, leading Jen to feel worthless – unless she is successful at tennis. It can be hard as a teenage athlete to find somebody safe to talk to. If Jen doesn't feel able to tell her parents, she might want to find a teacher she trusts to talk about how she is feeling.

We know that Jen has body image concerns and is struggling with eating and perfectionism. Research studies show that teenage athletes struggle with these types of problems more often than their friends might. It might be that if Jen has some help around her eating, body image concerns and other difficulties she might be able to get back her love of tennis and enjoy being a competitive athlete again.

Sometimes adults don't think about how a teenage athlete might be struggling because on the outside they can look so competent – especially if they are doing well at their sport. There can be huge physical pressure if there is lots of training and not enough rest, which puts teenagers at risk of injuries. It can be hard for coaches and parents to get the balance right between encouraging the teenager to do well, while at the same time caring about their wellbeing and whether they are having fun. It is important to spot problems like body image, eating concerns, perfectionism and low self-esteem.

Only a small percentage of high-school athletes will continue to compete as university athletes, and even fewer university athletes might go on to succeed at professional sports.

If you feel like Jen, it is important to find somebody you trust who you could talk to. Some teenagers will ask their parents to stop watching them when they do competitions. They might wish to do less of their sport, or to stop this particular sport and try something new.

Teenagers who are thriving on being a competitive athlete might also want to think about their self-esteem and make sure that they feel good about themselves as a person, not just because of winning at their sport.

Relative Energy Deficiency in Sport (REDS)

REDS affects male and female athletes in any sport and at many different levels. In REDS, athletes are not taking in enough energy to fuel energy requirements. In teenagers there are the energy demands for growth and development as well as for sport.

Athletes can show signs of REDS if they go for long periods without eating during the day or before or after sport. They might not always show weight loss.

> *'Ellaaaa!' I hear my mum shout. I sigh – what does Mum want now? She is being so annoying!*
>
> *'When did you last have your period?' she asks me – I have no idea and she needs to stop bitching about it. Who cares? – it's not a big deal.*

Ella

'Ella – I haven't bought you stuff for months now and it doesn't look used. I am making an appointment to see the doctor.'

I feel so irritated and embarrassed. Lots of dancers don't have periods. Why does she have to make a big deal about it? I think to myself, 'Honestly – that woman is tragic! Doesn't she have a life?'

Ella's mother takes her to the doctor, Dr Smith, who checks her height, weight and blood pressure. She also sends Ella to the practice nurse to have some blood tests. Dr Smith explains to Ella that not having periods is an unhealthy sign and can lead to health problems. She asks Ella about her health and Ella tells her doctor how healthy she is and how healthy her lifestyle is and that she is following a 'dancer's exercise programme'. Ella is proud of her body and her diet. She likes how she looks and isn't trying to lose weight.

When Ella's blood tests come back the doctor calls her back to explain the results to her. Her hormones are all low and she is not eating enough and weighs too little to be healthy. She explains that Ella has something that athletes sometimes get called 'Relative Energy Deficiency in Sport' and that it happens when not enough energy is taken in or too much goes out. She also tells Ella and her mother that without increasing her energy and getting her periods back she risks severe injuries and might need to stop dance. Dr Smith tells Ella that she would like to see her in a month's time and expects her to eat a balanced diet of three meals a day, three snacks a day and to have more high-energy foods in her diet.

Ella feels stressed and unhappy that she is having to change how she eats. What will her social media followers think about this? Ella's mum is very strict about it and tells Ella she has to eat with the rest of the family otherwise she will not take her to her dance classes. She speaks to the dance teacher, who suggests Ella stops some of her home workouts.

Four weeks later Ella has her period. Her dance teacher tells Ella she is dancing more freely and that her jumps are becoming stronger, and Ella realises that the changes she made to her nutrition and lifestyle have been helpful rather than disastrous as she initially thought.

Can boys get REDS?

Wes

I'm working harder than ever at the gym, and I think it's starting to pay off and I am looking more ripped. I'm writing down all my macros and focusing on the proteins. I've cut back the carbs and fats. Hopefully my hard work pays off and I become good enough to join the rugby academy. It's so frustrating though when my coach subs me before the end of a game.

Wes notes his appearance is changing and is pleased, but at the same time is struggling with muscle aches and pains and a shoulder injury. In Chapter 14 we will catch up with Wes and talk about his physio appointment – the physiotherapist felt his injury was due to working out too much and not having the right rest and nutrition. Wes was trying to gain muscle, but because he was cutting back on carbohydrates and fats he was missing out on the energy he needed.

Our bodies like to run on carbohydrates. When we do a long sports session our body will use fuel taken in before training but also from our own stores of energy in muscle and liver (glycogen) to fuel the activity. After glycogen stores are used up, our bodies will then start to digest muscle and protein to get enough energy.

There is a lot more awareness of REDS in athletes, but many forget that busy teenagers can be susceptible too, especially with growth spurts and busy school days, as well as walking or cycling to school and doing active lunch clubs.

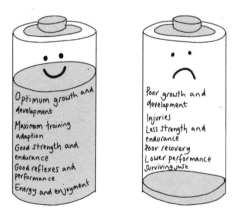

Having power in our batteries gives us the best chance of reaching our potential

REDS will affect every organ system in your body. Not only does it affect growth and development and the ability to put on muscle, it also affects your immune system (making you more susceptible to colds and other viruses), the gut (causing bloating and tummy discomfort), mood (causing low mood and higher stress levels), learning and sleep, and increases risks of injuries. REDS also has an impact on sports performance – muscle strength and endurance are affected, as well as decision-making, concentration and ability to improve from training.

When there are concerns about REDS it is important to try and get help from a professional who understands. There are many sports clinics your doctor could send you to; and although there can sometimes be a wait to be seen, it's important to address this issue and get it right.

We will talk about Wesley more in Chapter 14 where we think about how body image concerns present in many young men and boys. Chapter 3 gives more information on healthy eating and fuelling sport.

Summary

- Physical activity has lots of physical, psychological and social benefits and it is recommended that teenagers get at least an hour a day of activity to be healthy.

- Physical activity does not have to be a competitive sport – and you're more likely to stick to it if it's something you enjoy.

- It can be hard to become more active when you're not used to it, but doing something fun with friends can be a good way to start.

- Exercise can be unhealthy if it is done because of body image concerns or is the only way to manage stress.

- Over-exercise can be unhealthy for our bodies.

- If teenagers exercise but don't meet their energy requirements, they can develop REDS (Relative Energy Deficiency in Sport).

- Being a competitive athlete can be rewarding but also challenging; it is important to make time for friendships and leisure.

Chapter 14

Common Problems for Teenage Boys

My entire body aches but I'm so pleased about the rugby game this afternoon – my first year as captain and we beat a really good team. Everybody played well and I love how much the guys in the team look up to me; I even managed to score a try near the end which helped us win. Loads of people were watching from school – even Ella (who is too cool to react much) cheered for us. At the gym after the game, I'm a bit too sore to workout properly. I only do a few sets with some dumb-bells and then shower – today is supposed to be an 'Abs Day'. I feel a bit nervous about skipping my workout – I'm trying so hard to build muscle I don't want to miss any sessions.

When I go into the male changing room, it's pretty busy – I check myself in the mirror and reckon I look small and a bit pathetic. My abs aren't defined even though I'm at the gym every day. One of the personal trainers is getting changed and I notice that his arms are at least twice the size of mine – wow! – he looks shredded. I wonder what workouts he's doing and how he manages to bulk up like that. I wish I could look like that. I wonder what he eats and whether I could ask him for some advice. Maybe I need to take more supplements or train even more in the gym. I probably need to cut down some of my macros too. Mum makes all the wrong food at home.

I have some spots on my chin and I feel annoyed, and the happy feeling I had from scoring during the rugby match fades. I grab a protein shake from the shop before I go and get into the car with my dad. He asks about the game – sometimes I think that's all he cares about. I'm glad he didn't watch it because he always carries on about every little thing that I didn't do perfectly. All I can think about is my spots – and missing my workout.

Dad says I'm rude and ungrateful. I don't even bother to argue.

Wes

Today for PE we did dodge ball in the hall. I was the last to be picked for the team and nobody really wanted me. My glasses steamed up and fell off when the ball hit me in the face — everybody laughed. I hate being short and skinny and smaller than everybody else.

The boys were teasing me in the changing room afterwards. They kept saying 'Show me your biceps' and laughing at me. One poked me in the ribs and asked if my parents starved me.

I had to fight back tears and try hard to pretend not to care – the thought that I might have cried in front of everybody scares me. I'd never have lived that down.

I wish I didn't have to go to school, and I wish I would just grow. My dad says he only started growing when he was sixteen – I'm hoping I grow sooner than that.

Those boys who laughed at me asked for help in IT class today and then called me a nerd after I'd helped them. I wanted to punch them.

As I leave for my next class, I get tripped by someone and drop all my things. Everybody is laughing at me while I'm trying to pick everything up. Mr Grey, a teacher, comes past and helps me and then takes some of the boys into his office and seems pretty cross with them. I'm worried that they'll blame me if they get into trouble. I wish I could be invisible.

I can't face going into the canteen at lunchtime, so I don't bother to get lunch. I hate it there anyway – it's so loud and noisy with such strong smells. The dinner ladies also have a go at me for not taking vegetables and for having nuggets and chips every day.

Jake

What this chapter will cover:

- Issues for teenagers who identify as boys/young men.

- Unwritten rules in society around men and masculinity.

- Specific pressures that many teenage boys experience.

- Body image concerns in boys and men.

- Eating difficulties and eating disorders in boys and men.

Why a separate chapter for boys and young men?

Young men experience different pressures compared with those who identify as women. This can be in relation to puberty (early or late), eating, exercise and appearance. The way you experience these can have an impact on your life and how you feel about yourself.

In boys, experiencing puberty early is something that others may admire, whereas those who develop more slowly can have a rough time. In contrast, for girls, early puberty is something that can be associated with being teased and being called names.

At first glance, Wesley seems to have the perfect life – he is a successful athlete and respected by others. On the inside, however, he worries about not being good enough, successful enough or muscular enough.

Jake has a tough time – he is smaller and skinnier than his friends, needs glasses and as a result is teased and bullied at school. He struggles around fitting in and is quite fussy about what he eats.

Puberty

Teenagers start puberty at different times – some boys start developing into young men early in their teens. These early developers grow taller, broader and more muscular and their voice begins to change, while others in their school year develop and grow much later.

There isn't much you can do if you are a late developer – this is something that is influenced by your genes, passed down from your parents. Growth can also be slowed down or stunted if boys are not consuming enough energy, but often it just comes down to genetics. We know that boys who are late developers are more likely to be teased by peers, and can struggle with self-esteem and confidence as a result.

Research shows that teenage boys commonly worry about height, skin (and acne), their voice breaking (or not), muscularity, athletic success, penis size and appearance. Some of the physical changes that happen during puberty aren't always explained well, and it can be uncomfortable and embarrassing if you don't know what is normal. Boys often aren't sure who to ask for advice; older brothers might tease them, and it can feel risky showing vulnerability by asking friends.

Unfortunately, this means that many young men and teenage boys suffer in silence and struggle to know who to talk to. Some teenage boys who seem to be successful by society's standards might have questions but not want to embarrass themselves by asking. Boys might be insecure about a recent change in their bodies, but can also worry about a lack of change related to growth and puberty.

The unhelpful and unwritten social rules

There are many myths about masculinity

There are some unwritten social rules for boys and men which can affect wellbeing. Society tends to treat boys differently from the time they are toddlers, holding them up to certain 'masculine' values. These include stereotypes like 'boys are strong'. This gives the message that it is important for boys to be like the male heroes we see in movies, TV and books – strong, clever, smart and funny, or a combination of all of these. It includes values like not asking for help, or letting people know you might be struggling or don't know all the answers.

The rules suggest it is important to use these superhero abilities to be a great athlete, risk your life to save people in danger, or build up power and influence by making more money than other men. Some of the unwritten stories tell boys that they have to be the strongest/smartest/funniest/ hardest working in order to 'be somebody' or to 'be a man', and that competing against others (and beating them) can be more important than being a friend.

Does this mean boys should not show any feelings? Does it mean never letting anybody see you struggle or fail? Does it mean pushing through pain despite it causing a lot of discomfort? Does it mean putting yourself in dangerous situations just to be the hero? Does staying safe make you less than others? Does it mean having the prettiest or most popular girl as your girlfriend? What if you're gay – does that mean that you're less of a man?

It can all be very confusing, especially when coupled with expectations that masculine boys should be tough and in control. Boys can start to believe that toughness includes pushing through confusion and fear and pretending everything is fine. Over time this can make it hard to understand your own feelings or who you really are and what you want. This becomes even more frustrating when you need to explain how you feel and ask for advice, even if you want to.

Some people think that a way to become popular and accepted by friends is by looking muscular and strong, which must mean that you have really good athletic skills. How you look can then get mixed up with fitness, and somehow that muscular and shredded appearance is interpreted to mean that you must be better at sport and more successful in life. Thinking about Jake – what does it say about the boys in his class when they trip him up and call him names because he is smaller and less sporty? Are they doing this to try and feel more confident themselves? What about Jake's talents with IT? Is this something people could and should look up to?

Both Jake and Wesley try not to show their feelings or their worries. It can be hard for boys to share feelings with other boys (or girls) or even with their parents, and even harder to ask for help. Little niggles and worries can turn into bigger ones which can affect health, sleep, energy, friendships and schoolwork.

The other kids in Jake's class seem scared of standing up for him or standing up to the behaviour shown by some of the boys. How do they feel when they watch what is happening to Jake, but don't say or do anything?

Although society is changing, boys can still struggle to talk about feelings or what is bothering them or making them feel insecure. Perhaps we should look at it like this: what about the *bravery* to admit that you might be struggling with something? What about the *determination* to figure out how you think and feel? And the *strength* to talk about your feelings with a friend, which gives them the chance to share their feelings too?

Ask yourself:

- What are some of the things you wish you could talk about with your friends?

- Do you worry about how your friends see you and talk about you?

- Are there times when you have seen other boys being bullied – how do you feel thinking about this?

- Are there 'rules' about being a man that you have picked up from your family, teachers and friends?

- Are there men you look up to who are brave enough not to follow society's unwritten rules?

- Are there athletes who not only talk about their feelings but are not afraid to show them? Does this mean they are less strong and successful?

Mental health difficulties

Over the last ten to twenty years we have learned much more about mental health difficulties in boys. Although an increased number of boys are now being diagnosed with low mood and anxiety than in the past, mental health problems are often hidden and there can be barriers to talking about these problems or getting help.

Sadly, this means that some teenage boys hide their problems, and might only show them by becoming angry or irritable, misusing alcohol and drugs, or experiencing physical symptoms that miss the bigger picture. Boys aged fifteen to nineteen show a higher rate of death by suicide compared to teenage girls and this is thought to be partly because mental health problems are often hidden by the stigma of asking for help. This might be one of the reasons why boys and men turn to activities like excessive exercise to try and cope with difficult feelings.

Some research says that boys feel under more pressure to hide their feelings compared with girls, but that many wish that schools and those around them could encourage them to talk more and give them a chance to open up.

Things are starting to change – but maybe not quickly enough.

I've just read that online article where a premiership rugby player from my favourite team discusses his difficulties with his mental health and body image. He looks amazing and he's a really good player. He's always been so tough and strong.

It's weird that he describes feeling not good enough, or strong enough, and it's brave of him to talk about it. He talks about how he spoke to somebody and that now he's changed the way he thinks about things and how he feels.

Maybe just trying to get bigger and more muscular isn't the answer – but what will my friends think if I'm not maxing it out at the gym? I wonder if there is anybody I could ask? Would they even understand me?

Wes

More celebrities and athletes are speaking up about their mental health and about their feelings and the struggles they might have. It can be hard to talk about the tough stuff, but opening up a conversation about how you feel with someone you trust shows real strength. You might give someone else the courage to do the same, which can help you both to feel less alone.

Ask yourself:

- Do you and your friends ask each other 'Are you OK?'

- How do you answer when you are asked this?

- Are you able to open up to your friends about how you are feeling?

- Are they able to open up to you?

- What would happen if you let others know that maybe you weren't OK?

- Are you able to talk to them, or to an adult, if you are worried about them?

Tips for talking about difficult things

You might want to find a quiet time when there are just the two or you and perhaps start a conversation while gaming together or kicking a ball around. You might need to ask the question more than once, or start off with something that you've noticed. For example: 'I've noticed that you don't seem to be having a laugh as much as usual, and hanging out with us much less often. Are you OK?' You might also want to share something about yourself and how you have been, which can encourage your friend that it's OK to share. And finally – ask your friend if they would like to talk about it.

Self-esteem

All ages, sexes and genders show a drop in self-esteem during the teenage years. Males show a significant decrease from around fourteen to sixteen (for those identifying as girls it can be younger). This is worse for boys who feel they don't fit society's stereotypical masculine ideal of what it means to be a 'man' or who identify as gay or trans.

To read more about self-esteem have a look at Chapter 9.

Problems around exercise and body image

There is much less research about body image in young men but fortunately this is changing. What we are discovering is that many teenage boys don't feel they are muscular enough and that many play sport with the only goal of increasing their muscularity (the size of their muscles and leanness) rather than for enjoyment or to become a better athlete or to be healthy.

There is a lot of research about body image in girls and the pressures they can face with 'needing' to look a particular way. In the past, some researchers thought that boys might not be as affected, but we are now aware that boys also experience a lot of pressure based on appearance, and that this has increased over the last ten to twenty years.

People have looked at how action figures (toys) for boys have changed over time, as they have morphed to reflect society's ideal muscular appearance for men. These action figures now have huge and defined bodies which would be unachievable for any human.

Male body image research shows that being big, muscular and shredded can be seen (by both men and women) as meaning that the man is strong, powerful, successful and in control. Muscular men are also believed to be stronger and faster and better at sport. The downside for a muscular, athletic man is that any struggles with body image, eating or mental health are less likely to be noticed.

Finally, everyone has a different height, weight and build; in the same way that you have your unique appearance you also have unique personality, skills, interests and values. This is explored more in Chapters 5 and 10 on body image.

There are lots of male influencers on social media telling boys how to achieve a particular look or how to eat and exercise. Often these influencers are also selling a product of their own or are being paid by another company to promote their goods, which means that what they are saying may be untrustworthy.

Ask yourself:

- How much do you think about your appearance?

- Do your thoughts about how you look influence how you feel about yourself?

- How do the people you follow on social media influence how you feel about yourself?

- Are you spending a lot of money on supplements that promise to make you look a certain way?

Eating difficulties

I have carried on trying to become more shredded and I have researched the perfect supplements and macros. Mum and Dad don't understand and will just not buy me all the stuff I need to max my progress.

I think I'm starting to see improvements and my friends have all noticed and are joking about how I'll get all the girls.

I'm feeling pretty tired and down, though, and I'm not sleeping that well at the moment. I've got a really sore shoulder from a bad tackle during my last match and it's making my upper-body gym sessions impossible. Luckily Mum and Dad have made an appointment with the physio so that I can sort it out and get back to my training programme.

It is common for problems around eating in teenage boys to go unnoticed. Those who might be quite unwell with an eating disorder can miss out on treatment because the signs are less obvious in boys. They might be starving themselves, missing food groups and becoming unhealthy. But because they are driven to become more muscular, teachers, parents, coaches and even doctors may not realise they have a problem. We know that there is even more shame and embarrassment for a boy to be diagnosed with an eating disorder than for girls, and that parents, teachers and others can be misled by stereotypes about what an eating disorder *should* look like.

Boys can struggle with a variety of different eating problems – some of these are similar to those commonly seen in teenage girls, but others can show in a different way.

Disordered eating

Disordered eating is how we describe some of the early signs that eating problems are starting to develop, and this can look different in boys compared to girls. The most common problems in boys tend to involve strict rules around what foods can and cannot be eaten, when to eat, and obsessively weighing out and tracking different nutrients.

The nutritional information often comes from the internet or social media where fitness influencers encourage diets which involve eating huge amounts of protein but cutting back on the healthy carbohydrates and fats that teenagers need to grow, develop and be healthy. Using supplements can seem quite normal for teenage boys but these can have the wrong balance of nutrition, leading to a negative impact on growth and development and mental and physical health.

Some boys will cut out carbs and fats in an attempt to look leaner and appear more muscular, but these behaviours put teenage boys at risk of developing an eating disorder. These diets can harm their kidneys and have an impact on mood and energy. This way of eating (in an athletic boy) can also increase the risk of developing REDS, which is discussed in Chapter 13.

Studies have shown that up to a third of boys are taking protein powders and shakes, and one in ten might be using other supplements which promise to increase the amount of muscle. Boys can be tempted to use illegal and potentially harmful drugs to build muscle and are at a higher risk of using these if they are already using legal supplements.

Supplements sold by influencers may not give the results they claim, and will not magically make people end up looking like the influencer. Often these influencers look like they do because of genetics or because they use dangerous drugs like steroids. For more about healthy nutrition take a look at Chapter 3.

I've just seen the sports physio recommended by the rugby club. I had expected he would do some painful massage on my shoulder but instead he asked me a lot about what I am eating and my workouts. He has told me he thinks I have REDS (something about not having enough carbs and energy) and that maybe I need to see my family doctor to have some blood tests to see whether the way I'm eating is affecting my health. He has also said that looking shredded doesn't mean I'm faster and stronger – and if I'm not eating enough, I'm likely to get slower and get more and even worse injuries.

He asked if he could talk to my rugby coach and promised he'd help him understand what was happening but will also let him know that with some time off sport I will be back and maybe better than ever. He also said he would ask the coach to check how the whole team might be eating and talk to them about all the shakes we're having.

I cried during the appointment and am still really embarrassed about this. He did seem to really understand me and will see me again, but it will be so tough to stop the workouts and eat differently. I'm not sure what my friends will say, and I'm worried they will think I'm weak. Mum joined me at the end of the appointment and gave me such a lecture on the way home I wanted to scream. She did let me take the rest of the day off school and we had lunch together, and I slept a bit this afternoon.

There is often very unhelpful information about diet and exercise on the internet, and it is easy for teenagers to develop problems with their health and to get injured by following the advice online. The physio has been really helpful in figuring out what is going on with Wes's eating and exercise, but making changes might be hard.

Some boys will find it easy to make changes once they have the right advice and information, but for others, even with the correct information and facts, changing habits can be hard. If Wes really struggles, he and his family might need to think about whether he needs some support around this.

Read Chapter 8 for more information about building back healthier eating.

Picky eating

Picky eating, or being underweight due to not liking food and therefore eating too little, or not enough variety, is more common in boys than girls. This is something that tends to start in early childhood; while most boys outgrow this by the time they reach puberty, some can still struggle.

Jake is quite fussy about food: he tends to live on beige or white foods (pasta, chicken nuggets, chips) but can also forget to eat, especially when gaming or stuck on his computer. When he is having a bad day, he sometimes feels like not eating at all, and this is made worse by his mother nagging him to eat. Right now, the thought of trying new foods isn't high on Jake's list of things he wants to think about, but if he could start eating differently, his health will improve. Jake needs to have enough energy to grow and develop. He might also find that he feels less stressed and worried all the time and that he has more energy to talk to others.

To help Jake change the way he eats, he could start off by talking to the school nurse. She might have some ideas on how to help him eat lunch more regularly, especially if the canteen puts him off eating. Sometimes seeing a dietician can be helpful to identify ways to improve how regularly Jake eats, hitting all his food groups through some quick wins that he doesn't hate, to make food and eating easier. This can include taking a packed lunch and snacks to eat at break time and at the end of the school day. Jake might also want to make sure he is finding somewhere he feels comfortable and that he has enough time to eat.

Anorexia and bulimia

Boys can develop eating disorders such as anorexia nervosa, where they restrict food and lose a lot of weight. Very often it doesn't start with any idea or intention of wanting to lose weight, but with restricting food in a particular way to reduce body fat. Unfortunately, this can get out of control and lead to a situation where it gets harder and harder to eat and a significant amount of weight can be lost.

Similarly, boys can develop bulimia nervosa, which is where a person diets and restricts eating so much that they eventually end up bingeing and feeling out of control. If they have strict rules about what they allow themselves to eat, they

336 Overcoming Worries About Body Image and Eating

might try to get rid of or compensate for foods when they break those rules. This can involve making themselves sick or doing unhealthy amounts of exercise. When boys struggle with an eating disorder, they are more likely than girls to practise unhealthy levels of exercise.

Finally, research has also shown that when boys have difficulties with their eating, they often struggle with identifying and managing feelings. Addressing this is an important part of tackling the problem. Take a look at Chapter 7, which talks about identifying, understanding and managing feelings.

Ask yourself:

- How much time am I spending on social media thinking about appearance and what I should or shouldn't eat?

- Who do I want to be as an adult?

- What values are important to me?

- What choices would I make if I wasn't worried about how others would see me?

- Could I try to talk more about how I feel with my friends? Who would I speak to and what might I say?

- Do I ask my friends if they're OK, and what could I say to encourage them to talk more?

- How do I act when I see a boy from school being bullied – and is there something I could do differently?

Summary

- Boys and young men face pressures in adolescence regarding identity and unwritten social rules around what it means to be a man.

- Social media portray images of male body ideals, including being muscular and lean, which can contribute to concerns about eating and poor body image.

- Mental health problems occur in boys, but it can be harder for them to ask for help because of society's unwritten rules about men.

- Boys and young men get eating disorders too, but it may be harder to identify them.

- Stereotypes and unwritten rules about what it means to be a man are being challenged, but there are still barriers facing boys around asking for and getting help to tackle problems.

Part 3

Getting Help from Others

Chapter 15

Getting Help from Family, Friends and School

Zoe

I have known Jen since we were in primary school together. She has always been a great friend, kind, supportive, bubbly, funny. We spent a lot of time together chatting, laughing, telling each other stories, sharing ideas on clothes, hairstyles, boyfriends and lots of other things.

Now, everything has changed. I have noticed that she has become more anxious and is worried about her weight and what she's eating. She keeps saying she is too fat and needs to lose weight. I keep telling her that she is fine, but she won't listen to me. She has stopped hanging out with me as much, and even when she does she is no fun, we don't have the same laughs, she is so serious, quiet and lost in her own thoughts – she just doesn't seem to be really there. I have also noticed that she seems to be losing weight and have tried to talk to her about this, but she just ignores me. I just don't know how to help her.

Aisha

> *I felt really embarrassed when I started develop-ing problems with my eating. My parents have always really loved and supported me, and my mum makes tasty meals for the whole family. So I felt guilty when I couldn't eat the meals and began to make excuses. I told my mum I had eaten a big meal at school (when I hadn't eaten anything) and wasn't hungry, and in any case had homework to do. I began to lose weight and I knew that my parents were concerned about me. Eventually Mum had a chat when we were out for a walk and she asked me what was wrong. I tried to tell her that everything was fine, but she didn't believe me and I ended up crying and telling her everything. It was a relief to be able to talk to her about it and we agreed that she would go to the doctor with me.*

What this chapter will cover:

- The importance of family and friends.
- Accepting help from friends.
- Accepting help from parents.
- What about siblings?

It can be difficult to open up to family and friends if you have worries about eating or how you look. At the same time, they may be concerned about you and not know how to help. This chapter looks at the importance of family and friends and how you can let them help you. Siblings play an important part in this too. We will think about how you can keep connected with them while you are experiencing difficulties.

The importance of family and friends

Having problems with eating and body image can make you feel very much on your own: it can be hard to open up to others about what is going on. Yet, for many young people, family and/or friends are our biggest resource, and being able to turn to them when we have problems is a huge advantage. Even talking about the small things that bother you is a starting point to developing the sort of relationship where it is possible to talk about the big things.

Research has shown that your sense of connection to others will greatly influence how you move on from problems such as difficulties with eating or body image. Having friends or family who are supportive, understanding and kind can really help you in your struggles. However, we also know that friends and family can inadvertently make things worse: for instance, they can minimise or, alternatively, focus too much on your problems, make hurtful comments about your weight, tease you or make you feel ashamed of yourself. It can feel like they just don't understand, or they try to make out that their own problems are worse. So it's important to work out how best your family and friends can help, and to be clear with them about this.

Many young people who manage to overcome their problems say that connecting with friends and family again and sharing their concerns with others has been an important part of their recovery and getting back to normal. Having a secret can make you feel very much on your own, but when you share with others you realise that other people have problems too, that you are not on your own and can benefit from their support.

It is often the case that family and friends just don't understand what you are going through, particularly if they have never experienced anything similar, so helping them understand what your problems are can be a good first step.

Sometimes, people who you thought were your friends may start to ignore you if you have a problem, as they don't know what to say and how to help. If you share where you are at they can begin to understand why you are struggling. You may feel ashamed about your problems, or not want to burden others, but if you do summon up the courage to talk about what is going on, you are likely to end up feeling closer to your friends. This is what happened to Sam.

I just felt like my friends didn't understand the issues I was going through – my parents living apart, my mum being so busy with my younger siblings and my concerns about my gender. I felt really alone and began to keep to myself more and more. However, my best friend, Charlotte, suggested we might try a new youth club together. I said no to start with, but she kept on at me, so I eventually went with her. Once I started going, I surprised themself and actually enjoyed it and became a lot closer to Charlotte. I eventually plucked up courage and told her about the stress I was under at home. She was very understanding so I talked to her about my worries about my gender too. She introduced me to someone who had similar concerns, and this really helped me to feel less alone.

Sam

Accepting help from friends

Zoe was really concerned about her friend Jen and tried to talk to her, but Jen brushed her aside. Sometimes, it is hard to accept that our friends are concerned about us and want to help, and it is easier just to ignore what they are saying.

However, taking them seriously is important. It is an important sign of friendship that someone is concerned enough to want to talk to you about what they have noticed. Try to listen to what your friends are saying and see things from their perspective.

Having a chat with friends that you trust – where they share their concerns, and you share your perspective – can be a first step to getting the right sort of help. Friends often want to help, but don't know how, or what to say. You can brainstorm together some things they could say or do to help you. Boyfriends/girlfriends may also want to be supportive and keen to work out how they could help.

If you are not feeling good about yourself, one of the most important things you can do is to continue meeting up with your friends. This will help to build your life away from any concerns about body image or eating. Spending a lot of time on your own can make you more and more focused on your body image and less confident in yourself. Spending time with friends helps you develop confidence and a sense of who you are, as well as getting back some fun and joy in your life.

Zoe was able to tell Jen that she was concerned about her. Jen was initially a bit defensive and tried to say that she was OK, but as the conversation continued, she realised that Zoe was really trying to help. She began to share with her how awful life had become. They worked out together that it would be helpful to meet up regularly in the local park.

Sometimes young people worry about burdening their friends and may feel uncomfortable talking about their problems. It may be enough to just spend time together doing fun things such as watching a film or going for a walk, which can take your mind off your difficulties.

Ask yourself:

- Would it help to spend more time with your friends?

- What can your friends do to support you with your problems?

- Who could you talk to about this?

Accepting help from parents

When young people develop problems with eating and body image, they can become quite secretive. It can be hard to tell your parents that you have a problem. It may feel shameful to admit what is going on. At the same time, your parents may be concerned about you and not know the best way to approach you. So you both end up avoiding the issues and not talking about the things that matter.

However, parents usually want to help even though they may not know the best way to connect with and support you. When teenagers have worries about eating or how they look, parents can be vital in supporting them to make changes and feel good about themselves again.

It really helps if you can be honest with your parents, letting them know what your worries are and making it clear what would be either helpful or unhelpful. See if you identify with any of the following:

Check it out: Unhelpful and helpful things that parents sometimes do

Unhelpful

- Commenting on how you look: the worst thing is when you are told you have put on weight, or lost weight, or that you need to go on a diet.

- Jumping in with advice before really listening.

- Telling you to snap out of it and that you don't really have a problem.

- Being negative about small things you get wrong.

- Not noticing how hard you are trying.

- Commenting on your snack choices or eating habits.

- Blaming or shaming you, telling you the impact it has on them, or making it all about them.

- Not keeping calm during a conversation – anger or high emotion never helps!

Helpful

- Listening well with their full attention to what you have to say.

- Trying to understand even the smallest problem.

- Working out with you how they can help.

- Staying calm in the conversation.

- Not rushing in to try to change or fix things.

The aim is to have more of the helpful responses, but unfortunately, parents don't always know whether they are helping or making things worse. Having a conversation and letting them know what helps or doesn't help is often needed. It can be tempting to stay quiet when your parents say unhelpful things, but try to speak up and let them know – they need to be told!

Spending time with parents doing activities you both enjoy, such as watching a film together or going out for a walk, is a good way to build a relationship. It then makes it easier to discuss difficult topics.

Ask yourself:

- What do your parents do or say that you find really unhelpful?
- What can your parents do or say differently to help you feel better about yourself?
- How would you like your parents to support you?
- Do you feel able to talk to your parents about this?
- When would be a good time to talk this over with your parents?

Siblings' relationships and reactions

Getting on with your sibling depends on lots of things – your ages, whether you are the same gender, share the same interests or have the same sort of personality. Most siblings have times when they get on, and times when they really hate each other. Overall, a sibling tends to be concerned if things are not right for their brother or sister.

When someone in the family has an eating problem, siblings may sense that something is not right. They may feel worried but not able to talk about it.

Rashmi
Aisha's
sister

I always used to get on well with Aisha, but then she started to keep to herself and didn't want to play games with me. I was really upset by this and started to get cross with her. She also became angry with me. It was difficult and I couldn't understand what had happened to Aisha – she seemed so different. I talked about it with Mum who said it was probably because she was growing up. However, I noticed that Aisha didn't look very well and seemed to have lost some weight. Also, family meals became a real pain. Aisha was constantly arguing with Mum and Dad, I couldn't wait to finish my meal and leave the table. Family meals used to be fun; Mum cooks great meals and we used to chat about things and have a good laugh. That all changed and the whole family seemed to become really tense.

As time went on, I became more and more worried about Aisha. I even thought she might die because she looked so unwell, but I couldn't talk to her and didn't know how to help. I was so relieved when Mum told me that she had been to the doctor and was going to get some help.

Siblings can find it bewildering if their sister or brother starts to develop problems with eating. Their whole personality seems to change, and they find it so much harder to relate to them. They can also be concerned about the physical health of their sibling and may even worry that they are going to die. There may be tension within the family, and usual family activities may have stopped.

Jen

When I started going to the eating disorder service they suggested that my whole family came along for one of the appointments, including my younger brother. I realised that I had become quite distant from them, even though I knew they were worried about me. I really wasn't sure about Ben coming along. How could I possibly talk about things in front of him? However, Mum and Dad reassured me that there would still be a chance to talk on my own. In the end I found it helpful having him there as he understood much better what I was going through, and we were able to work out ways in which he could support me. I know that he really wanted to help. It was a relief when we started to get on better again.

Research has shown that most young people with eating problems find it helpful to have siblings involved in supporting them to get better.

Ask yourself:

- Has anything changed in your relationship with your sibling(s)?

- How could things be different?

- How would you like your brother/sister to help?

- Is there a good time to talk to your sibling?

Getting help from school/college

Teenagers spend a lot of time in school or college and their teachers/tutors get to know them well. They may be the first to notice that a young person has changed in some way; for example, not contributing in class, keeping to themselves, appearing unhappy or starting to get poor grades. They may approach you to ask if things are OK. This is a good chance to open up about your difficulties. Your teacher may be able to work out with you who might be able to help; for example, a school counsellor or school nurse.

Even if they don't approach you, try to think of a staff member that you get on well with and ask if you can have a chat with them. Most school/college staff are very happy to listen to any concerns.

Sometimes, it will be your friends who approach a member of staff, letting them know that they are worried about you. You may feel betrayed by this, but remember that they genuinely are concerned and want to make sure that you get some help.

In some schools it is possible to refer yourself to the school counsellor for some help. This might be easier for some teenagers, rather than talking to a teacher first.

Aisha's teacher noticed that she had become very quiet and withdrawn, not like her usual bubbly self. She took Aisha aside and asked her if anything was wrong. Aisha's first reaction was to say, 'Everything's fine', but the teacher gave her time and just sat with her for a few moments. Aisha plucked up courage to say that she wasn't sleeping well and felt dizzy and really low in energy a lot of the time, making it hard to concentrate at school. The teacher suggested she should talk to her parents about this and offered to be with her when she did so. Aisha found this very supportive and agreed to a meeting with the teacher and her parents.

Ask yourself:

- Is there a member of staff at school or college who you would feel comfortable talking to?
- When would be a good time to talk to them?
- How could you start the conversation?
- How would you like them to help?

This chapter has focused on how to get help from those people who are closest to you. You may feel anxious about the idea of talking to people about your problems, but sharing how you feel can make you feel less isolated and be the first step to getting back on track with your life again.

There are lots of people who could help Aisha. Accepting help from people around you is a bit like having a safety net, with people there to stop you falling.

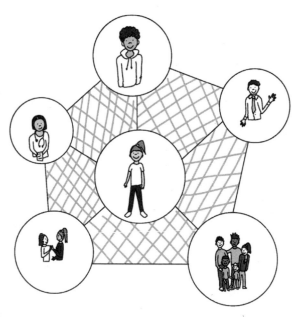

Friends, family, school and clubs can
all be part of your safety net

Summary

- Friends and family may be concerned about you but not know how to help.

- Having an eating problem can be very lonely.

- Getting connected with family and friends in small ways can help you feel less isolated.

- Talking things over with friends and family can be helpful.

- School staff can be supportive too.

Chapter 16

Getting Professional Help

Jen

I was thinking about food all the time and was just miserable. I stopped seeing my friends and was very snappy with my parents who I know were trying to help. Each meal was a real struggle as I felt so full and uncomfortable even though I was hardly eating anything. I had no energy for tennis and my coach suggested I take some time off. One day, I felt I'd just had enough and couldn't eat another mouthful at suppertime. My parents tried to encourage me to eat but my tummy hurt, and I felt awful. The next day I couldn't manage breakfast either, and didn't have the energy to go to school. My parents were really worried and said they were going to take me to the doctor. I didn't want to go, but I had to. I broke down and cried when the doctor spoke to me.

What this chapter will cover:

- How will you know if you need professional help?

    ° Symptoms that suggest an eating disorder.
    ° Symptoms that suggest depression.

- How do you get professional help?

    ° Referral routes.
    ° What help is available.
    ° Voluntary organisations.

- What can you expect from professional help?

    ° Assessment.
    ° Community treatment.
    ° Inpatient treatment.

- How to work with professionals.

- How to stay well.

As with Jen, it can sometimes be difficult to get through a problem with eating, even with help from family or friends. This is when you might need professional help. You can continue to use those strategies in this book that you have found helpful, but you may also need a therapist or a specialist team to help you through this particularly difficult patch in your life.

This chapter will discuss how to tell if a difficulty with eating is becoming more serious, what sort of help is available and how to access it.

How will you know if you need professional help?

Jen was really struggling with her eating, was getting tummy pains, and feeling miserable. It was at this point that her parents suggested that she should see a doctor.

Here are some of the signs that might indicate that you need more help:

- When weight loss has an impact on your health:

    ◦ Feeling weak and having no energy.
    ◦ Fainting.
    ◦ Not being able to concentrate.
    ◦ Feeling breathless, especially when exercising.
    ◦ Losing muscle strength.
    ◦ Noticing your skin, hair and nails becoming drier, and hair and nails more brittle.

- When your mental health and wellbeing has suffered:

    ◦ Feeling low in mood.
    ◦ Experiencing high levels of anxiety.
    ◦ Becoming isolated from friends and family.
    ◦ Having thoughts about self-harming.
    ◦ Feeling so preoccupied about your body image that it is hard to concentrate on anything else.

- When you have serious problems with eating and weight:

    ◦ Losing a lot of weight, especially in a short space of time.
    ◦ Feeling that your eating is out of control.
    ◦ Being unable to eat sufficiently to give you enough energy for the day.
    ◦ Being unable to stop bingeing and vomiting.
    ◦ Absence of periods or delay in their onset.

If you are experiencing any of the above it may be that you need to see your doctor or nurse practitioner. It is helpful if you can discuss this with your parent or carer. They may help you set up an appointment and go with you. If you don't feel able to talk to a parent/carer, or you live independently, you may want to talk things over with a trusted friend or an adult you know well.

Another helpful point of contact is a school nurse or school counsellor, if available. Meeting with the school nurse is a good chance to talk over any worries you may have. They will know the best course of action to take, which might be seeing a school counsellor, making an appointment with your doctor or continuing to see the school nurse on a regular basis.

Your doctor will listen to your concerns and may do a physical examination and refer you for blood tests. They may suggest that you are referred to a service specialising in eating disorders. If you are under eighteen years old, this will generally be a service specifically for children and young people. If you are over eighteen this will be an adult mental health service. Some eating disorder services accept direct referrals from young people or parents, but going to the family doctor first can be helpful as they can take a wider view and check out whether a physical illness is causing your symptoms. Not everyone with an eating disorder will be underweight: rapid weight loss, regular vomiting and missing meals, alongside worries about your weight and shape, can be just as serious as being very underweight.

If you are aware of any struggles or anxieties about your gender, you may need additional help from a service that is specifically experienced in this area. Your primary care doctor may be able to point you in the right direction.

Feelings you might experience at the point of getting help

It's normal to have a mix of feelings about the idea of seeking help. Some teenagers might feel ashamed that they have developed this problem and can't get out of it; they may be uncertain about whether they need help, or even feel that they don't need help; they may feel embarrassed that they have let their family or friends down; relief that they might be getting help; frustration that no one listens; exhaustion because of having to think about eating and weight all the time; anger with their parents for making them eat; or feeling really scared about making changes. You may experience a mix of all these emotions, and even others too. You might be unsure how to feel – things have been difficult for you for some time now, and you might be starting to feel a bit numb. These feelings are all quite normal, and the mental health team will understand what's going on for you.

You may also be aware of others' feelings. For example, you may notice your parents being worried or frustrated or even angry with you.

Ask yourself:

- What emotions might you feel if your eating problem has got out of hand?

How do you get professional help for an eating disorder?

Once a referral has been received by the mental health team, they will work out whether you have been referred to the right place and how urgent it is for you to get help. Some teams like to have a chat with you (and your parents) over the phone to check out how you are doing and work out the next step.

Mental health services try to see people as soon as they can, but there may be a waiting list. So, what can you do while you are waiting?

It is usually helpful to have a chat with your parents to see what they might be able to do to support you. Self-help books can be a good starting point while you are waiting to see a clinician (see the resources section at the end of the book for some recommendations).

There are also voluntary organisations which can be very helpful for young people with eating disorders – have a look at the resources section for organisations in different countries. Be wary of unhelpful social media influencers who claim to be giving expert advice.

What can you expect when you are referred for help?

Once the service has accepted the referral, you will be sent an appointment for an assessment. If you are under eighteen, your parents or carer will usually be invited too, and sometimes your siblings. The reason for this is that if you have an eating disorder, your family are likely to be very important in helping you get back to full health again.

If you are eighteen or over, you will be sent an individual appointment and it will be up to you whether you take your parents or carer along as well. Many teenagers and young adults find it supportive to have their parents/carer present, and you are likely to have some time during the appointment talking with the clinician on your own. Most eating disorder services have websites so you can check out what they offer, and what the process is going to be like, in advance.

Assessment

Your first meeting with the professional team will be an assessment (either on your own or with your family). This involves checking out your concerns, and working out what you would like to be different. They will want to find out about your background (including your growth and development throughout childhood), who you are living with and how you get on with your family, what's going on at school or with your friends, as well as your physical and mental health. This is really important to help build up an understanding of you as a person and how the difficulties you are experiencing have developed over time – and become stuck.

At the end of the assessment your clinician will discuss with you their understanding of the issues and whether they feel you have an eating disorder. They will also discuss the next step, which may mean starting some treatment within the service.

Jen

Once I had seen the doctor, I was sent an appointment for the eating disorder service for a few weeks' time, and went along with both my parents. I felt really anxious at the assessment, wondering what was going to happen and whether they might suggest I should be admitted to hospital. I was also scared they would tell me I needed to eat more; I just couldn't imagine doing this.

However, the psychologist made me feel at ease and I was able to talk about some of my worries and my fear about having to eat more. She seemed to understand how difficult things were for me.

So what treatments are available? How do services help young people with eating difficulties take charge of their life again? And, importantly, do you really want to accept help?

Building motivation

At the point of getting help, you may have a mixture of thoughts about what you want. Part of you might be relieved that you are getting help, but another part might just want to be left alone. It is hard to stop what you are familiar with and to embark on the unknown. What will help be like, will they listen to me, will they take away all my choices? Even if you know deep down inside that you want to get over this, it may feel really scary.

How do you weigh up what you want?

It can be helpful to make a list of the pros and cons of accepting help. Jen felt really uncertain at this stage but, with the help of her therapist, wrote a list of the pros and cons of accepting help for her eating disorder:

Pros	Cons
• I'll have the energy to go out with my friends again.	• It is easier to keep things as they are.
• I won't have to think about food all the time.	• I am afraid that I will be told what to do.
• I'll be able to concentrate better on my schoolwork.	• I'm embarrassed to talk about myself.
• I'll get on with my family again.	• Basically, I don't want to put on any weight.
• Hopefully, I will feel better about myself.	• I know that I will have to eat more, and I just can't do it.

Jen's pros and cons for accepting help

Ask yourself:

- What are the pros of getting help for your eating difficulties?

- What are the cons of getting help for your eating difficulties?

It's understandable to feel uncertain about getting help and making changes

Accepting help

You may be wondering what sort of help is available. There are several types of therapy that are offered to people with eating disorders, but an important starting point will be monitoring your physical health and keeping you safe.

Physical health monitoring

The priority, whatever your age, is to assess and manage your physical health. You may also be given dietary advice. A decision will be made as to whether your physical health is stable enough to manage at home or whether you need more intensive help in hospital or a day care setting. Monitoring may include checking your blood pressure and pulse regularly, monitoring your level of hydration, checking your muscle strength and weight. You may also have blood tests, and a scan of your bones. Females may have a scan to check how their uterus (womb) is developing. This monitoring is likely to be done by a nurse, a doctor or another professional trained to do these tests.

Psychological treatments

If you are under eighteen and have an eating disorder, you are likely to be offered *family-based treatment (FBT)*. Your family will be involved right from the start. Research suggests that involving your family in this sort of treatment will give you a better outcome. You may also be offered *multi-family therapy*, where your family will attend a four-day treatment with other families to increase understanding of eating disorders and to work out with the whole group what is needed to make changes.

If you are over eighteen you will generally be offered *cognitive behavioural therapy (CBT)*. Young people under eighteen may also be offered CBT either at the start, if it seems the best approach for you, or at a later stage in treatment.

You may be offered *adolescent-focused treatment (AFT)*, where you are helped to work towards personal goals – there is some evidence that this treatment can be effective for some teenagers. If you are over eighteen you may be offered the *Maudsley Model of Anorexia Nervosa Treatment for Adults (MANTRA)*, which is an outpatient treatment for adults that addresses the thoughts, feelings, relationships and biological changes that keep people stuck in their eating disorder and gradually helps them to find alternatives and more helpful ways of coping.

Other treatments that are sometimes offered are *interpersonal therapy* (where the focus of treatment is on your relationships) and *dialectical behaviour therapy (DBT)* where you are encouraged to develop your skills in dealing with distress, managing your emotions and developing positive relationships. Whatever treatment you are offered, it is likely that your physical health will be monitored carefully, including regular checks of your weight, blood pressure and pulse rate, as well as blood tests. You are also likely to see a dietician who will discuss your nutritional needs and help you plan your meals.

All the eating disorder-focused treatments will involve physical health restoration as well as help for emotional difficulties.

Some teenagers may be offered group treatment where they can meet with other young people with eating disorders and discuss topics such as managing stress, coping with mealtimes or building an identity separate from the eating disorder. Your parents also may be invited to join a group with other parents to help them understand eating disorders better and discuss how best to help.

If a teenager is very unwell, a health professional may recommend that you are admitted to hospital for a while so that you can be taken care of while you recover. See below for more information.

> **Check it out: The main treatments for eating disorders**
>
> - Community:
>   - ° Physical monitoring and dietary advice
>   - ° Family-based treatment (FBT)
>   - ° Cognitive behavioural therapy (CBT)
>
> - Inpatient treatment

Here are details of the two main community-based eating disorder treatments (FBT and CBT).

Family-based treatment (FBT) is an approach where the family is closely involved in helping you recover from an eating disorder. Generally, twenty sessions will be offered, weekly to start with and then less frequently as progress is made. There are three stages of FBT:

Stage 1: Support from parents At the start of treatment, your parents will be encouraged to support you with your eating. This will involve cooking your meals, serving them and supporting you while you eat. The reason for this is that it may have become too difficult for you to manage this on your own. Parents can find this approach really hard as they are used to you eating independently, but at this stage you may need lots of support to get back on track with your eating again. Siblings may be invited to attend treatment sessions to make sure they understand what is going on and to help them work out the best way to help you; for example, by distracting you during or after meals. If you are unwell physically you may need to have some time off school. The aim is to help you get back to normal regular eating and improve your physical health and wellbeing.

Although it might feel very difficult for teenagers to have their parents helping to make decisions about the food they eat, most young people look back at the end of treatment and say that this has been helpful as they couldn't do it for themselves.

Stage 2: Taking responsibility again Later in treatment your parents will gradually help you to take back responsibility for preparing, serving and eating your meals. This will be done at a pace that you can manage, with lots of discussion between you, your parents and the therapist. Often, young people want to get on with this and take back responsibility quickly; however, others find this anxiety-provoking. It is important to do this at a pace that is manageable.

Stage 3: Staying well At the end of treatment, you will be helped to get back on track with your usual activities (schools, friends, interests, etc.). Your family will be helped to manage any difficulties in relationships that may have arisen, and get back to being a normal family again. You will also prepare to finish treatment and work out how to continue to stay well.

So, I went with my mum and dad to the eating disorder clinic and we were all seen together. This was really hard to start with as my parents agreed to supervise my meals and I really hated this as I didn't want to put on any weight. I was pretty angry at the beginning, but as time went on, I got used to my parents helping me at mealtimes and I began to have a bit more energy and to sleep better at night. That meant that I was able to get back to school and go out with my friends again.

Cognitive behavioural therapy (CBT) Eating-disorder-focused CBT is the main recommended treatment for those over the age of eighteen and may also be offered to those under the age of eighteen either following a period of family-based treatment or as an alternative to FBT, or during an inpatient stay (see below). The programme is twenty sessions (or more if weight is very low to start with), with the young person being seen twice weekly to start with, then weekly, and finally every couple of weeks.

To make the most of CBT, it is important that you are able to collaborate well with the therapist and be prepared, with their help, to make some changes. The therapist will help you to develop some curiosity about how you have become stuck in an eating disorder. In CBT you and the therapist work out together how you can make changes and you take a lot of responsibility yourself, so you need to be happy to be in control of the process. Neither the therapist nor your family are going to do it for you, but they are there to help and support you. CBT is structured with four different phases, as described below.

1 *Understanding your problems and returning to normal eating* The main aim is to help you make the changes needed to return to regular eating. You and your therapist will work together in partnership to discover what keeps your eating disorder going. This is done with the aid of a diagram (called a formulation – see below) which helps explain what keeps you locked in the eating disorder and what you might need to do to break out of the cycle. You will be asked to keep a diary of what you are eating, the circumstances and your accompanying thoughts and feelings. Identifying patterns of eating helps you and your therapist to work out where any changes might be helpful.

For Jen, feeling bad about her weight and body led her to try and change her body shape by skipping meals and eating smaller portions. To start off with, Jen felt good about the changes, and received some compliments from some of her peers. This motivated her to keep going with eating less. However, as her body became more malnourished, other symptoms emerged, like feeling low in mood, losing interest in other activities and feeling full all the time. When Jen experienced these, she had thoughts such as *'I'm so lazy'*, *'if I feel this full, I must be eating too much'*, which increased her worries about weight and shape and kept the cycle going.

The diagram below shows how Jen became trapped in an eating disorder.

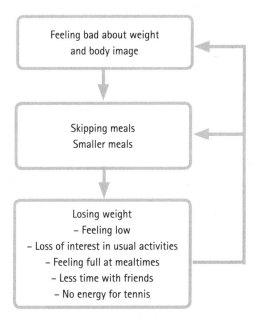

How Jen became trapped in an eating disorder

During the first part of treatment, you will be encouraged to get back to regular eating and your weight will be monitored regularly. Important people in your life such as a parent, grandparents or your boyfriend/girlfriend (if appropriate) may be involved to support you. If you are low in weight to start with, the first part of treatment will need to be longer.

2 *Reviewing your treatment* In the middle of treatment, your therapist will give you a chance to review how far you have progressed and work out a plan for the rest of treatment.

3 *Addressing the factors that keep your eating disorder going*

- **Continuing weight restoration** If you are still low in weight, you will be supported to continue to put on weight until you are healthy again.

- **Body image** This will help you to find out what keeps your negative view of yourself going and how to be more accepting of your body.

- **Rules around eating** If you have rules about eating, for example, what to eat, when to eat or how to eat, you will be supported to challenge the rules.

- **Managing mood and stress** If stress and life events have an impact on your eating, then you will be helped to find ways of managing this.

- **Dealing with setbacks and mindsets** Learning to identify when an unhelpful mindset creeps in and how to displace it.

Some people might benefit from additional support in the following areas:

- **Relationships** Identifying what the problems are in your relationships and finding ways to get on better with your friends and family.

- **Self-esteem** If you suffer from low self-esteem, you may be offered some therapy to help you develop a more positive sense of yourself.

- **Perfectionism** If this is a problem, you will be helped to develop a mindset that is not about being perfect in every way but accepting yourself for who you are and being realistic about your goals and achievements.

4 *Working out how to stay well* Finally, you will work with the clinician to create a plan for the future to help you keep well. This will include looking at how the eating problem developed, what kept it going, what has helped you to get over it and how you can stay well in the future.

Inpatient treatment

If there is concern about your physical and/or mental well-being and you are not getting better with treatment in the community, your team may recommend an inpatient admission, either in a psychiatric or a general hospital. This is to provide you with more intensive treatment (including psychological and medical) in a safe environment. All decisions will have the young person's best interest in mind. The aim is to keep them safe and well, while also taking into account their opinions.

Working with professionals

When you start treatment for an eating disorder, you may experience different voices or thoughts in your head suggesting what you should do. The healthy voice that is on your side may tell you that you need to have treatment to get well and back on track with your life. However, the eating disorder voice may tell you that you don't need treatment so you may be reluctant to start and, even when you do start, may resent the treatment and find the sessions really difficult.

It helps if you can be honest with your therapist about what you are finding difficult and what helps. The outcome is generally better if you can work together with your therapist and with your parents: working together is the most effective way to fight the eating disorder. If you give it time and say honestly how it all feels, then you have the best chance of building up trust with your therapist.

Your therapist won't be perfect: sometimes they get things wrong or don't understand what you are trying to say. It is best to be honest and let them know what is helpful and what is unhelpful.

Ask yourself:

- How could your therapist be more helpful?
- Would you be able to tell them this?

At the start of treatment, it may be hard for you to make your own decisions, and the therapist might take an active role in helping you to change. As time goes on you will be able to take more and more responsibility for yourself. It is helpful if you can say when you are ready to take more responsibility. Professionals are there to help and want the best for you, but it is also up to you to engage and take responsibility yourself.

They can't do it for you, but they can give you support and the necessary tools.

When treatment starts, things may get tricky before they get easier: the eating disorder may feel threatened and do all it can to make sure you don't progress. This is the moment when you need all the support you can get from family, friends and the professionals looking after you.

Towards the end of treatment, it is important to discuss with your therapist when you are ready to be discharged. Being ready is not just about whether eating and weight have improved, it is also about how you feel about yourself, and whether you are able to get on with other aspects of your life, such as school and seeing friends without the eating disorder getting in the way.

Follow-up

Once you have been discharged from the service, you may be offered a follow-up in a few months' time to check on your progress. Not all services are able to offer this, so you may need to book an appointment with your family doctor to review how you are doing.

Staying well

Here are some ideas for staying well once you have recovered from an eating disorder:

• Make sure you eat regularly.

- Take regular exercise that you enjoy.

- Make sure you keep in contact with your friends.

- Keep going with your interests (hobbies, clubs, arts and craft, music, etc.).

- Try to have a balance between work and relaxation.

Good luck on your journey to overcoming your difficulties and being able to live your life to the full!

Summary

- Some teenagers may need professional help.

- Your family doctor can help you access the right service for you.

- Treatment will be worked out with you according to your needs.

- There are different types of treatment depending on how unwell you are, your age, or what would work best for you.

- Inpatient treatment may be necessary if you have a serious problem that is not getting better in the community.

- Having a good relationship with your clinician really helps.

Chapter 17

A Chapter for Parents and Carers

Wesley's dad

I feel really concerned about Wesley. He comes back late from school and is very secretive about where he has been. In the evening he hides away in his room and all we can hear is pounding and banging. He is very cross when I try to go into his room to see how he is and what he is doing; he just shouts at me, saying he wants to be left alone. I really care about him but can't work out how to get through to him. We both know that he isn't happy but just don't know how to help.

Aisha gets up late and then doesn't eat anything for breakfast. She says she's in a hurry to get to school and will have a snack when she gets there, but I am not at all convinced that she's doing this. In the evening she makes excuses not to join family meals – and when she does join us, she just sits there picking at her food, not saying anything, then slips away quietly to her room. She used to love playing family games and going out with the family but doesn't seem to enjoy doing things with us anymore – and she's really irritable with her younger brother and sister, which upsets them. It's difficult to know if this is her just 'being a teenager', or if something is wrong. I feel really concerned, but don't want to draw attention to what is happening in case I make things worse.

Aisha's mum

What this chapter will cover:

- Navigating the teenage years:

  ○   Dilemmas and challenges.
  ○   Role of parents.

- Helping to create a positive relationship to eating and body image.

- Early difficulties with eating and how to help.

- Getting professional help.

- Looking after yourself.

Many parents face similar situations and can feel at a loss as to what to do. This chapter is aimed at parents/carers and how they might be able to help. The ideas and suggestions are informed by research as well as through discussions with parents and teenagers about strategies that they find helpful. If your child is developing a problem with eating it can be hard to know whether you have cause to worry and need to do something active, or whether to leave things alone – is this just part of being a typical adolescent, or a phase they are going through?

We will start by thinking about the ups and downs of normal adolescence and how to help your teenager through this stage and feel good about themselves, before focusing on the particular challenges you face if your child develops problems with eating and body image. Each family is unique, and you may want to adapt these ideas to suit your own situation. As a parent or carer, the aim is to find your own way to communicate with and support your teenager.

Navigating the teenage years

What are the dilemmas and challenges?

The teenage years are a time of transition. Not only is the body changing rapidly as the young person enters puberty, they are also learning to be independent, fit in with friends, work out who they are and cope with school life, exams and career choices. In addition, teenagers can be impulsive and emotional, and not too good at thinking through issues logically (see Chapter 1). Most teenagers get through this phase without too much difficulty, but mental health problems, including depression, anxiety and obsessive compulsive disorder (OCD), as well as eating disorders, increase during these years – and some young people are particularly vulnerable. Most teenagers look to their parents for direction and advice, and there will be lots of times when you don't agree with each other. Disagreement is a normal and healthy part of parent/teenager interaction. It enables the teenager to practise and acquire skills such as how to express opinions, how to respect the views of others even if they are different, and how to manage conflict.

Coping with the increasing independence of teenagers can be a tricky time for families. Conflict often arises as teenagers try to work out who they are and what they want to do.

When they express angry feelings towards parents it may be no more than part of their struggle to 'stretch their wings'.

In addition, the teenage years often coincide with parents managing multiple demands, including careers, social life, leisure interests and caring for other family members, for example, elderly relatives. This can make it harder to notice how your young person is feeling. However, you may observe that your teenager is becoming more withdrawn from the family, losing energy or motivation for usual activities or isolating themselves in their bedroom, spending long periods of time on the internet or not joining in with family activities or meals. These can be signs of normal adolescence – part of growing up and developing one's own identity – but may also signal that your teenager has concerns or is struggling with their eating. You may wonder whether you have cause to worry and need to do something active or whether it's best to leave things alone.

Try to work out if these behaviours are becoming more frequent or are having a marked impact on family or peer relationships or are causing significant distress for the individual or affecting their functioning at school. If any of these are the case, it may be right to be concerned and to explore what is going on for your teenager.

Helping our teenagers through this period of life may bring up issues that were a challenge for us at their age. This can help us identify with them but may also bring up painful memories. It can be useful to remind yourself of what helped you at this stage in your life.

Ask yourself:

- What things were important to you during adolescence?

- What was your own journey through puberty like?

- What did you learn then that might be useful now?

Role of parents in the teenage years

So, what can parents do? Although teenagers may want us off their back at times, parents have a crucial role during this phase of life.

Staying connected

Even though your teenager is growing up and learning to be independent it is still important to spend time with them to build up your relationship. It is great if your teenager can suggest things that you can do together, such as going to the cinema, going for a walk or bike ride, playing a family game, having a pizza evening or watching a film together. You might need to suggest an activity; initial resistance will often give way to pleasure in doing something together. Sharing an activity can create space to talk and gives a strong message that you care. Your teenager needs to know that even if they are cross with you or tell you to get out of their lives, you are still there for them and are ready to support them. Having a secure, reliable base to come back to gives them the confidence to grow up.

Keeping lines of communication open

This is something that most parents and teenagers struggle with at times. However, keeping dialogue going and being there when your teenager needs help and support is so important. A hug or a smile may be all that is needed at times. Taking an interest in your teenager's views and allowing them to express themselves without judging or belittling them helps them develop confidence in who they are and what they think. It is all too easy to be judgemental or critical if you think they have made a wrong decision or done something which they might regret, but it is important to respect where they are and allow them space to reflect. Some teenagers may find it hard to think through issues logically, so having space to talk things over can be really helpful (even if they tell you at times that you are useless!).

You may need to broach difficult subjects, particularly if you are concerned about your teen's eating habits. So how can you do this?

Where Teenagers like their private space, but grabbing moments when you are together such as on a car journey, taking them shopping or to football practice, can provide an opportunity to talk over any concerns.

How There are different ways to approach difficult topics, ranging from direct questioning to more indirect gentle approaches, depending on how you relate to your teenager.

A useful model for effective communication is known as the OARS model, developed by Miller and Rollnick (see the reference section at the end of the book). OARS stands for Open-ended questions, Affirming, Reflective listening and Summarising.

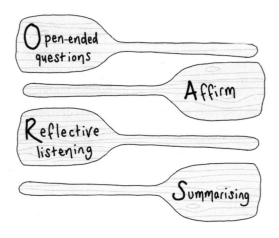

OARS can help you to communicate effectively with your teenager

Open-ended questions Using open-ended questions that don't require a yes/no answer works well as this opens up the conversation and helps you understand what is going on for your teen. However, sometimes you may need to use a closed question to find out about specific things.

Check it out: Examples of open-ended and closed questions

Open-ended questions

- 'How are you feeling today?'

- 'Tell me how your day went?'

Closed questions

- 'Do you feel depressed?'

- 'Did something happen at school today which upset you?'

Sometimes you may need a combination of open and closed questions, using either a more direct approach or a gentler indirect approach – depending on what works best for your teen.

Check it out: Examples of direct and indirect questioning

Direct questioning

- You seem a bit down at the moment– what's going on?'

- 'I notice that you're not your usual self – is there something worrying you?'

- 'Sorry you didn't join us for the walk today. Is there something the matter?'

- 'I noticed that you didn't come down for breakfast this morning. Is anything upsetting you?'

- 'You don't seem to be going out with your friends as much – is anything wrong?'

Indirect questioning

- 'How are things going at school? What are the things you enjoy doing?

- 'Is there anything you are finding difficult at school?'

- 'What can I do to help you with this?'

- 'How are you getting on with your friends?'

Affirmation Learning to acknowledge and affirm your teenager's feelings without being patronising, being able to notice small things to praise (even when they are angry or silent) and respecting their skills and strengths are all skills worth honing with teenagers. In the table below we have listed some examples of positive affirmations. You may think of others which fit better for your own teenager. The important thing with a positive affirmation is neither to jump into giving advice nor be defensive, which is all too easy! Look at the examples below and have a think about what your initial automatic response might be. Try out different responses.

Teenager	Possible affirming response
'I got my results for the exam today. I did really badly. I am a complete failure and may as well give up'	'I'm glad you told me; that must feel disappointing, especially after the work you put in last night'
'This meal is really disgusting; I can't eat it'	'Just as well you told me. What are the foods you like best?'
'You're the worst parent in the world. I wish I wasn't part of this family'	'It's good you can be honest with me'
'I have decided to give up Biology A level and do Art instead'	'It sounds like you have been thinking hard about this. Do you want to talk it over?'
'I called my friend today to arrange to go out'	'That's great you did this, as I know you were anxious about it'

Reflective listening Just think for a moment of the last time you had a conversation with someone when you felt really listened to. What was it about the experience that made this so special? Perhaps it was their undivided attention, making eye contact with you and letting you speak without interruption or judgement. Or was it that they let you express what you wanted to say, not jumping in to give advice, reflecting on what you were feeling or saying to make sure they understood you correctly? All of this is active or reflective listening, which is very different from the experience we all have at times when we don't feel listened to. Sometimes we get the feeling that the other person is just waiting for us to finish so that they can express their opinion or offer advice or, even worse, pronounce judgement.

There are many advantages of this type of listening with our teenagers. It helps them feel safe while they explore their own feelings and gives a clear message that we care about them. It also means that they learn the skills to resolve their own problems.

However, being a good listener is a skill that needs practice. We can easily cut in too quickly with our own ideas for what they should do, or let judgement creep in, particularly as we have the advantage of a more mature adult brain. It is important to remember that the teenage brain is less developed, and our child may be struggling to work out what to do or how to think. When we listen, we need to take into account the age and stage of development of our adolescent.

Giving undivided attention can be hard at times when we are preoccupied with our own issues – a tricky problem at work, or wondering about what to cook for supper. But the benefits of listening with undivided attention without judging or needing to offer a solution are huge, and can make a big difference to the quality of your relationship.

Summarising It can be helpful when speaking to your teenager to summarise what they have said and check back with them to make sure you have understood their perspective and that you both know what might happen next. Is there a plan of action? Will you talk again? Do they need any help?

Encouraging independence within broad boundaries

Managing the transition into independence is a journey for both parents and teenagers.

It can be difficult knowing how much freedom to give teenagers. Having no boundaries can be anxiety-provoking, but too many restrictions can impair the development of independence. Some teenagers need more boundaries than others, so it is important to work out what is appropriate and possible for your teen, taking into account their development, and then be clear and consistent about the rules and non-negotiables.

As parents it can also be anxiety-provoking allowing our children to take their steps of freedom, but this is a necessary part of growing up and we need to be able to do this, while both acknowledging and aiming to minimise the risks.

Young people tend to challenge boundaries – it is a natural part of growing up. They appreciate you listening to their views as you set boundaries for their use of social media, what time they come home, whether they join family meals, where they can go, how much homework they do, and so on. You may need to be prepared to compromise and meet them halfway or take gradual steps to move from the parental position to where the teenager wants to be. The aim is to be supportive, kind and firm, adapting flexibly to the growing maturity of the young person – easier said than done, and we all get it wrong at times. Remember, we only need to be 'good enough', not perfect, parents. See the reference list at the end for some good books on parenting adolescents.

> *Aisha is very grumpy with her parents when they insist that she joins family meals, but there is a side of her that really wants to be part of the family. Although she grudgingly joins the meals, she discovers that she actually feels less isolated.*

Helping your teenager to develop a positive attitude to eating and body image

Conflicting messages about diet and weight can be very confusing for young people and parents. The media portrays images of models with perfect bodies – which many teen-agers aspire to – and adverts for diets are everywhere. The teenage years are when calorie needs are highest, but at the same time the healthy eating culture (including public health messages about obesity, physical health and exercise) emphasises the importance of making healthy food choices, including reducing fat and processed foods. So, what are the nutritional needs of growing teenagers? How does this need to be balanced with exercise? Is it wrong to eat crisps and cake? Is it abnormal to be obsessed about weight? How can you help your teenager feel good about their body?

There are lots of questions to think about as a parent, and it can be hard to know how to talk to your child about these issues. Most teenagers will experience some concerns about eating, weight or body shape as they go through puberty. Some of these concerns will be mild, others more serious. However, it is important to be aware of them early on and help your child develop healthy eating habits and feel good about themselves as they grow up. The first step in having these discussions is to find ways of building a positive relationship with your teenager. This will have huge benefits for both of you.

Here are some ideas on how to help your teenager to develop a positive attitude to eating and body image.

Modelling healthy eating habits

One way to support a positive relationship to eating and body image in your teenager is to model it yourself. If we feel comfortable about eating and the way we look, this will influence our children just as much as what we say. Seeing that we eat a range of healthy foods, including treats, in a relaxed way without being preoccupied with calorie levels, and are comfortable with ourselves, can have a profound effect on their choices (see Chapter 3 for more information).

Research shows that growing up in an environment focused on weight and shape can increase the risk of developing eating disorders. This can be tough if you are struggling with an eating disorder yourself or don't feel happy about your weight. Try to avoid discussing your anxieties with your teenager and consider getting support for yourself.

Family meals

Mealtimes can be an important time for families to get together and catch up with each other. However, it is all too easy for regular mealtimes to get eroded in our busy lives and it may be difficult for some families to eat together. There are lots of activities to fit in, with family members wanting to do different things, and eating together can be a challenge. It may be unrealistic to eat together every day, but planning in some regular mealtimes together can make a huge difference to family life. Try making them fun times where the family communicates and laughs together. Eating round a table, if that is possible, and switching off the TV or mobile phones, makes this much easier. Mealtimes are not just about eating; they are also a time to connect.

Going out for meals as a family can be an opportunity to do something enjoyable together in a different setting.

Celebrating special occasions with a meal out is something children will remember. It can be tempting to make comments about what your teenager is ordering or eating in a restaurant. Conversations about healthy eating are best had at another time so that family meals become times that are enjoyable and not about the rights and wrongs of eating.

Planning menus together can be a good way to involve your young person in family meals.

Encourage healthy eating

Regular meals and hydration Eating regularly is important for adolescent growth and development. This is the time of life when calorie needs are at their highest and it is normal for teenagers to eat more during this period, perhaps raiding the fridge when they get home from school. If teenagers skip meals, they will become hungry and may end up bingeing or feeling out of control with their eating habits. Make sure your teenager has breakfast before leaving for school, or at least takes a cereal bar and fruit to eat on their way to school if they get up late (the natural pattern for teenagers is to go to bed late and get up late). Lunch is important too and gives them energy in the middle of the day. A packed lunch may be needed if there are lunchtime activities that prevent them from sitting down to a school meal.

Teenagers may need to be reminded that the recommendation is to drink at least 1.5 litres of fluid a day to keep well hydrated. Snacks between meals can help prevent fatigue and improve concentration, so encourage your teenager to eat some food at least every three hours. It is healthy to eat a wide range of foods and not exclude anything. If you ban foods, you can end up craving them.

How much your child eats will also depend on the amount of exercise they are doing. Some teenagers will need to eat huge meals if they are very active. It is important to make sure that the food your teenager eats provides sufficient energy for their activity, as well as for rapid growth. Many packaged foods now display calorie values, but focusing on calories is not helpful. The important thing is to ensure that they eat regularly, respond to hunger cues and stop eating when they have had enough.

At the same time, it is also common for some teenagers to eat more than they need, particularly if they are bored, when snack foods may be consumed in large quantities. If this is the case, you might need to support your teenager in noticing this and finding other ways to relieve boredom.

Portion sizes in restaurants have increased over the last decade, which can be a pressure when eating out, and many menus in restaurants also provide calorie values for different meals. Try to encourage teenagers to make choices determined by taste and preference rather than calorie levels. It helps to model healthy portion sizes at home and avoid discussion of calorie levels.

Nutrition The main principle when feeding your children is to ensure variety, regular eating and a balance of nutrients. Meals that look good are more appealing to eat. Home-cooked meals are great, but not everyone has the time or inclination for cooking; there are lots of healthy ready-cooked alternatives.

Young people tend to eat what is in front of them or what is readily available, so make sure that there is a variety of healthy foods in your home. It can be helpful to get your children involved in shopping, cooking and planning meals.

Discourage dieting Dieting is very common in adolescents and many teenagers go on a diet at some point. They might do this to try and lose weight, build muscle or to fit in with their peers' lifestyle choices. Research shows that up to 50 per cent of adolescent girls go on a diet during the teenage years. When they start dieting, teenagers may get positive comments from others about weight loss, which makes them feel good about themselves. However, dieting increases the risk of developing an eating disorder, particularly if young people are vulnerable in other ways such as having low self-esteem or anxiety. In the long run, dieting is not a good way to lose weight and can even lead to an increase in weight. It can also be unhealthy at this stage of life as energy is needed for growth and development.

If your teenager tells you they are going on a diet, try not to over-react. Ask them what they mean by 'diet'. Check out why they feel they need to go on a diet and ask them about any concerns they have about themselves. Remind them of their positive qualities and reassure them that they are valued in ways other than how they look. Discuss with them the pros and cons of dieting and let them know that you are there to support them. It is helpful to find out where your teenager is getting their dieting information from. Many of the tips on dieting websites are designed for adults who are no longer growing and are overweight. Adolescents are not within this target audience and have very different needs.

Sometimes, teenagers decide to change their diet to vegetarian or vegan. As a parent you may need to check that they are still eating a balance of the main food groups as well as the vitamins and minerals that are important for growth and development. It is particularly hard with a vegan diet to ensure a healthy range of foods. Teenagers who decide to go vegetarian or vegan sometimes progress to restricting their food intake excessively. Getting the advice of a dietician may be helpful.

Encourage regular exercise

Exercise is an important part of a young person's life. Research shows that it promotes physical health and can lift mood and help to manage stress, as well as improve posture and body image. It is also a very good way to connect socially with others. Encourage your teenager to have regular exercise that is enjoyable. If they are exercising a lot, they will need more food to give them enough fuel for the exercise.

Occasionally, a young person may start to exercise in an obsessional way, either exercising very frequently or appearing upset/distressed if they can't exercise. They may be exercising with the aim of weight loss. If you notice that your teenager is going to the gym for long periods or for long runs or cycle rides on their own, you may want to gently encourage them to focus on enjoyable/social exercise. Exercise can become addictive, and it may be helpful to discuss with your teenager how their level of exercise affects their life.

On the other hand, many teenagers need to be encouraged to do more exercise. It is helpful if they can integrate activity into their social life and do exercise that is fun. Enjoying doing exercise together as a family can be a great way to connect and stay fit. Going for walks together is a really good start. See Chapter 13 for more information.

Internet and social media

Teenagers can get a lot of pleasure from gaming, films and online activities with friends. However, there are downsides too. The internet provides easy access to unhelpful websites that present an unrealistic expectation about an idealised life, as well as chat rooms that can encourage young people to feel dissatisfied with their appearance and try to lose weight. Excessive use of social media can lead to comparison with others and deterioration in body image. Spending large amounts of time online can leave less time for other interests, schoolwork or exercise, which may be detrimental. Cyberbullying has increased and can be very distressing for young people; research shows it can be linked to low mood and self-harm.

We need to be aware of what our young people are watching, teach them to ask questions about what they see and hear, and encourage them to make wise choices about their internet use. Various programmes have been set up on the internet to build positive body confidence and self-esteem and can be readily accessed by teenagers (see the resources section at the end of the book). Teenagers can be sensitive to comments about their social media or internet use, but opening up discussion in a non-judgemental way about how social media might be affecting us all can be helpful. See Chapter 12 for more information.

Responding to 'fat talk'

Although we are surrounded by messages about healthy eating and having a perfect body size and shape, 'junk food' is everywhere. Portion sizes in restaurants have increased, while also displaying calorie values on the menus. Eating is also often used to manage stress. So, what can we say to young people? How can we help them to be more accepting of their body and adopt a healthy lifestyle? What do you say when your teenager says to you, 'I feel so fat, I'm going to go on a diet'? Just reassuring them doesn't always work. Here are some suggestions which you may like to try out:

- The most important thing is to make it clear to your young person that you love them for who they are and not how they look.

- It can be helpful to remind young people that body image is not consistent – our view of our body changes, depending on what we are doing, who we are with and how we are feeling.

- Try to explore with your young person the things that make them feel better about themselves and what makes them feel worse about themselves.

The table below gives some ideas on the sorts of things that can either improve your body image or make you feel worse about yourself. Are these things that your teenager notices too?

Check it out: Things that can improve your body image – or make it worse

Improve body image

- Taking some exercise.
- Doing things which improve your mood.
- Spending time with close friends.
- Developing your interests and unique style in clothes, hairstyle, shoes, etc.
- Eating a healthy balanced diet.

Make body image worse

- Looking in the mirror a lot and judging yourself.
- Weighing yourself frequently.
- Worrying about yourself and how you look.
- Comparing yourself to others.
- Going on a diet.

Despite appearances, teenagers may be looking to parents as role models. Feeling comfortable about your own body is an important message for children. What they see you do and hear you say influences them hugely. It is best to avoid commenting on the weight or body shape of your child, or of anyone else.

Encourage positive mental health and wellbeing

Positive mental health can diminish the chances of developing eating problems and there are a number of things that parents can do to encourage this (see also Chapter 6 and Chapter 7).

Sleep It is important to make sure that your teenager has sufficient sleep. Research shows the benefits of sleep on physical and mental health. This may mean limiting the use of mobile phones late in the evening or after they have gone to bed.

Self-esteem As parents you can help to build up self-esteem in your teenagers. Try to avoid personal comments about their size or shape. Instead, focus positive comments on their personal qualities and their efforts. Remind them of their positive qualities, for example 'You are really caring to your friends' (see also Chapter 9).

Persist with family meals If your child is developing difficulties with eating, they may avoid sitting down to meals with the family. However, it is important to try to keep these family meals going (see the section on family meals earlier in this chapter).

Coping with stress Encourage your children to develop positive ways of coping with stress by doing the following (see Chapter 7 for more ideas):

- Sharing problems with others

- Problem-solving

- Learning to relax

- Connecting with friends

- Communicating with family

- Developing an absorbing interest

- Prioritising sleep

Friendships and peer relationships Encourage friendships that help your child feel better about themselves, rather than worse. Be aware of the influences of friends and peers. For example, is your teenager engaging in discussions about weight and dieting with friends? Is there a lot of body comparison talk? Is your child being bullied about their weight? Talking about eating can sometimes include an element of competitiveness in unhealthy peer relationships.

Perfectionism Research suggests that perfectionistic personality traits are associated with eating disorders. Striving to do well is important in order to achieve work goals, pass exams and accomplish tasks. However, excessive perfectionism can be unhelpful and make it harder for us to achieve what we want (see Chapter 11).

Check it out: The downside of perfectionism

Behaviour	*Outcome*
• Working late into the night to perfect an essay.	• Too tired the next day to concentrate on schoolwork.
• Can't decide the perfect answer to an exam question.	• Don't write anything. • Losing weight and becoming unwell.
• Trying hard to look like perfect models in the media.	

As parents we need to help our teenagers know when they have done enough and not let perfectionism get the upper hand. Here are some strategies for managing perfectionism:

- Make sure that your teenager knows you love them for who they are, not what they have achieved.

- Try to resist the desire to be overambitious for your children.

- Praise them for their efforts rather than results.

- Help your child to develop a positive sense of themselves and who they are (see Chapter 9).

- Try to model having a balance between work and time for relaxation and enjoyment.

Although teenagers may write off our views as old-fashioned, they generally seek the approval of parents and want to know our opinion. They appreciate parents taking an interest in what they are doing. This helps to build their self-esteem and confidence.

Early difficulties with eating and how to help

How common are eating difficulties and body image problems?

Eating difficulties and concerns about body image have been on the rise in the last decade or so. These difficulties increased even more with the COVID-19 pandemic when young people became stressed and isolated from friends, with more time to become preoccupied with eating and body image.

Obesity has become an increasing problem for young people. Approximately 15 per cent of teenagers are over-weight and many more are at risk of becoming overweight – with all the physical and mental health consequences that this can bring. Additionally, if you are obese as a child or teenager it can increase your risk of developing an eating disorder such as anorexia nervosa or bulimia nervosa, as well as adult obesity.

Around 50 per cent of teenage girls go on diets or use strat-egies to control their weight, for example, skipping meals.

As we mentioned in Chapter 4, diets are generally ineffective and may lead to weight gain in the long run, and those who diet are at increased risk of developing an eating disorder. Around half of teenage girls and a quarter of teenage boys have problems with their body image.

Around 0.3 per cent of teenage girls will develop anorexia nervosa during adolescence and 0.9 per cent will develop bulimia nervosa (see Chapter 4). Anorexia nervosa and bulimia nervosa are more commonly identified in girls, but we know that boys can develop eating disorders too. Although prevalence rates are lower for males than females (studies show that about one in ten of those with identified eating disorders is male), this may be partly because of difficulties identifying and accessing treatment for eating disorders (see Chapter 14).

Once an eating disorder is established, it can be hard to resolve, and teenagers can miss out on normal adolescent development while they struggle with it. So how do you spot these problems early on, in order to prevent the more serious difficulties developing?

Aisha had started skipping the family meal in the evening, telling her mum that she had eaten a large snack at school and was full. Her mum noticed that she was spending a long time in the bathroom and was often quite moody and irritable.

Signs that your child may be developing an eating disorder

Sometimes, it can be hard to spot an eating disorder developing. Some young people may lose weight (particularly if they are anorexic) but it may be a while before you notice the change. Other young people may be of normal weight or even overweight (particularly if they have bulimia nervosa or binge-eating disorder), yet still have an eating disorder. Eating disorders may go unnoticed for a long period as the young person may be ashamed of what they are doing and try to keep the behaviours secret. They may wear baggy clothes to conceal the fact that they have lost weight.

Other changes may be noticeable, such as a drop in mood, as well as specific changes of eating behaviour. For example, a bubbly twelve-year-old turning into a grumpy thirteen-year-old may suggest there is something going on in their life.

As a parent, it can be hard facing up to the fact that your teenager may have an eating problem. Feeding your child is a basic instinct from birth, so acknowledging that your teenager is not eating properly can be undermining and make you feel guilty and ashamed about your role as a parent. It can be particularly hard to notice signs in teenage boys as it is less common and not expected.

It is important for parents to realise that they are not to blame for an eating disorder in their teenager; eating disorders are illnesses and no one's fault. However, parents/carers can be very much part of the solution when it comes to helping their teenager get over it.

These are some of the signs relating to eating and weight that may alert you to the possibility of an eating problem:

Eating behaviours

- Making excuses to avoid eating with the family.

- Skipping meals, eating very little at meals or becoming very selective or fussy with food.

- Throwing away their packed lunch or bringing it home in their lunch box.

- Eating more junk food than normal – you may notice that packets of biscuits or crisps disappear from the cupboard, or they spend lots of their money on chocolates or sweets.

- Becoming more interested in food and how it is cooked or prepared, or wanting to be in control of preparing meals.

- Spending a lot of time in the bathroom after a meal.

Physical signs

- Losing weight or rapidly gaining weight.

- Looking pale or unwell.

- Complaining of lack of energy.

- Feeling cold or wearing extra layers of clothes.

- Irregular or missing periods.

- Dry skin around their mouth or callouses on their knuckles (these can be signs that they are making themselves vomit).

- Dental problems.

Exercise

- Going to the gym frequently or exercising intensely in their room.

- Feeling stressed if they can't do their regular exercise.

Body image

- Weighing themselves more often.

- Checking themselves for long periods in the mirror.

- Telling you that they are too fat.

- Expressing fear of gaining weight.

- Comparing themselves with others.

- Wearing baggy clothes.

Other signs

- Poor sleeping.

- Becoming withdrawn.

- Spending a lot of time in their room.

- Losing interest in things they previously enjoyed.

- Avoiding going out with friends, especially if food is involved.

- Getting angry or irritable.

If a number of these signs are present, it may be that your child is developing difficulties with eating or their body image. However, some signs, such as loss of weight or loss of interest in usual activities, may also indicate that a young person is suffering from stress, anxiety or depression or might be physically unwell (rather than having an eating disorder). It is helpful to check out whether they have other physical symptoms or are feeling low or worried about something. If you are not sure what is going on for your teen, it may be helpful for them to be checked out by their family doctor. Teenagers might be resistant to this, and if that is the case, it can be helpful to explain to them your thought process in suggesting they see a doctor.

Check it out: What to say to your teen if you are concerned

- Are you worried about anything?
- Do you have any concerns about your health?
- How is your sleeping?
- What are your energy levels like?
- Are you concerned about your eating?
- Would it be helpful to get checked out by the doctor?

How do you help your teenager get on track with eating again?

There are lots of things parents can do to help young people with eating difficulties. Here are some ideas – and you may have others, too.

Nourish your relationship with your young person

- Take an interest in what they are doing.

- Take time to do enjoyable activities together, e.g. watch a film.

See also the section earlier in this chapter on staying connected.

Model regular eating and normal meals

- Your teenager will notice what your own eating behaviour is like, so try to make your own meals normal, regular and relaxed.

- This may be difficult if you also have concerns about eating, so you may need to show your teenager that you are trying to address this yourself.

- It is good to be upfront and honest about any of your own eating problems and explain what you are doing to tackle them as this can help your teenager to find the courage to do the same.

Help your child feel good about themselves and their body

- Help them to be aware that the way we view our body can change from day to day depending on the context – it is not a fixed thing.

- For example, how you feel about your body when you are having a good day may be very different from how you feel when you are stressed.

See also the section earlier in this chapter on self-esteem.

Check if your young person is worried about anything

- Make some time to talk to your teenager when you are not going to be interrupted.

- Talking while walking or in the car together works well as you don't have to be face-to-face.

- You might start off talking about general issues before focusing in on problems.

  ○ How are things going at school?
  ○ How are things going with your friends?
  ○ Is there anything that is worrying you?

    * At school?
    * With homework?
    * At home?
    * With friends?

Encourage ways to manage stress

- Talking over concerns.

- Taking time to relax and be mindful.

- Having enough sleep.

- Getting out for some exercise.

See Chapter 7 for more information.

Find out if your child has any physical health symptoms

- If your child appears to be losing weight, suggest they have a check-up with the family doctor.

- Help them book the appointment and go with them, if at all possible, to provide support.

- It's OK for you to share your concerns about your teenager with your family doctor, even if your teenager is reluctant for you to do so.

Sit down to meals together on a regular basis

- Try to make family meals fun and a time to connect with your young person.

Ask your child if they have any concerns about their eating

- Reassure your child that you are there to support them, not to judge them.

Discuss with your child their nutritional needs

- Help your child be aware of the impact of inadequate eating on their social, emotional and physical wellbeing.

- Explain that teenagers need to eat a variety of foods of a sufficient amount to grow and develop, have energy and ensure that their brains are working effectively.

Support your child to finish their meals

- Be with them for the meal.

- Sit with them after meals as they may be stressed about what they have just eaten.

- Engage them in a game or activity to help distract them.

- Let your young person know that you want them to be safe and healthy.

Wesley's parents notice that he is exercising obsession-ally and beginning to lose weight. They spend more time with him, even though he is reluctant at first. Over time, he begins to open up about the effect that the exercise is having on his life. He admits that he is spending a lot of time in the gym and hardly has time to see his friends.

Worries beginning to impact your teen's life - Take action. Support

Worries about body and eating starting - Keep communicating, Keep alert

Normal adolescence - open communication

Be alert to the temperature changing and take action when needed

Getting professional help for your child

> *Jen was struggling with her eating and beginning to lose weight. Even when she knew she should eat, she felt uncomfortably full and couldn't manage to finish her meals. She found it hard to speak to her parents about what was happening and started hiding herself away in her room. Her parents were increasingly concerned but did not know how best to help.*

Sometimes, with the best will in the world, it can be difficult to get your teenager on track with eating again. Your child's eating problem may have become serious enough to seek professional help. If this is the case, the sooner you get help the better as there is a risk that habits can become entrenched.

Check it out: Signs indicating the need for professional help

- Refusal to finish meals, despite encouragement.
- Rapid weight loss.
- Feeling that food/weight/shape dominates their life.

- Making themselves sick:

    ◦ Vomiting causes the body to lose vital salts, which can affect the heart.

- Taking drugs to lose weight, such as laxatives or diet pills:

    ◦ These can unbalance the level of salts in the blood and can cause serious heart problems.

- Loss of menstruation or failure to start menstruation (in females) or delayed puberty/growth in males.

- Worries about losing control over their eating.

- Believing that they are fat even when they are thin.

- Unable to stop bingeing.

- Fainting.

- Your child is persistently unhappy.

Eating disorders are hard to fight alone, and your child will need you on their side to help with the struggle against the illness. The first step is a visit to the family doctor, where your son's/daughter's physical state will be checked out, including height and weight.

After excluding physical illness, a referral may be made to the local Child & Adolescent Eating Disorder team or mental health team where your child will be assessed. There are well-researched and effective treatments to help young people overcome eating disorders (see Chapter 16).

Sometimes, teenagers and their parents decide they want to have independent private help. You need to make sure that the therapist is experienced in working with eating disorders in teenagers and is properly qualified. It is important to make sure they are giving the right sort of help, i.e. focusing on helping your teenager to improve their eating and physical wellbeing as well as addressing their emotional state.

Getting support for yourself

It can feel very lonely if your child is developing an eating disorder. As well as being really worried, you may feel guilty or embarrassed. It is important to remember that it is not your fault and that there is support for parents in this situation. There are a number of helpful websites and online forums where parents can get information and talk to other parents in the same situation (see the resources section at the end of the book).

One of the most important things you can do is to make sure that you look after yourself, which may mean taking time out, accepting support from family and friends and setting aside time for nurturing activities such as enjoyable exercise, going out with friends, having a relaxing bath, watching a film, listening to music, and so on. If you don't care for yourself, it is hard to have the energy to care for other family members who need your help.

Summary

- Keep communicating with your teenager.

- Make time to do enjoyable activities together.

- Encourage family meals.

- Notice and act on changes in your teenager.

- Get support for yourself.

Chapter 18

Summary – What Happened Next?

Jen

I feel that I have been on a long journey with ups and downs. It has been pretty hard at times, particularly when I couldn't face seeing my friends and began to get lonely and sad. But the fact that my friends stuck by me has really helped. I know that I still struggle a bit at times and need to make sure I share my problems with others and accept the support of my friends and family.

What this chapter will cover:

- What happened to the teenagers?

- What did they learn?

- Further ideas to remain well and feel good about yourself

You may have realised by now that eating difficulties and worries about body image are common in young people. Most get over it and can get on with their lives feeling confident about themselves, but others find it a challenge.

We have followed seven teenagers throughout this book and you may well be wondering what has happened to them all. Let's see what they have to say:

Ella

I've been through a rough time, and am not totally through it. Looking back, I think I have always been very conscious of my appearance, just like the rest of my family, but things got worse when I took up dancing. I felt under pressure to keep very slim so that I looked good for dancing. There are full-length mirrors in the dance studio which means I get to study myself in detail while I am dancing. I became very aware of every little bit of weight I put on and was always determined to lose it again. I began to change my diet to a very healthy one to make sure that I kept my weight low. Then I hit on the idea of posting photos of my meals on social media. To my surprise I soon began to get a big following, and although this felt very good to start with, I soon found that I had to keep posting new meals to keep my following. It began to feel like another pressure, even though it was nice being admired. I also posted my exercise routines online and was flattered when so many people liked them. It made me feel quite special.

The shock came when I began to feel tired, stopped having periods and seemed to lose the energy for dancing. I went to see the family doctor and she told me that I wasn't eating enough and that it was bad for my health to keep dancing unless I increased my food intake. This really made me think. I didn't want to give up dancing, yet the thought of giving up my small healthy meals filled me with dread. How was I going to explain this to my followers?

In the end I talked things over with my mum. She thought that all the posting on social media was taking a lot of time and making me feel moody. I didn't like to admit it, but I think she was right. So over time, I just posted less and less till I seemed to lose the urge to keep posting. At first, I really missed that feeling of looking at my phone and seeing all the likes and comments. However, I had a lot more spare time and began to do things I enjoyed such as talking to my friends and listening to music. Once I had stopped obsessing about my food portions my eating became more relaxed, I put on a little weight and my periods started again. So that's where I am at now. I still do my dancing and love it, but I try not to obsess so much about my food and exercise routines.

I think I have learned that social media posting can take a lot of time and can make you feel worse about yourself. Friends mean a lot to me, and it is important to make sure there is enough time to spend time with them. Eating healthily doesn't mean having excessively small portions. It is easy to lose weight, even if you don't intend to, and harder to put it back on again.

Chloe

Chloe

I've always been shy and worried about fitting in, so when my body started growing and changing before everyone else's, I just felt so self-conscious. All my friends are so small and pretty and I felt like I was this massive female hulk! I just didn't feel comfortable in my body. Then when my parents started arguing, I stopped feeling comfortable at home too. Mum was so upset all the time, and I didn't want to put any more stress on her by telling her how I was feeling or asking about dinner. It was just easier to grab whatever food I could from the kitchen to escape the arguments. Eating also helped to distract me from what was going on downstairs. But one biscuit would lead to another, and before I realised it I'd eaten a whole packet. Then I'd feel terrible, especially when I looked at the pictures of salads and smoothies that Ella was posting online. I promised myself that I wouldn't do it again and would make up for it by skipping breakfast and lunch, but when the next day came, I found myself falling into the same pattern of missing meals and then bingeing on whatever I could get my hands on at home.

It all came out at parents' evening. My form tutor had apparently noticed that I seemed unhappy and my parents told her they were getting divorced. My form tutor suggested I had a few sessions with the school counsellor. I was a bit reluctant at first – loads of kids' parents get divorced and they seem to manage it, but both my mum and form tutor were really insistent. So I went along, and actually found it was helpful to talk about how I was feeling. With the help of the counsellor, I realised that I was using food as a way of coping with what was going on at home and how I felt about myself. The counsellor was really helpful, and she taught me some ways to manage anxiety. We also talked about self-esteem, and she suggested some things I could do to feel better about myself.

My parents are divorced now, and Mum has moved into a new flat. I split my time between my parents' homes. It's a bit strange but I'm getting used to it and I'm glad they aren't arguing anymore. Now that things have settled down, I am eating more regularly and help out with preparing meals. I'm not bingeing anymore, but I do enjoy having chocolate and biscuits a few times a week!

Wesley

This last year has been tough. Everyone has expected so much of me. I got into the first rugby team, which was great, but then I felt I wasn't fit enough so I started going to the gym regularly to work out. This became an obsession: every day after school I would go to the gym for a couple of hours and then tell my parents that I had been doing my homework at school. Even at home, I would secretly do exercises in my room, hoping my parents wouldn't hear me. I began to post my workouts on social media and got lots of likes. But I was still worried that I wasn't doing enough. I started taking protein shakes to try to build up my muscles, but this didn't seem to work, and I started to lose weight. I began to go to bed later and later, so that I could pack the exercise in, but this resulted in me being really tired during the day. I spent less and less time with my friends and then one day my girlfriend said that I wasn't much fun any longer and asked me what was wrong.

This really got me thinking and I realised that my life had become pretty boring, just rugby and the gym, no time to meet my friends or do fun stuff. My parents were getting concerned about me too – they tried to talk to me, and I know I was really irritable back at them. Even worse, my performance at rugby had really slipped. I just didn't have the energy.

Eventually, my physio asked me if I was OK, and I told him about the exercise and how worried I was that I wasn't good enough for the team. He said I was a great player and that I didn't need to do all the extra training, in fact he felt it probably made things worse. He said I should build up my energy again by eating regularly and getting enough sleep. I agreed that he could contact my parents, and once they knew what the problem was, they helped me to reduce my exercise. It was hard, but I found that I had more time for other things and my performance on the rugby field improved too.

Jake

Jake

It has been hard for me as I have always felt quite different from others. Everyone else seemed to have lots of friends and they met up after school to do stuff together, but no one invited me to join them. I used to get anxious in class because I worried that I would be teased. I have always found eating a challenge as I can only eat food of the right colour or texture – I have no idea why, but it doesn't feel right when I eat certain foods. When I am anxious it gets even worse, and then I start to feel sick and unwell. I know that my parents have worried about me because I never seem to be hungry and stay quite thin. I would like to do more sport, but worry that I am not as good as the others in my class.

However, Harry suggested that I might like to do taekwondo. I was anxious when I went for the first time, but someone I knew had also started going so I plucked up courage to go along. Surprisingly, I really enjoyed it and found that I was quite good at it, despite being small. I made a couple of friends there and discovered that they have the same interest as me in gaming, so we meet online as well. I have also joined a coding club at school and am pretty good at it!

I have become a bit more confident at school and can speak up in class which I was never able to do before. I don't worry as much about my food and my parents think I have put on a bit of weight and look healthier.

Jen

I have always been fairly slim and sporty and not worried too much about my weight. I took up tennis and was soon achieving at county level and hoping to get into the national team. But things really fell apart for me when I was told by my coach that I had put on some weight and my game wasn't as good. I began to worry about my weight and started dieting in a serious way. I started to lose weight, but my tennis didn't improve. In fact, it really suffered as I just didn't have enough energy. It was as if I had fallen into a black hole and couldn't get out of it.

At school, my academic grades began to fall off. I was beginning to despair, but I wasn't able to tell anyone, and things went from bad to worse. I think the change came when I plucked up courage to tell my friend Zoe about what was happening. I was really anxious about telling her as I didn't want to burden her, but she listened to me and was very supportive. It felt a relief to be able to tell someone about what was happening to me. She told me I had to speak to my parents about what was happening. I didn't want to, but my mum approached me first and said she was really concerned about me.

She insisted I went to the doctor. Things followed quickly from there. I was referred to the Child & Adolescent Eating Disorder team and began to see a therapist regularly. It felt really weird starting to talk about myself as I have always been quite a private person. At the start I was resentful – I just didn't want to go, and didn't like the therapist. However, she encouraged me to say what was helpful and what was unhelpful, and we began to get on better. Now I think she is brilliant: she has really helped me to feel better about myself, as well as helping me to be healthier. I really hated my parents at the start for making me go through with it all, but as time went on, I realised that they were really trying to help me, even when they seemed to be forcing me to eat. Actually, the most important thing for me was being able to talk to my family and friends properly again. One thing I learned was how important family and friends are. I am much closer to Zoe now as we have been through a lot together.

I had to take some time off school initially as I was so unwell. But now, I'm back at school and doing much better with my schoolwork. I feel much more confident about myself and have started to play tennis again, but it is no longer obsessional, and I make sure I still have time for friends and my other interests. I decided that I didn't want to continue tennis at a national level, since it was putting me under too much pressure. It was scary telling my parents as they have spent so much money on my coaching and trips to tennis matches. However, they were really supportive and just seemed to want the best for me. I now really enjoy tennis – and actually my game has improved!

Aisha

I have been through a difficult time, but I feel that I am now able to get on with my life again. My parents and aunts and uncles are all a bit overweight, and I was always terrified of putting on weight myself. When I went into puberty I put on some weight and decided that I had to take action. I went on a strict diet, without telling my mum. I pretended that I was eating my meals, but in reality, I was throwing lunch away and skipping the evening meal. I started to feel more and more distant from my family and friends. All I could think about was how I could get through the day without breaking my rules about eating. I started to lose weight and began to feel really tired with no energy.

Aisha

Eventually, one of the teachers said she wanted to see me and asked if I was OK. I just blurted everything out to her – it was such a relief.

My teacher thought it would be a good idea for me to see the school health nurse so I went to see her and she advised seeing the doctor for some blood tests. My teacher also suggested I talked to my parents about what was happening. At the same time, my friends started to tell me they were worried about me. So I plucked up courage and talked to my mum. She hugged me and said I looked really unwell and tired and she was concerned about me. She went with me to the doctor who did blood tests and found that I was anaemic. We got some advice from a dietician who suggested a meal plan to get me healthy again. Mum made sure that I ate all my meals. I also saw the school health nurse a few more times as she wanted to keep an eye on me.

I was referred to the school counsellor who helped me to talk about my problems and work out how I could feel better about myself. I began to have laughs again with my siblings, Rashmi and Aadesh – first time for ages.

What I learned most was the importance of sharing your worries with someone else.

Sam

For a while I have felt uncomfortable with the gender I was assigned to at birth, and I've been really anxious recently of becoming more feminine as I go through puberty. I reduced my food intake to try and stop myself growing and developing. However, I started to lose energy and became more and more preoccupied with concerns about my gender, losing sight of all the other things about me. I withdrew from my friends and family and became very isolated. Reducing my food intake just gave me more problems to deal with.

When my best friend asked me to go to a new youth club with her I initially said no, but she persuaded me and things started to change.

I began to open up to her and told her initially about how difficult things were in my family. I eventually took the leap in speaking to her about the thoughts and worries I've been having about my gender identity. She listened to me and was really supportive. She also knew of someone else who had similar feelings and introduced them to me, which has helped a lot. I made a plan to go back to eating normally and to try to connect with like-minded people in school. I hope to share my feelings about my gender with my family soon.

All seven teenagers had struggles and challenges in different ways. Jen ended up needing to be referred to the Child & Adolescent Mental Health Service and, although she really didn't want to go initially, she found it was helpful talking about her problems, learning how to manage stress, getting a better balance in her life and regaining her energy. Aisha saw a school counsellor who helped her work out ways to manage her anxiety and feel better about herself.

An important thing for all these teenagers was acknowledging that they had a problem and accepting help from family and friends, and in some cases professionals too.

It is interesting to hear what they learned from the experience. A common theme was that they ended up feeling more confident as they had built skills to keep themselves emotionally and physically healthy.

So, what can teenagers do to remain well and continue to gain in confidence and self-esteem? See the top tips below.

Check it out: Top tips for staying well

- Look after yourself:

    ○ Make sure you get enough sleep and time to relax.

    ○ Take regular exercise.

    ○ Eat regularly and listen to your hunger signals.

    ○ Work out ways to manage stress and practise strategies that help.

- Make time for the things you enjoy doing.

- Make time for friends and family.

- Share your worries with others.

- Think carefully about how much time you spend on social media.

- Focus on your positive qualities.

If you have read to the end of this book, you have done well! Good luck with your journey.

Ask yourself:

- What have you learned from reading this book?

- What are you going to try out?

- Who are you going to share things with?

Summary

- Eating difficulties are common in adolescence.

- Most eating difficulties resolve, but they can develop into eating disorders.

- Eating disorders can have a negative effect on your physical and emotional wellbeing.

- Looking after yourself in adolescence is important.

- Eating healthily, sleeping well and managing stress are all crucial in order to grow and develop.

- Keeping contact with friends and communicating with your parents can help you to get through difficulties.

Resources and References

Normal development in teenagers – and how to get through the teenage years

Resources

The Art of Being a Brilliant Teenager Andy Cope, Andy Whittaker, Darrell Woodman and Amy Bradley (2023) Capstone

Blame My Brain: The Amazing Teenage Brain Revealed Nicola Morgan (2013) Walker Books

Cognitive behavioural therapy (CBT)

Resources

Feeling Better CBT Workbook for Teens Rachel Hutt (2019) Althea Press

Thinking Good, Feeling Better Paul Stallard (2015) Wiley

Websites

Living Life to the Full https://LLTTF.com

Self-care

Resources

The Self-care Kit for Stressed-out Teens: Healthy Habits and Calming Advice to Help You Stay Positive F. Young (2021) Vie

Healthy eating

Resources

Eat Well and Feel Great: The Teenagers' Guide to Nutrition and Health Tina Lond-Caulk (2022) Bloomsbury Publishing

The Intuitive Eating Workbook for Teens: A Non-diet, Body Positive Approach to Building a Healthy Relationship with Food Elyse Resch (2019) New Harbinger

It's Not What You Are Eating, It's What's Eating You Shari Brady (2018) Skyhorse Publishing

No Weigh! A Teen's Guide to Positive Body Image, Food and Emotional Wisdom Signe Darpinian, Wendy Sterling and Shelley Aggarwal (2018) Jessica Kingsley Publishers

Websites

The British Nutrition Foundation website has lots of information about the role of minerals and vitamins in the body https://www.nutrition.org.uk

Specific information about minerals and vitamins in the teenage years can be found by searching for minerals and vitamins at https://www.raisingchildren.net.au

References

Das, J. K., Rehana, A. S., Kent, L.T. et al. (2017) Nutrition in adolescents: physiology, metabolism and nutritional needs. *Annals of the New York Academy of Sciences*, 1393 (1) 21–33

Eating disorders

Resources

Beating Your Eating Disorders: A Cognitive-behavioural Self-help Guide for Adult Sufferers and Their Carers Glenn Waller, Victoria Mountford, Rachel Lawson and Em Gray (2010) Cambridge University Press

Although this book is written for adults, it has lots of useful tips on how to take back control over your eating.

Overcoming Binge Eating Christopher Fairburn (2013) Guilford Press

Although the title of this book suggests a focus on binge eating, it has an approach that applies to anyone with an eating disorder and describes the impact of an eating disorder on your body and mental state and what changes you can make to take control of your eating.

Overcoming Anorexia Nervosa Patricia Graham and Chris Freeman (2019) Robinson

Overcoming Bulimia Nervosa Patricia Graham and Peter Cooper (2024) Robinson

An Introduction to Coping with Eating Problems Gillian Todd (2017) Robinson

These last three books are also written primarily for adults but have very helpful strategies that teens can use too.

What's Eating You?: A Workbook for Teens with Anorexia, Bulimia and Other Eating Disorders Tammy Nelson (2008) New Harbinger Publications

Websites and helplines

BEAT: a website and helpline for sufferers, and also for carers of people with eating disorders https://www.beatingeating disorders.org.uk

Butterfly Foundation: support for eating disorders and body image issues https://butterfly.org.au

National Eating Disorder Association: based in America, this organisation is devoted to preventing eating disorders, providing treatment referrals and increasing the education and understanding of eating disorders, weight and body image https://www.nationaleatingdisroders.org

References

Dalle-Grave, R. and Calugi, S. (2020) *Cognitive-behaviour Therapy for Adolescents with Eating Disorders* Guilford Press

Fairburn, C. (2008). *CBT-E for Eating Disorders* Guilford Press

Galmiche, M., Déchelotte, P., Lambert, G. & Tavolacci, M. P. (2019). Prevalence of eating disorders over the 2000 – 2018 period: a systematic literature review. *The American Journal of Clinical Nutrition*, 109 (5), 1402–1413

Keegan, E., Waller, G. & Wade, T. D. (2022). A systematic review and meta-analysis of a 10-session cognitive behavioural therapy for non-underweight eating disorders. *Clinical Psychologist* 26 (3) 241–254

Exercise

Resources

Eat Like a Champion Jill Castle (2015) AMACOM

I Can: The Teenage Athlete's Guide for Mental Fitness Josephine Perry (2021) Sequoia Books

References

Aira, T., Vasankar, T., Heinonen, O. J. et al. (2021) Physical activity from adolescence to young adulthood: patterns of change and their associations with activity domains and sedentary time. *International journal of behavioural nutrition and physical activity* 18:85

Bennett, K. (2022) *Treating Athletes with Eating Disorders: Bridging The Gap Between Sport and Clinical Worlds* Routledge

Jayanth, N., Pinkham, C., Dugus, L. et al. (2013) Sports specialisation in young athletes. *Sports Health* 5(3) 2510257

Mountjoy, M., Ackerman, K. E., Bailey, D. M. et al. (2023). International Olympic Committee's (IOC) consensus statement on Relative Energy Deficiency in Sport (REDS). *British Journal of Sports Medicine,* 57, 1073–1097

Thompson, R. A. and Trattner Sherman, R. (2014) *Eating Disorders in Sport* Routledge

Stress and Anxiety

Resources

A Still Quiet Place for Teens: A Mindfulness Workbook to Ease Stress and Difficult Emotions Amy Saltzman (2016) New Harbinger

Dealing with Stress and Anxiety Stress Reduction Workbook For Teens Gina Biegel (2017) Instant Help Books

Mindfulness for Teen Anxiety Christopher Willard (2021) New Harbinger

Mindfulness for Teens in 10 Minutes a Day Jennie Marie Battistin (2019) Rockridge Press

Overcoming Social Anxiety and Building Self-confidence: A Self-Help Guide For Teenagers Eleanor Leigh, Emma

Warnock-Parkes, Elyse Brassard and David M. Clark (2024) Robinson

Stick Up for Yourself: Every Kid's Guide to Personal Powers and Positive Self-esteem Gershen Kaufman and Lev Raphael (2019) Free Spirit Publishing

The Complete CBT Guide for Anxiety by Roz Shafran, Lee Brosan and Peter Cooper (2013) Robinson

Although this book is written for adults it has lots of useful ideas that can be applied to teens.

Websites

Headspace app (mindful meditation) accessible at https://www.headspace.com

A site for meditation and sleep.

https://www.calm.com

A free site for learning and practising mindfulness.

https://www.smilingmind.com.au

References

Segal, Z. V., Williams, M. G., Teasdale, J. D. (2013) *Mindfulness-based Cognitive Therapy for Depression* (2nd edition) Guilford Press

Teigen, K. H. (1994). Yerkes-Dodson: A law for all seasons. *Theoretical Psychology* 4(4) 525

Low self-esteem

Resources

Banish Your Self-esteem Thief: A Cognitive Behavioural Workbook on Building Positive Self-esteem for Young People Kate Collins-Donnelly (2014) Jessica Kingsley Publishers

The Overcoming Low Self-esteem Handbook: Understand and Transform Your Self-esteem Using Tried and Tested Cognitive Behavioural Techniques Melanie Fennell (2021) Robinson

Body image

Resources

Banish Your Body Image Thief: A Cognitive Behavioural Workbook on Building Positive Body Image for Young People Kate Collins-Donnelly (2014) Jessica Kingsley Publishers

Body Brilliant: A Teenage Guide to a Positive Body Image Nicola Morgan (2019) Franklin Watts

The Body Image Workbook for Teens Julia Taylor (2014) Instant Help Books

Websites

Changing Faces is a very helpful website for everyone who has a visible difference on their face or body: it provides support and promotes respect https://www.changingfaces.org.uk

Perfectionism

Resources

Failosophy for Teens: A Handbook for When Things Go Wrong Elizabeth Day (2023) Red Shed

Overcoming Perfectionism: A Self-help Guide Using Cognitive Behavioural Techniques Roz Shafran, Sarah Egan and Tracy Wade (2018) Robinson

Social media

Resources

The Social Media Workbook for Teens: Skills to Help You Balance Screen Time, Manage Stress and Take Charge of Your Life G. S. Bocci (2019) Instant Help Books

Teen Mental Health in an Online World: Supporting Young People Around Their Use of Social Media, Apps, Gaming, Texting and the Rest V. Betton and J. Woolard (2018) Jessica Kingsley Publishers

References

Brandtzaeg, P. B., Luders, M. (2021) Young people's use and experience of the internet during COVID-19 lockdown: Well-being and social support. *First Monday* 26(12)

Browne, G. J., Walden, E. U. (2021) Stopping information search: an FMRI investigation. *Decision Support Systems* 143: 113498

Copp, J. E., Mumford, E., Taylor, B. (2021) Online sexual harassment and cyberbullying in a nationally representative sample of teens: Prevalence, predictors and consequences. *Journal of Adolescence* 93(1) 20–211

Qutteina, Y., Hallez, L., Raedschelders, M. et al. (2021). Food for teens: How social media is associated with adolescent eating outcomes. *Public Health Nutrition*

Men and boys

Resources

Boys Will Be Human: A Gut-Check Guide to Becoming the Strongest, Kindest, Bravest Person You Can Be Justin Baldoni (2022) Harper

What is Masculinity and Why Does it Matter? Jeffrey Blakey and Darren Chetty (2019) Wayland

References

Nagata, J. M., Brown, T. A., Murray, S. B. & Lavender, J. M. (2021) *Eating Disorders in Boys and Men* Springer

Issues of diverse gender

Websites and forums

Clinics and resources for trans and non-binary people Terence Higgins Trust https://www.tht.org.uk

Guide for parents on gender identity and mental health available at Young Minds https://www.youngminds.org.uk

Mental Health and being LGBTIG+ Information available at https://www.mind.org.uk

Parents and carers

Resources

Anorexia and Other Eating Disorders. How to Help Your Child Eat Well and Stay Well Eva Musby (2014) Aprica Publishers

ARFID Avoidant Restrictive Food Intake Disorder: A Guide for Parents and Carers Rachel Bryant-Waugh (2019) Routledge

Eating Disorders: A Parents' Guide Bryant-Waugh (2004) Routledge

Help Your Teenager Beat an Eating Disorder by James Lock and Daniel Le Grange (2015) Guilford Press

I'm Like, So Fat! Dianne Neumark-Sztainer (2005) Guilford Press

Raising Body Positive Teens: A Parent's Guide to Diet-Free Living, Exercise and Body Image Signe Darpinian, Wendy Sterling and Shelley Aggarwal (2022) Jessica Kingsley

Websites and forums

BEAT: a website for sufferers, and carers of people with eating disorders https://www.beatingeatingdisorders.org.uk

Dove Self-esteem project https://www.dove.com

FEAST: global support and resources for families affected by eating disorders https://www.feast-ed.org

Maudsley Parents: a site for parents with information on family-based treatment for anorexia and bulimia http://maudsleyparents.org.uk

References

Eisler, I., Le Grange, D., Lock, J. (2015). Treating adolescents with eating disorders. In Thomas Sexton, Jay Lebow (eds.) *Handbook of Family Therapy*, pp387–406

Goodier, G. H. G., McKormack, J., Egan, S. J., Watson, H. J., Holles, K. J, Todd, G., Treasure, J. (2014). Parent skills training treatments for parents of children and adolescents with eating disorders: a qualitative study. *International Journal of Eating Disorders* 47, pp368–375

Miller, W. R. & Rollnick, S. (2002). *Motivational interviewing: preparing people for change* (2nd edition) Guilford Press

Glossary

ADHD Attention Deficit Hyperactivity Disorder. This is a condition where a young person may have a reduced attention span, find it hard to sit still and a tendency to be impulsive.

Amygdala The part of the brain that deals with emotions.

Anorexia nervosa An eating disorder in which the person is over-concerned with their body weight or shape and tries to lose weight to feel better about themselves, even though they may be told that they are too thin.

ARFID Avoidant Restrictive Food Intake Disorder. This is when a young person avoids certain foods or types of food and ends up eating less than they need. This is due to anxiety about certain types or textures of food rather than a desire to lose weight.

ASC   Autistic Spectrum Condition, where a young person may struggle with communication, relating to others and flexible thinking, but often have strengths such as intense interests and a detailed knowledge in subjects.

Avoidance   A type of safety behaviour where we don't do something because we are worried something bad will happen if we do. Avoidance stops us from finding out what really happens in a situation and so tends to keep our worries going.

Behaviour   What we do or the actions that we take.

Behaviour experiment   A way of testing out your thoughts to find out what actually happens when you drop your safety behaviours or do the things you are worried about.

Binge-eating   Eating a larger amount of food than is normal in a short space of time and feeling a sense of loss of control over eating.

Body image   The thoughts and feelings you have about your body and your physical appearance.

Bulimia nervosa An eating disorder where the person is concerned about their body weight or shape and restricts their diet, but ends up bingeing and tries to get rid of the calories they are eating by, for example, making themselves sick.

Carbohydrates One of the main food groups, formed of sugars, starch and cellulose and releasing energy in the body.

Cognitions The mental processes in the brain, including thinking, attention, reasoning, memories and learning.

Cognitive behavioural therapy (CBT) A therapy which seeks to help people overcome their problems by looking at the link between their thoughts, feelings, physical sensations and behaviours.

Emotions Feelings which arise from different circumstances or in relationships with others.

Fasting When you stop eating for a period of time.

Fats One of the main food groups which are essential for health. They consist of oily substances such as glycerol and fatty acids and give us energy, insulate our body and help us to absorb certain vitamins.

Glycaemic index (GI) A rating for foods containing carbohydrates which shows how the food affects your blood sugar when it is eaten on its own. GI can change if different foods are eaten together.

Hippocampus   The part of the brain which is involved in learning and memory.

Macros (macronutrients)   Carbohydrates, fats and proteins: the three basic components of our daily food intake.

Melatonin   A hormone that is produced in the pineal gland and helps to regulate sleep. The body produces melatonin just after it gets dark and is at its highest during the early hours of the morning, reducing during the daylight hours. Being exposed to light at night can reduce melatonin production. Some young people take additional melatonin in tablet form to boost their body supply.

Metabolism   The chemical reactions in our bodies that keep us alive and functioning. The main functions are to convert energy in food to energy needed by the body to keep our cells working and enabling us to be active.

Minerals   Naturally occurring elements such as calcium and iron that are found in food and are essential for our bodies to function properly.

Parasympathetic nervous system   The part of the nervous system that relaxes the body by slowing the heart and relaxing muscles in the digestive tract. It balances the action of the sympathetic nervous system.

Proteins

One of the main food groups. They contain amino-acids and are essential in developing healthy muscles, skin, bones and hair.

Puberty

The period of life when adolescents grow and develop and reach sexual maturity. They experience physical and hormonal changes that mark a transition into adulthood.

Purging

When people try and get rid of their food after they have eaten, either by vomiting or by making themselves poo more.

REDS

Relative Energy Deficiency in Sport occurs when people are active in sport but don't eat enough to fuel the energy they need. They can end up losing weight or becoming unwell.

Rules for life

A type of thought or expectation, based on our experiences, culture and values, which tells us how we should think or act. These can be unhelpful if they are rigid, extreme or unrealistic.

Safety behaviours

Behaviours that help us to become less anxious (keep us safe) but actually make us more anxious in the long term because we don't address our fears: for example, avoiding speaking up in class or continually asking for reassurance about how we look.

Self-esteem The thoughts and feelings you have about yourself, and how much you value yourself.

Sensations How we feel in our body.

Sympathetic nervous system Controls the fight or flight response. It prepares the body for strenuous physical activity by increasing the heart rate, blood pressure and breathing rate.

Thoughts A type of cognition which is constantly going through our heads and helps us to make sense of our experiences by telling us what we think about ourselves, other people and the situations we are in. We often assume our thoughts are true, but thoughts are only opinions, not facts.

Vicious cycle When thoughts, feelings, sensations and behaviour work together in an unhelpful way which keeps us stuck in a difficult situation or inadvertently makes the situation worse.

Virtuous cycle When thoughts, feelings, sensations and behaviour work together to make the situation better.

Vitamins   Essential nutrients contained in food that our bodies need to function and stay healthy. They boost the immune system, help cells and organs to work properly and support normal growth and development.

Acknowledgements

Many of the ideas in this book have been gleaned from working over many years with teenagers with difficulties with eating and body image, and with their parents. We have learned a lot from them and are enormously grateful.

In writing this book we have drawn on ideas and models from leading researchers in the field, particularly the following:

- Chris Fairburn, Zafra Cooper, Roz Shafran, Rebecca Murphy and Suzanne Bailey-Straebler for developing and disseminating Enhanced Cognitive Behaviour Therapy for Eating Disorders (CBT-E) and Riccardo Dalle Grave for adapting CBT-E for young people. CBT-E is the main evidenced-based treatment for eating disorders. We describe this in Chapter 16 on getting help, and draw on their ideas extensively throughout the book.

- Glen Waller, Tracy Wade, Hannah Turner, Madeleine Tatham, Victoria Mountford, Ella Keegan and others for their CBT model of working with eating disorders, including a brief model of treatment.

- Melanie Fennell for her work on self-esteem which forms the basis of Chapter 9, with adaptations for young people.

- Ros Shafran, Sarah Egan and Tracy Wade for their models of perfectionism (Chapter 11), which we have adapted for young people with eating difficulties.

- Ivan Eisler, Jim Lock, Daniel Le Grange and colleagues for developing and disseminating a family-based treatment for eating disorders. This is described in Chapter 16 on getting professional help.

- William Richard Miller and Stephen Rollnick for the OARS model of communication skills described in their book on motivational interviewing. This model is used in Chapter 17 on supporting parents.

- Zindel Segal, Mark Williams and John Teasdale and others for their work on mindfulness and mental health.

We would also like to say a huge thanks to the young people who have contributed ideas and helped us by reading and providing feedback on the different chapters of the book.

Daniel Kaye, Tallulah Self, George Mycock and Oliwia Dziwisz have read through the whole book and made very helpful comments. We are grateful to other young people and parents who have looked at particular chapters for us, particularly Kate Jenkins, Ella Jenkins, Iris Pittard, Elsie Waite, Aiden Hughes and Finley Hughes. Your feedback at all stages of the project has been invaluable. Not all of you are named here, but you know who you are!

We would also like to thank colleagues, family and friends who have read specific chapters and given extremely useful feedback, including Melanie Fennell, Zafra Cooper, Rebecca Murphy, Sally Burne, Meinou Simmons, Ruth Baer, Mel Venables and Mary Bennett. Robin Stewart read many of the early drafts of chapters and gave helpful feedback on the language and comprehensibility.

Our editors, Polly Waite and Andrew McAleer, have been enormously helpful and patient throughout the whole process. We are grateful for the invitation to write the book and for their encouragement, expert advice and belief in the project. In preparing the final draft for publication we are grateful to Sue Viccars, copy-editor, and Peter Jacobs, project editor, who have helped to transform our draft into a book.

We are very grateful to our illustrator, Juliet Young, who has put our ideas into pictures in an engaging way.

Finally, we would like to thank our families for all their support and encouragement throughout the writing of this book.

Index

Note: page numbers in **bold** refer to diagrams.

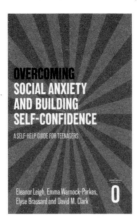

OVERCOMING SOCIAL ANXIETY AND BUILDING SELF-CONFIDENCE

A SELF-HELP GUIDE FOR TEENAGERS

Eleanor Leigh, Emma Warnock-Parkes, Elyse Brassard and David M. Clark

Anxiety about embarrassing yourself in social situations is common, particularly amongst teenagers.

Whilst for most these worries are mild, for some young people they are more troublesome and persistent. If you are spending a lot of time feeling shy or worrying about social situations, this can be overwhelming and can have a big impact on your life.

The aim of this book is to help you to understand a bit more about these worries, what you can do about them and how you can reduce your social anxiety and build self-confidence.

Written by clinicians with many years of experience working in services that treat anxiety disorders in children and adolescents, this book follows an approach called cognitive behavioural therapy (CBT), which is a really useful way of helping us to make sense of our experiences and overcome the difficulties that we face. CBT is an evidence-based approach, which means that lots of research has been done to evaluate it and show that it can be helpful.

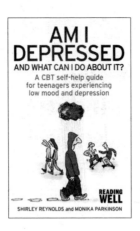

AM I
DEPRESSED
AND WHAT CAN I DO ABOUT IT?
A CBT self-help guide
for teenagers experiencing
low mood and depression

READING
WELL

SHIRLEY REYNOLDS and MONIKA PARKINSON

Available Now

Depression is one of the most common mental health problems and is estimated to affect around 15% of people at some point during their life. For many people depression is a life-long disorder which starts during the teenage years around 10% of teenagers are estimated to have an episode of depression and many more experience persistent low mood.

This is an accessible, engaging and age-appropriate self-help guide based on current research and best practice (NICE, IAPT treatment pathways, Books on Prescription, all of which promote CBT) for young people aged 13 to 17 who experience low mood and depression, and their friends, family and health professionals. The book adopts a narrative approach with graphic elements, incorporating case studies and including some interactive exercises. It provides an essential bridge for young people who have not yet asked for professional help as well as support for those who are waiting for treatment.

Available Now

Growing up is a juggling act. Our bodies and hormones change, usually at the same time as important decisions about our future need to be made. We often put extra pressure on ourselves, compare ourselves unfavourably to others and excessively worry about what other people think. Add in exams, interviews, relationships, social media, peer pressure, celebrity culture and everyday stressors, and it's no wonder our wellbeing can take a nosedive.

The Kindness Workbook is a modern-day guide to help people navigate such complex times and combines amazing ideas and practices from a variety of therapies including: Acceptance and Commitment Therapy, Cognitive Behavioural Therapy, Compassion-Focused Therapy, Counselling and Expressive Therapy.

Using creative exercises, examples and prompts, *The Kindness Workbook* teaches the skills of problem-solving using guided imagery, mindfulness, mind maps, vision boards, letter-writing, music, physical activity, drama and art. It has a number of icons to help signpost different sections and has eye-catching illustrations and worksheets, all of which aim to give your wellbeing a boost.

A must-have book for young people and anyone working with young people to enhance wellbeing. Your kindness journey starts right here. So, it's time to become your own best friend, instead of your own worst enemy.

Available Now

The way you think about yourself affects how you live your life.

In *The Psychological Toolkit*, you will learn how to use psychology on your journey to knowing your true self. It is so important to take the time to understand how you view yourself, and to understand that your most important relationship is the one that you have with yourself.

This workbook will guide you through the development of your own positive theory and view of your unique self and identity. You will learn how to think about yourself on a deeper level through honest, non-judgemental questioning and based on what is of value to YOU. You will also:

–   Learn to engage proactively with the world and those around you
–   Develop new thinking skills and resources
–   Improve your autonomy and ownership of your thoughts, feelings and behaviours
–   Develop a strong understanding of your own identity and on-going 'story'
–   Take control of your wellbeing, resilience and mental health
–   Increase your self-esteem and self-awareness
–   Improve your pro-social and citizenship behaviours to make a more positive impact in the world
–   Connect to your inner voice and become your own personal advisor

Available Now

Each of us has thoughts that are painful at times; sometimes the pain is sadness, sometimes worry or anger or shame or grief or some feeling that you don't even have words for.

If you are a young person struggling with your emotions, you do not want to be told that 'everyone feels like that' or that 'you will grow out of it'. You want to feel that your emotions are valid and that the person offering help truly understands how painful life can feel at times. With a strong emphasis on validation and compassion, *Stuff That Sucks* encourages you to accept your emotions rather than struggling against them. It also shows how to reconnect with what is really important to you, giving you the tools to help clarify your personal values and take steps towards living a life where those values can guide you in your day-to-day behaviour.

Available Now

Did you ever want to become a superhero? Did you ever wish you could get magical powers or travel through the universe, across time and space?

This dynamic new self-help book is designed to help heroes who are struggling with anxiety, depression, anger, shame and trauma.

Written by Dr. Janina Scarlet, the leading advocate of superhero therapy, a new technique that helps you to recover from common psychological and emotional problems by showing your concerns are mirrored in the stories of extraordinary superheroes from fiction. The book takes you through the core concepts of Acceptance and Commitment Therapy (ACT), which will better arm you to face the challenges of your superhero quest.

Illustrated by talented comic book artist Wellinton Alves, this book tells the tale of a group of troubled heroes enlisted at the Superhero Training Academy (inspired both by fictional characters and real-life people who have benefited from this therapy), learning to overcome their problems using the techniques of ACT. This will appeal to readers with a geeky side to their nature, or anyone just seeking to find their inner superhero.